1982

CHILD CARE, FAMILY BENEFITS, AND WORKING PARENTS

CHILD CARE, FAMILY BENEFITS, AND WORKING PARENTS

A STUDY IN COMPARATIVE POLICY

SHEILA B. KAMERMAN
ALFRED J. KAHN

New York
COLUMBIA UNIVERSITY PRESS
1981

This book is printed on permanent and durable acid-free paper.

Library of Congress Cataloging in Publication Data

Kamerman, Sheila B
Child care, family benefits, and working parents.

Bilbliography: p.
Includes index.

1. Family policy–Europe.   2. Family policy–United
States.   3. Children of working parents–Government
policy–Europe.   4. Children of working parents–
Government policy–United States.   5. Child welfare–
Government policy–Europe.   6. Child welfare–Govern-
ment policy–United States.   I.   Kahn, Alfred J.,
1919–   joint author.   II. Title.
HQ612.K35   362.8'2   80-39690
ISBN 0-231-05170-0   AACR1

Columbia University Press
New York   Guildford, Surrey

WITH THE COLLABORATION OF
THE COUNTRY TEAMS

FEDERAL REPUBLIC OF GERMANY

STUDY DIRECTORS

Dr. Ursula Lehr
Psychologischen Institute der Universität Bonn
Dr. Max Wingen
Bochum University

TEAM MEMBER

Mr. Philipp Stephen Schrankel

FRANCE

STUDY DIRECTORS

Dr. Mira Stambak
Dr. Olga Baudelot
Dr. Evelyne Burguiere
Section de Recherche de l' Éducation Spécialisée et de l' Adaptation Scolaire
    (SRESAS)
Institut National de Recherche et de Documentation Pédagogique
Ministère de l'Éducation, Paris

TEAM MEMBERS

Dr. Michelle Berthoz
Ms. Monique Breaute
Ms. Nicole Lantier-Rafalovich

GERMAN DEMOCRATIC REPUBLIC

STUDY DIRECTOR

Dr. Anneliese Sälzler
Des Institutes für Hygiene des Kindes- und Jugendalters, Berlin

TEAM MEMBER

Dr. Gerda Neibsch

HUNGARY

STUDY DIRECTOR

Dr. Julia Szalai
Institute of Sociology
Hungarian Academy of Sciences, Budapest

TEAM MEMBER

Dr. Agota Horwath

SWEDEN

STUDY DIRECTORS

Mr. Ingemar Lindberg
Landsorganisationen I Sverige
Mr. Søren Kindlund
Socialdepartmentet, Stockholm

TEAM MEMBER

Ms. Lena Nordenmark

UNITED STATES

STUDY DIRECTORS

Dr. Sheila B. Kamerman
Dr. Alfred J. Kahn
Columbia University School of Social Work, New York

TEAM MEMBERS

Ms. Ellen Galinsky
Ms. Phyllis Silverman
Ms. Louise Silverstein

CONTENTS

PREFACE

This report offers the results of a six-country study which approximates a natural experiment. It deals with one of the major family policy questions facing industrial urban societies, or perhaps *the* major question: what is the optimum response, or what are optimum response alternatives, to a situation in which parents are in the paid labor force, want to have children, and want to rear them successfully? Modern societies have a stake in both childbearing and successful child rearing, but the consequences of different policy responses have not been given detailed, systematic examination.

After surveying fourteen country patterns, we selected six countries which have adopted different approaches. The options represent a continuum, with those in the middle involving different mixes. The group also includes a "no policy" option. We have studied social benefits in support of an at-home option, as well as child care services. We have placed all this in societal context, given an overview of where children under three actually are during the day, and assessed the debate and interest group positions in each country. There is a secondary review of research on costs, effects, prices, and who pays. Current trends are depicted.

The work was carried out in each country by teams following jointly developed research instruments. The team met several times to develop guidelines and to assure a combined effort. The study directors visited programs and met with officials in all countries. Two U.S. reporting meetings in Washington in May 1979 and a conference in Copenhagen (cosponsored by the European Regional Office, World Health Organization, and the Danish National Institute of Social Research) helped focus the presentation. At the Copenhagen sessions, the team members also had an opportunity to add to and to update their reports and to help clarify the implications of the study.

Needless to say, no matter how careful the work and cooperative the collaborators, problems do arise in assuring data comparability and completeness in such an effort. Nonetheless, we do believe that the results have sufficient specificity and rigor to be of interest—and to justify some significant policy learning. For this we are grateful to the country teams, and to the officials in several countries who cooperated throughout and educated us in the course of our several visits to each country in the period from 1976 to 1979. A full description of our study method is given in Appendix B.

We are especially grateful to the German Marshall Fund of the United States, which supported the work financially, and to Robert Gerald Livingston, president, and Peter Weitz, program coordinator, whose "other" contributions, in the form of hard questions, were of significance as well.

CHILD CARE, FAMILY BENEFITS,
AND WORKING PARENTS

One

WORKING PARENTS

WORK, FAMILIES, AND SOCIAL CHANGE

A social revolution has occurred in all industrialized countries during the last twenty years and the consequences are only just beginning to be felt. This revolution has been described in different terms over the years, often reflecting what appeared to be the most immediate—or most visible—cause of social change. Thus, the 1960s saw repeated mention of "the changing role of women in society" as more and more women entered the paid labor force. During the 1970s, the issue was more often described as "the changing roles of men *and* women," as it became clear that if more women, especially married women with young children, entered the labor force, there would be inevitable consequences for men—male coworkers, husbands, and sons. Now, as we enter the 1980s, it has become increasingly apparent that what is occurring is more than just a change in male and female roles with consequences for each domain in which these roles are carried out. Instead, what we are confronting is a variety of internal and external pressures on two of the most central institutions in society: the family and the workplace.

The result may well be a major reorganization of work and family life, in particular a restructuring of the relationship between these two domains. Indeed, there are some who would say that some such change *must* occur if industrialized societies are to survive.

It is within this context that we discuss the developments in six countries experiencing these changes, and analyze the implications for the industrialized world in general.

Childbearing and child rearing continue to be the core functions of the family in our society, and child care continues to be the most important family responsibility carried by employed women. If women are to bear and rear children at the same time as they participate in the labor force, traditional assumptions regarding women bearing sole or primary responsibility for child care and child rearing become increasingly untenable. Even as there is more shared responsibility between husbands and wives, the pressures on the time and energy of working parents—and especially on single parents—increasingly demonstrates the need for some sort of response and adaptation by the society at large as well.

The question of what this response should be has already emerged as a central issue in family—or social—policy in many countries. The primary source of concern may vary. There may be worry about the decline in birth rates as women enter the labor force. An anticipated decline in population may lead to apprehension regarding the growing burden of retirement and old-age pensions on a contracting productive population. There may be interest in encouraging or discouraging (depending on the country) work by women. There may be some desire to assure women greater equality with men. There may be a search for improved approaches to child development and socialization, or for ways to improve the quality of life for all. Efforts at addressing any or all of these concerns must be balanced against problems of resource limitations and scarcity. Yet whichever concern is primary, the problem of caring for the very young child touches them all. *The central question remains: can adults manage productive roles in the labor force at the same time as they fulfill productive roles within the family—at home?*

There are serious differences of opinion on such important questions as What is best for the child? What is best for women—as well as men? What is best for the family unit? For the society at large?

The *immediate* policy choice has to do with whether the mothers of very young children should be expected to remain home and care for their children, should be expected to work, or should be permitted to choose either option, and be helped to implement their choice by a supportive policy.

The *ultimate* policy choice—for societies which need children and need them to be well cared for if the society is to survive—must reflect concern not only with women and child care, but with the income of families with children, the availability of jobs and the nature of work, the allocation of time to work and home. In other words, the ultimate concern must be with the development of alternative ways for adults, regardless of gender, to manage both family and work roles simultaneously, without undue hardship for themselves or for their children.

The two-parent, two-earner family has emerged now as the largest single family type in all the countries studied except for the Federal Republic of Germany. Furthermore, in several countries the growth in female-headed families during the last decade indicates another significant change in family life styles. Thus, just as adults are increasingly likely to experience a lifestyle in which they will be coping with both work and family responsibilities, children will in all probability be born and reared in families with a sole or two working parents. Some difficulties are inevitable regardless of the age of the child, but clearly these difficulties are most intense where there are very young children. Nor is there clarity, wisdom, or knowledge as to what is the "ideal" response by society. Yet, obviously, there must be a response.

THE TRIGGERING FACTORS IN INITIATING CHANGE

THE SEPARATION OF WORK AND HOME

The separation of work and home—or work life and family life—has long been identified as one of the most significant characteristics of industrialized societies.[1] The weekend father, the commuting husband, and communities populated by women and children during the work week, have emerged as popular stereotypes of contemporary life, dramatizing this separation. The negative consequences, including isolation and depression for the at-home wife, the absence of positive adult role models for children, and the increase in concomitant family stress, are well known.[2]

Recently, there has been growing discussion in the literature regarding the work-family dichotomy.[3] Some analysts view the problem as having been inaccurately defined. In other words, the problem is not the separation of work and family but the overwhelming pressures that work puts on family life. Others insist that the picture is far more complicated and urge more research directed at the interface of the two domains.

Some people have suggested specific remedies, usually focused on ways to expose children more to adult role models and work experience, to bring them closer to the "real world" of work.[4] There have been recommendations to reorganize work or to provide counseling so as to alleviate the stress. The recent increase in female labor force participation is viewed by some observers as contributing still further to family stress and disorganization: children are inadequately cared for or supervised while mothers work; family routines are disrupted or ignored; working women with independent incomes are more likely to dissolve unsatisfactory marriages; changes in women's roles inevitably lead to change in men's—or to tension and conflict.[5]

Our own perspective is a rather different one. That is, the conflict between work and family life resulting from the separation of work and home under industrialization, though a source of continuing stress, may be tolerable as long as one family member remains at home. Once most adults, regardless of sex, are in the labor force, complete separation of work and home becomes increasingly untenable—if there are to be children and if they are to be reared satisfactorily. An entirely new situation emerges, with important ramifications for family, for work, and for society in general.

Thus, it is our hypothesis that the entry of women—especially married women with children—into the labor force in the last half of the twentieth century is what is making the whole question of the relationship between work and family life the central family policy issue in Europe and in the United States for the coming decade.

Before exploring the policy implications of this development, however, we offer a brief overview of the situation of women in the labor force. It is, after all, the change in female labor force participation rates that is the most significant factor in stimulating what we and others are describing as a major phenomenon in social change.

WOMEN IN THE LABOR FORCE

The entry of women into the labor force emerged as a dominant characteristic of all industrialized countries after World War II. For some the trend emerged almost at once, while for others it became a significant development only in the 1960s. Regardless of when it began, by the mid-1970s labor force participation was the modal pattern for adult women in almost

TABLE 1.1

Female Labor Force Participation Rates (FLFPR) in the Study Countries (1975)

Country	Age Range	FLFPR	Percentage Full Time	Male Equivalency Rates	FLFPR in the Prime Middle Years (25-54) 1977/78
France	15-64	48%	85%	80%	54%
FRG	15-60	52	60	85	50 (est.)
GDR	15-60	85[a]	68	—	87
Hungary	15-55	75[b]	Almost 100	85	75
Sweden	18-64	69	50	90	70
U.S.	18-64	56	67	88	60

NOTE: Data relate to how the productive years for women are defined in each country.

[a] At work or in training, but excluding 16-68 year olds in school.

[b] Includes women home on child care leave; otherwise the figure would be 66%.

all the industrialized countries. The extensiveness of this development, the rapidity with which it has occurred, and its consequences for families and for society have led some social commentators to describe it as the most significant phenomenon of the twentieth century.

Between half (F. R. Germany) and 87 percent (German Democratic Republic) of the non-aged adult women in the countries to be discussed here were in the labor force in 1978, constituting between 38 percent and 50 percent of the total labor force. (For comparative purposes, in order to obtain data for the same year in all countries given occasional lags in data collection, our standard data refer to 1975. However, in the text, where it may be of special interest, we present more recent data.) Since the definition of productive ages varies, precise comparisons are difficult. Typically, labor force participation for the prime "middle years" (25-54) constitutes the best and most comparable overall picture. For this group, the German Democratic Republic, with 87 percent female labor force participation, is probably at close to maximum possible rate, with Hungary (75 percent) and Sweden (70 percent) not too far behind. Current U.S. figures are 60 percent for this age group; projections for 1990 are 70 percent, about equal to Sweden's present rate, although lower than the present rates of Hungary and the German Democratic Republic. In both France and the Federal

TABLE 1.2

Women as a Percentage of Total Labor Force (1975)

France	38%
FRG	38
GDR	49
Hungary	49
Sweden	43
U.S.	41

Republic of Germany, over half this age group is working. (For comparative purposes, we note that female labor force participation rates for this age group in Denmark are about the same as in Sweden, while the British rates are more like those of the FRG.)

Historically, for obvious reasons, labor force participation rates for women with very young children have been the lowest in all countries. Childbearing and child care require time and women have had to withdraw from work to fulfill these roles. Moreover, there has also been a strong belief in many places that children are damaged if their mothers leave them when they are young. Conventional wisdom has been that women can enter the labor force more easily when children are old enough to go to school (five, six, or seven depending on the age of compulsory schooling in different countries), and the school, as an institution, can assume child care and supervision along with education and socialization.

Yet in the last ten to fifteen years in the Western industrialized countries there has been an extraordinary growth in labor force participation rates of women with preschool-aged children. This development occurred earlier in many of the Eastern European countries. Not only have single mothers with young children entered the labor market, but the major growth has been attributable primarily to the entry of young married women, living with their husbands, with young children.

The trend began first with women with the "older" preschool children: those aged three to compulsory school age. Although Hungary and the GDR experienced high labor force participation rates for women in this category soon after World War II, in Sweden, France, the FRG, and the United States, this development has occurred primarily since the middle and late 1960s. Regardless, by the mid-1970s, in all except the FRG, close to half—or more—of mothers with children of this age were in the labor force;

TABLE 1.3

Percentage of Children Aged 3–5 in Preschool Programs

Country	Percentage
France	95%
FRG	75
GDR	85[a]
Hungary	78
Sweden[b,c]	28
U.S.[c]	64

NOTE: Data are for 1975 or 1976.

[a] In 1977, 90% of the children of this age were in preschool programs.

[b] Compulsory school entry is at 7; but these data cover 3–5 since compulsory school entry is at 6 in all the other countries.

[c] Includes preschool programs, day care centers and family day care homes.

in the United States, the labor force participation rate for these women has doubled since 1960, and has come close to tripling for women with children under three. And the numbers continue to increase.

Paralleling this development was the enormous growth throughout much of Europe in the 1960s and 1970s of preschool programs for children aged three to six, which expanded the availability of out-of-home child care for this age group in all the European countries discussed here.[6] Except for Sweden, where there are relatively even fewer available places than in the United States (although almost all publicly funded in contrast to the extensiveness of private provision in the United States), between 75 percent and 95 percent of the age group three to six is already in a preschool program in each of these countries. And Swedish public policy is explicitly directed toward achieving comparable coverage. One consequence, as can be seen from a comparison of labor market trends, is that there is a growing similarity between the patterns of work of women with children three to six and of those with school-aged schildren. (Here, too, we would note the complexity of the issues. Although the patterns are somewhat comparable, there is no direct correlation between female labor force participation and extensiveness of preschool coverage. Other factors enter into the ultimate policy decision, as will be seen in the subsequent discussion.)

The pattern for women with still younger children, however, remains

TABLE 1.4

Labor Force Participation Rates of Women by Age of Child (1976)

Country	0–3	3–6	School Age
France	43%	44%	48%
FRG	32	34	41
GDR	80	85	85
Hungary	82[a]	75	75
Sweden	58	64	78
U.S.	35	48	56

[a]33% excluding women home on child care leave; 82% if women home on child care leave are included.

very different. Out-of-home child care arrangements are far less extensive, and even more important, much less consistently supported. Yet at the same time, mothers of very young children are the most rapidly expanding group entering the labor force in all the Western countries. Indeed, in the United States, married women with children under age three are now entering the labor force at a faster rate than any other group.

Women appear to be in the labor force to stay. Labor force participation rates of women have increased despite periods of rising unemployment. Families may need the woman's income just for survival, either because she is the sole support or because total family income is low. Family aspirations for an improved standard of living may require supplementary income. And some women work for the many other noneconomic reasons that some men do. Countries need female labor, too. Apart from extensive importation of foreign labor, which generates its own problems, albeit of a different category, little can be done to redirect current labor force trends for women generally.[7]

Although experts may differ as to its rate, few doubt that the increase in female labor force participation will continue.[8] Furthermore, it seems clear that the major future growth will continue to occur among married women with children, especially among those with young children. And while arrangements for the care of preschool or school-aged children aged three to ten when school is closed may present problems for working mothers, this is generally acknowledged as requiring attention and is not viewed as a debatable need. Indeed, only with regard to the mothers of children under the age of three is there still significant question raised about what the dominant work and child care patterns will be or should be.

THE POLICY OPTIONS—AND THE COUNTRIES IN WHICH THEY EXIST

Undoubtedly, we would all agree that there has been a major change in individual and family lifestyles in all our countries. But changes in society seldom evoke an immediate policy response—there is always a social policy "lag." Mothers of preschool children entered the labor market before there were adequate child care policies, before the world of work had assumed any responsibility for adapting to this new source of labor, and before there was any redefinition of social risks. Yet despite the policy lag, some countries have already selected one of several policy options. Most others are clearly at the crossroads, debating which option—or options—to choose.

In the following pages, we shall present a description, analysis, and comparison of the full range of policies and programs already in place or currently proposed and debated regarding care of the very young child while a single parent or both parents work. Rationales for policy choice, costs, and the overall implications for each country will be reviewed and assessed.

Our objective is to increase knowledge and understanding regarding different policy options and the implications and potential consequences of each. Our ultimate goal is to provide a background for decision making on this most critical issue.

THE COUNTRIES

The countries discussed here are France, the Federal Republic of Germany (FRG), the German Democratic Republic (GDR), Hungary, Sweden, and the United States. They were selected because 1) they have relatively high levels of industrialization (as compared to the developing world); 2) they have high, and for some still rising, rates of female labor force participation; and 3) in an initial exploration they appeared to represent distinctive contrasts among the available policy options. As will be seen, each of the countries is involved in a series of dynamic adjustments, with consequent modifications emerging regarding earlier policy positions.

We concentrate on labor force participation of women with family responsibilities, in particular those with children under the age of three—for many people, the most significant and demanding of all family responsibilities—and the implications of this for the relationships among work, family life, and the society at large. More and more of these women are working. What are the variations in policy and program responses among the different countries to this most critical issue involving women, work, and family? What combination of policy choice and societal context leads to the specific policy/program models in each country, why, and with what consequences and implications?

The countries—and our original reasons for their selection—are described briefly below. As will be seen, the story is more complex than these initial characterizations suggest.

The German Democratic Republic was selected as representing the purest example of a country supporting organized, group, out-of-home care of very young children. In 1977, over 48 percent of the children under age three (primarily those aged one and two) were already in day care centers. (We use terms "day care centers," "day nurseries," "*crèches*," "preschools," "*Krippen*" interchangeably.) If one eliminates children under twenty weeks of age, whose mothers are covered by paid maternity leaves and who are not admitted to center care, the coverage rate becomes 60 percent. It is worth noting that this is full-day care (8–12 hours, depending on parental needs), that there is extensive research in the GDR regarding the effects of group care, and that there is continuous monitoring of these programs by health and child development research personnel.

The Federal Republic of Germany was selected primarily because of the interesting comparison it provided with the GDR, and because of its very different position regarding such child care. Both countries began at the same point, yet there was, in the FRG, very limited organized child care for the under-threes, and little enthusiasm for it other than a few pilot, demonstration projects experimenting with and studying the effects of supervised family day care. Instead, a child caring allowance (*Erziehungsgeld* or *Familiengeld*, technically a child rearing grant) was being suggested for all women remaining at home to care for children up to age one (and eventually, up to age three) regardless of whether these women had been employed previously. In effect, the proposal debated in the FRG as the study began is what has been called earlier in policy discussions a "mothers' wage" for the mothers of very young children.

Hungary was selected as representing the policy position opposite that of the GDR. In Hungary, women who have had at least a brief working experience are given a generous cash allowance to remain home and care for their child up to age three. This policy has been in effect since the late 1960s, and thus provides much material for study and analysis.

France was selected because of the government's continuing effort to support a neutral position. The official policy is to provide neither incentives nor disincentives for women to work or to remain at home, but rather to offer support for both options, permitting women to choose whichever course of action they prefer without (or with a minimum of) economic hardship.

The major objective (not yet achieved) is to assure the low-income mother the same option as the middle-income mother. France has more very young children in organized, subsidized, low-cost, licensed family or center-based care than any other Western country. Furthermore, its current plans are to expand such care. Yet at the same time, the French government provides a significant means-tested cash benefit (*complément familial*) for mothers of very young children, regardless of whether they remain at home and care for their own child or purchase out-of-home care.

Sweden was selected because the official government position is to maximize women's equality by providing child care arrangements making it possible for women to work outside the home, and to facilitate increased care of children by both parents by subsidizing a shorter workday for parents of children under age three. Plans in Sweden involve the expansion of day care centers and a proposal to shorten the workday to six hours for some parents of very young children, with the difference in income to be provided as a social insurance benefit for a limited period of time.

THE SITUATION AND CONTEXT IN EACH COUNTRY

Clearly, the policy choice in each country is made in a context that includes labor force participation rates of women and whether or not they are increasing; per capita GNP or wealth of the country; the availability and extent of resources to support alternative policy choices; demographic trends and the response to them, including whether there is particular concern about population patterns and declining birth rates; social trends and the extent to which, for example, equality of men and women is viewed as a desirable goal or changes in traditional family structure and roles are seen as detrimental to the fabric of society. Intermingled with these factors are existing approaches to child policy more broadly defined, as well as attitudes toward the role of government in society. All these variables were seen as clearly operative in each of the countries during initial explorations. Whether there is any one definitive causal pattern remains to be seen.

We begin first with an overview of the GDR and Hungary. These are the two countries in this group with the longest history of high labor force participation among women with very young children; yet they have taken very different approaches in responding to this development. We continue with the remaining four countries.

GDR

The GDR has the most extensive female labor force participation rate among the countries described here—a rate among the highest in the industrialized world. Eighty-seven percent of all women between the ages of fifteen and sixty were in the labor force in 1978, and about two-thirds worked full time. Full-time work is defined as 43.75 or more hours per week. Women represent 50 percent of the labor force. Women's median wages are about 65 percent of male wages.

The GDR has had a history of employed women since the end of World War II when women were needed in the labor force to compensate for the loss of males during the war. In contrast to Hungary, which began with a similar pattern, the GDR has had a consistently tight labor market since then, in which every adult was needed in the labor force. And in contrast to the FRG, the approach in the GDR has been to employ women to meet their needs for increased labor rather than to import foreign labor. (Importation of foreign labor has increased significantly in recent years, but not to a degree that affects female labor force participation.) The GDR did not question the fact that women would be working, and concentrated on the improvement of out-of-home child care facilities in order to eliminate—or at least attenuate—any problems created as a consequence. A great deal of money and research has gone into improving these facilities, with results that the country is deservedly proud of today.

At the same time, however, the GDR has become increasingly concerned about its declining birth rate, its decreasing population, and the increased percentage of the elderly in its population. The total population in 1975 was 17 million people, representing a steady and significant decline from the peak of 19 million reached in 1947. There is some indication of a slight reversal, and an increase in population, since 1975.

Crude birth rates per 1,000 population declined steadily until 1974. Indeed, the GDR was first among the four European countries (Austria, Luxembourg, FRG, GDR) which have already gone below replacement rate; that is, these countries have more deaths than births each year.[9] In 1975, the birth rate in the GDR was 10.6; the death rate 13.5. In the same year, the size of the cohort aged 0-3 (532,000) was significantly smaller than it was five and ten years earlier. In addition to its very extensive provision of out-of-home child care programs, the GDR has a substantial variety of social benefits for mothers, in part in response to growing concern about a declining birthrate. These have been expanded in the last few years.

At present, the GDR is reporting a significant increase in its birth rate (11.6 in 1976; 13.3 in 1977); the major increase is attributed to the birth of "second" children, in a country in which for some time many women had only one child. The following shows the more recent pattern of increased births:

1975	182,000
1976	195,000
1977	223,000
1978	232,000

While the numbers of first children (and third children) have remained the same, the numbers of second children have increased steadily:

1975	30.7%
1976	32.3%
1977	35.7%

If one were to identify a major theme in GDR child care policy, it would be as follows: to assure children an optimum environment for growth and development and reduce the steady decline in fertility, while maintaining high and essential female labor force participation rates.

HUNGARY

Hungary, like the GDR, has had a long history of attempting to deal with extensive labor force participation of women. Seventy-five percent of all women between the ages of fifteen and fifty-five are in the labor force, if one includes those women at home on Hungary's special child care leave; 66 percent, if not. (The child care leave, granted to women at the conclusion of their maternity leave until their child is three years old, is explained in detail in the next chapter.) Most of these women work full time, which is defined as forty or more hours per week. Women represent 49 percent of the labor force, or 44 percent if those on child care leave are excluded, and women earn about 62 percent of male median wages. Furthermore, as in the GDR, wage levels are such that in most cases two wages are needed to assure adequate family income.

There has been a steady increase in the participation of women in the labor market since 1960, as can be seen from the following data.

Women as a Percentage of the Labor Force
(excluding those on child care leave)

1960	35.5
1970	41.2
1973	42.7
1975	43.7

Moreover, the data suggest that the most important development has been in the increase of married women in the prime childbearing and child rearing years. Thus, the years 1949-1973 witnessed a decline in labor force participation of the youngest cohort (15-19) from 53 percent to 47 percent and an even greater decline among the oldest cohort (55 and over), as the younger women were increasingly likely to be in school and the older women more likely to be receiving pensions. In contrast, for the cohorts aged twenty to twenty-nine and thirty to thirty-nine, who were likely to be out of the labor force in 1949, labor force participation rates were 68 percent and 75 percent, respectively, in 1973 (or 86 percent and 79 percent, if women home on child care leave were included).

This trend, however, has been influenced by the establishment of a child care grant which permits mothers to take an unpaid leave from their jobs (without loss of seniority or fringe benefits) and receive an allowance from the government, until their child is three years old. The consequences of this policy for labor force participation of mothers are shown in table 1.5.

Of the close to 550,000 children under age three in 1976, about 120,000 had mothers who were actually at work.

TABLE 1.5

Hungary: Labor Force Participation Rates of Mothers with Children Under the Age of 18

	Women in Labor Force	
Age of Youngest Child	Excluding those on Child Care Leave	Including those on Child Care Leave
All women	64%	75%
Under 3	33	82
3–6	75	–
School–aged	74	–

NOTE: Labor force participation is defined as a minimum of 90 days work in the previous year.

In the mid-1960s, certain significant changes occurred within the Hungarian economy. The previous rapidly increasing annual growth rate slowed down, and the predictions, based on a variety of standard evaluations, were that growth would be still slower in the coming decade. At the same time there was an expansion in the supply of manpower as the "baby boom" population began to enter the labor market. Given Hungary's commitment to full employment, these young people would have had to be provided with expanded opportunities for further education and training or be offered job oppportunities. But neither of these could be accomplished, given the state of the economy at that time. A final factor leading to what ultimately emerged as a social policy innovation in the child care field was the inadequacy of existing child care arrangements for very young children and the high cost of providing good quality care—as well as the time needed to do so.

Thus, an increase in the numbers of unskilled young people entering the labor force, a decrease in economic growth and the rate of employment and labor market growth, discomfort with the consequences of existing group care for very young children—and concern with the costs of high quality group care—led Hungary toward a policy of subsidizing a short-term at-home role (and labor force withdrawal) for young women with young children.

A problematic consequence of this policy has been that as the rate of economic growth increased somewhat in the 1970s, industries with extensive female labor found themselves in tight labor market situations. There have also been other developments.

The total population of Hungary in 1975 was 10.5 million. Fifty-five percent are in the productive ages (15-55 for women; 15-60 for men). The population has been relatively stable over the last decade, although the birth rate had been declining for some time. Hungary is among a group of ten countries that have been expected to reach or fall below zero growth within the next few years.[10] Concern about a declining birth rate led the Hungarian government to institute a series of pronatalist policies in 1974. As a consequence, the steady decline in births seems to have been stayed, at least somewhat.

Crude Birth Rate per 1,000

1974	17.7
1975	18.4
1976	17.4

No. of Live Births

1974	179,472
1975	188,385
1976	180,307

Under-3 Cohort Size

1965	381,583
1970	444,100
1975	518,728
1979 (projected)	512,300

In part as a consequence of these policies and other actions initiated in 1967, by 1976 children under age three consituted 21 percent of all children under the age of eighteen, a significantly higher figure than in any of the other countries discussed here.

We would note that the average age at first marriage (23.3) and average age at first birth (24.2) are not very different than they are in all these countries. On the other hand, 94 percent of the births in 1974 were to married mothers (husband present); only 7 percent of all families with children are one-parent female-headed families; half of all first births occur within one year after marriage; and the divorce rate is 1 in 4 marriages.

If we were to characterize the major theme of Hungarian child care policy, it would be that of maintenance of high female labor force participation, subject to—and modified by—changing needs of the economy, and without assumption of concomitant high costs of high-quality child care for the very young child.

SWEDEN

Women, especially married women, poured into the labor market in Sweden during the 1960s, just as they did a little later and in slightly smaller relative numbers in the United States. Indeed, since the mid-1960s married women have constituted the major part of the growth in the labor force, and since 1970 most of this expansion has occurred among women with preschool-aged children. Developments over the last two decades have been particularly rapid. In 1930 less than 10 percent of the married women were gainfully employed; in 1950 the figure was 15 percent. Today the figure is close to 70 percent, although only half are working full time.

Women constitute 43 percent of the labor force, while 69 percent of the women between the ages of 18 and 64 are in the labor force (and 90 percent of the men of this age). Labor force participation is defined to mean at least one hour of paid work per week. Full-time work means thirty-five hours per week or more. Only 50 percent of Swedish women in the labor force work full time, the lowest full-time rate in any of these six countries. In 1976, 69 percent of all mothers with children under age eighteen worked. The rate was somewhat lower for mothers with young children: of those with children ages three to six, 64 percent were at work; of those with children under age three, 58 percent were at work. Women earn, on average, 69 percent of what men earn, a far higher percentage of male median earnings than in any other of the countries discussed here.

Women's work has been needed in a tight labor market. Plentiful jobs and relatively high wages, in proportion to male wages, have offered an incentive for women to enter the labor force. Furthermore, passage of new tax legislation for 1970, instituting individual taxation in place of joint tax assessment, made it still more worthwhile for women to work.

At the same time, other factors have affected the Swedish woman's tendency and ability to earn her own living: age, number and ages of her children, marital status, her husband's income, her educational level, place of residence, availability of out-of-home child care services, and so forth. Older women and those in rural areas are less likely to work, as are women with very young children or several children. Highly educated women are more likely to work, even when their husbands' incomes are high.

Women tend to work in a limited number of occupations, usually those described as "female" and thus low-paying. Although, as mentioned earlier, women receive on average 69 percent of men's hourly wages, 67 percent of all individuals receiving extremely low pay are women. Despite the increase in higher education of women, women continue to be rare in high income brackets or in high-level executive positions.

Both official and popular concerns with the inequities experienced by women have led to increasing stress on equality for women as a primary goal for public policy. Despite much discussion of the importance of child programs and stress on high-quality care, the number of places available in such programs remains rather low. On the other hand, in 1974, the statutory provision of maternity benefits was changed to provide parent insurance. In 1975, legislation was passed authorizing the expansion of preschool programs. In 1979 a shorter work day for parents of very young children became a right, although without full compensation.

Sweden has a relatively homogeneous population, which is now very close to zero population growth. Its population in 1970 was 8,076,903 and in 1974, 8,176,691. The birth rate has been declining steadily for some time, and the cohort of children under age three reflects this trend:

Under-3 Cohort Size

1965	335,560
1970	330,799
1975	323,463
1976	313,650
1977	298,000 (est.)
1979 (projected)	288,000

No. of Live Births

1972	103,116
1973	110,407
1974	109,940
1975	98,250

Although average age at marriage is only a little higher than in the other countries (24), the percentage of women who are married is smaller in

Sweden than elsewhere. In 1974, 63 percent of the women aged sixteen to sixty-four were married. Only about one-third had children under seventeen. Eighteen percent had children under seven (compulsory school age in Sweden). The number of children per marriage is low, too. Half of those families that have children have only one, while one-third have two. Twenty-seven percent of the children born in 1974 were born to single mothers. Sixteen percent of the children under age eighteen are under age three.

Thus, to discuss child care policy in Sweden is to discuss 300,000 children in a country with a declining birth rate and an increasing percentage of women—especially women with very young children—in the labor force, even though many of these work part time. Characterizing Swedish policy, we would say that it is directed at making it possible for women and men to participate equally at home and in the society at large—making it possible for all adults to combine work and family responsibilities (especially child care)—while providing the greatest help for families with the greatest needs.

FRANCE

The overall French female labor force participation rate (48% of the women aged 15–64) and the rate for all mothers (45%) is lower than that in the United States. However, the percentage of women with children under age three who work (43%) is somewhat higher, and almost all work full time. Full-time work is defined as forty hours or more per week, and only 15 percent of employed women work less than full time. Women represent 38 percent of the labor force. Productive adults equal 63 percent of the population.

French female labor force participation rates are unusual in this group of countries because 1) there has been relatively little growth in the overall rates since the early 1960s (from 42.5% in 1962 to 48% in 1975); and 2) the rates are relatively high for women with young children (43% for mothers of children under age three; 44% for mothers of children three to six). However, better jobs have become available and the level of wages has improved. Women now earn, on average, 65 percent of median male earnings.

At least 800,000 children have working mothers. It is estimated that there may be still more, because some low-wage-earning women may not record part-time work so that they may continue to receive their income-based single wage-earner allowance; and some foreign women work illegally— without work permits—and this labor too is unrecorded.

Thus far, there has been no active effort at increasing labor force participation by women. Nor, despite the recent increase in unemployment, has there been any concerted effort at encouraging women to leave the labor market.

France has a population of approximately 52.7 million persons, and is among the five countries now approaching zero population growth. (Among the countries discussed here, the GDR and FRG are below zero growth— for these countries, deaths outnumber births. Sweden, France, and Hungary, in that order, are among the top ten countries approaching zero growth. The United States is eleventh in the list of countries approaching zero population growth, immediately behind Hungary.) The French birth rate has declined steadily since the early 1960s:

Crude Birth Rate per 1,000

1964	18.0
1974	15.3
1975	14.1
1976	13.6
1977	14.0

No. of Live Births

1968	832,847
1970	850,400
1973	857,200
1975	745,100
1976	720,400
1977	745,000

Under-3 Cohort Size

1968	2,560,000
1975	2,529,000
1978	2,183,000

France has long had a very extensive system of family allowances, and its basic family allowance—a universal, cash benefit provided for each second and subsequent child in a family—is among the highest in Europe. Although the family allowance was established and supported initially as a pronatalist policy, the French birth rate has fallen steadily over the last thirty years, except for the brief post–World War II baby boom, similar to that in all countries. Most French view individual fertility decisions as based upon far more complicated factors (the economy generally, employment, housing, individual preferences) than the availability of a cash benefit. On the other hand, inadequate family income creates unnecessary and potentially harmful stress on families with children. Thus, the French strongly support income maintenance policies designed to reduce the financial burdens of families, especially those with very young children.

Supplementing this is the most extensive provision of out-of-home child care services in any Western European country. First, there is an extraordinary free public preschool system (nursery school), which serves 95 percent of the children aged three to six (and 32 percent of the two-year-olds) on a voluntary basis, whether or not their mothers work. A substantial portion of the schools attended by children of working parents also include some sort of care arrangements for before and after normal school hours, at lunch, and on school holidays. Second, there is an unusually high coverage for children under age three, in a combination of preschool programs, day care centers, and family day care.

The debate in France is not over the expansion of these programs, but rather over which type of program offers the optimum environment for early child development: a group experience or a family-like, surrogate-mother experience. Most French view a group experience as essential for good child development from age two on, regardless of whether the child's mother is working; the debate has to do primarily with the still younger child. Of course, policy is also affected by costs, and the way in which they are distributed.

What makes France unusual is that labor market issues seem to play a far less important role in setting French child care policy than in any of the other countries in the group, although the labor force trends are comparable. Moreover, although population policy concerns are important in France, it is not clear that they are determinate in setting child care policy.

Indeed, if there is an identifiable theme in the French policy it would seem to be that income redistribution to benefit low-income families with children is primary, and that some concern for developing child care policies and programs that are good for children is essential.

FRG

The FRG has the lowest rate of female labor force participation among these countries, lower than in the United States. With current concerns about unemployment, the FRG is more interested in discouraging women from working than in encouraging them.

Historically, traditional family roles are supported and encouraged here. Foreign labor was actively imported in the 1960s, while other countries fostered the employment of women. There is extensive political support for the "woman at home" role, intensified by current anxiety about the low birth rate. Despite all this, FRG women are working in greater numbers than ever before.

As in France, 48 percent of the women aged fifteen to sixty-four are in the labor force. (The productive years are defined as fifteen to sixty-four and 65 percent of the population are in this group. For women, the ages are fifteen to sixty, and 52 percent of this age group are in the labor force.) However, unlike the situation in France, the percentage of mothers who are working, especially mothers of young children, is very much lower. Thirty-two percent of the women with children under age three worked in the FRG in 1976, the lowest rate for all our countries. Moreover, it is the only country in the group where female labor force participation actually declined, albeit by very little, between 1975 and 1976. (The long-term projections continue to indicate growth, and probably extensive growth, in female labor force participation rates.)[11]

The major change in labor market behavior over the last decade, however, has been the increase in labor force participation by married women:

Labor Force Participation of Married Women

1961	33%
1966	34%
1970	36%
1975	39%

In 1975, one-third of the children under age three (541,000) had working mothers. Although somewhat more mothers work part time among those with very young children, in general over 60 percent of the FRG women who are in the labor force work full time (40 or more hours per week).

The population of the FRG is 62 million. As has the GDR, the FRG has already gone below zero growth. Indeed, its rate of population decline was second only to the GDR, and now may be greater than that of any other country. Its birth rate is declining steadily, and the greater part of the decline is due to reduced fertility among the German population. If it were not for the birth rate among children born to foreigners (the "guestworker" population), the FRG's birth rate would show an even greater decline:

Crude Birth Rate per 1,000

1973	10.3
1974	10.1
1975	9.8

No. of Live Births

1972	701,214
1974	626,373
1975	600,512
1976	602,851

Under-3 Cohort Size

1965	3.1 million
1970	2.6 million (2.5 million German)
1975	1.8 million (1.5 million German)

A variety of pressures influenced the expansion of preschool programs, so that legislation was passed aiming at 75 percent coverage in kindergarten for children aged three to six. This rate has been reached, even though the kindergarten day is short (as is the elementary school day), from 8:00 A.M. to 1:00 P.M. However, at least half the kindergartens now offer care to 4:00 P.M. if needed, and there are increasing numbers of all-day elementary schools at which children may remain until 5:00 P.M. As in the United States no systematic provision exists for caring for infants and toddlers, and family day care is preferred, if one can talk of preferences in a country where less than 5 percent of all very young children—and 15 percent of the children under three of working mothers—are in any kind of out-of-home child care. Here grandmothers are still the primary child care institution, caring for almost half (46 percent) the children of employed women.

Given the FRG's attitude toward the traditional family, and its current concerns with unemployment, low birth rate, and the state of the economy generally, it is understandable that the only widely discussed current policy and program proposals are 1) to provide an income-tested cash benefit to mothers who remain at home to care for their infants, and 2) to experiment with high-quality family day care especially for the children of low-income women.

We would characterize the FRG child care policy as a policy in ferment in which conflicting values (to encourage natality; to draw women out of the labor market; to respond to deprivation, poverty, and family problems within a context of limited resources for social programs; to cope with a growing tendency toward two-earner couples) result in a stand-off, for now.

UNITED STATES

The entry of women into the labor force occurred with astonishing suddenness and rapidity in the United States, as it did in several other countries. And as in those countries, the pattern is noteworthy because it is characterized by the growth in labor force participation of married women living with their husbands, and increasingly, of those with preschool-aged children.

The participation rate of women in the labor force increased from about one-third in 1950 to almost one-half (48.1 percent) in 1976.[12] At the same time, primarily as a result of earlier retirement, the participation rate of men in the labor force decreased from 86 to 78 percent. Sixty-nine percent of the population is in the productive years (18–64). Participation rates for men between the ages of twenty-five to fifty-four, the peak years of family responsibilities, are a little above 90 percent. Among women, 67 percent of those in their early twenties and close to 60 percent of those aged twenty-five to fifty-four are in the labor force. This trend is expected to continue, with still more women entering the labor force during the next decade, and with a projected participation rate in 1990 of 67 percent for those aged twenty-five to fifty-four. Two-thirds of these women work full time, which is defined as thirty-five or more hours per week.

Since World War II, the trend in labor force participation of women has been clear-cut. The first cohort to expand its participation rate consisted of those women aged forty-five to fifty-nine who had largely completed their child rearing responsibilities. Since the mid-1960s, however, the greatest labor force increases have occurred among women under age forty-five, especially married women living with their husbands. Thus, the proportion of married women in the labor force with school-aged children nearly doubled between 1950 and 1976, and the participation rate of wives with preschool children tripled. Moreover, the proportion of mothers participating in the labor force grew at a faster rate than for all other women; by 1977 half of the mothers of children under eighteen (50.7 percent) were in the labor force, as against 48 percent of women generally. By 1979 these rates were 54 and 51 percent, respectively.

Since 1970, the greatest labor force increases have occurred among married women under age thirty-five, with children under age three. Furthermore, the long-term pattern, in which large numbers of women withdraw from the labor force in their twenties to rear children, has apparently ended. Not only were close to 60 percent of the twenty- to twenty-four-year-olds in the labor force in 1970, and 67 percent in 1977, but for the first time there has been no significant decline in labor force participation for women aged twenty-five to twenty-nine, the prime childbearing years. This suggests increased commitment of women to permanent labor force attachment and work behavior increasingly similar to that of men.

Finally, we would note two more developments: 1) Among women aged twenty-five to fifty-four the effect of higher education on labor force participation is particularly pronounced, with the labor force participation rate for women college graduates being over 70 percent. Given the rapid and steady increase in women's educational attainment since 1950, there is great likelihood of higher overall rates for women. 2) Women with one or two children tend to work more than those with three or more. The long-term trend toward fewer children should contribute still further to this growth of the female component in the labor force.

In short, women are working in growing numbers and there is increasingly less difference between the labor market behavior of mothers and that of all women, and between women and men. Moreover, responses to national surveys regarding women's attitudes toward work indicate that they, like men, view work as central to their identities and would continue to work even if they could live comfortably without earned income.

Still, women, like men, work primarily for economic reasons. Forty-three percent of the women in the labor force are single, divorced, separated, or widowed. Another 25 percent are married to men earning less than $10,500 per year. (Median family income in 1976 was $15,923; it rose to $16,009 in 1977.) Women who work full time, all year, contribute 39 percent to family income.

U.S. society has changed, and the two-earner family has emerged as the dominant family type. Over half of all families and nearly half of all two-parent families include an employed woman. Over half of the mothers in the United States are now in the labor force. In 1979, the figures were 62 percent for mothers of school-aged children, 52 percent for mothers of children aged three to six, and 41 percent for mothers of children under age three. Nearly 4 million children under age three had mothers in the labor force in 1976.

The United States had an estimated total population of 220,000,000 in 1978. The birth rate has been declining steadily for some years and at present the United States is approaching zero population growth.

Crude Birth Rate per 1,000 Population

1970	18.2
1974	14.9
1975	14.7
1976	14.7

No. of Live Births

1974	3,166,000
1975	3,149,000
1976	3,165,000

Under-3 Cohort Size

1965	11.6 million	
1970	10.6 million	
1975	9.4 million	
1979 (projected)	9.5 million (median)	10.8 (high); 8.6 (low)

In spite of the implications of these figures, the United States thus far has taken a "do nothing" approach. The growth in female labor force participation has been largely ignored until the last few years when the mass media have begun to identify this development as harbinger of a major social revolution. There has been nothing done by the government that in any way would indicate a policy response. Indeed, one might say the reverse has been true. Participation in preschool programs by the three-to-five-year-old children of working mothers has increased significantly, but most of this has been in private programs and much goes unnoticed. Thus far, there has been only a small expansion of public preschool programs. Although many parents use the terms "preschools" and "day care" interchangeably, the U.S. debate still tends to separate the two into educational and social welfare programs. Infant and toddler care was not recognized as a distinctive child care mode until very recently either in discussions or in regulations. Nor was the need for such care acknowledged. Many are convinced that any care other than a mother's own is harmful, although clearly many children are not now being cared for by their mothers. There has been some provision of cash subsidies for very low-income single mothers with young children (AFDC), but most support has been contingent on labor market withdrawal (or has provided a disincentive for labor force participation), not the reverse. There has not been any significant policy regarding low-income, two-parent families.

The United States has neither an explicit labor market policy regarding women nor an explicit population policy. Furthermore, although rhetorical statements are made regarding children, the United States has no explicit child care policy and certainly none for families with very young children. Indeed, the U.S. policy seems to be that the absence of any policy is a good way of avoiding dealing with any possible value conflicts.

Yet the result of having no explicit policy is that as more and more women with young children are working, more and more children are being cared for in varied, disparate, and complicated ways, with consequences for families, children, and society that we have yet to realize.

SUMMARY

Thus far, we have identified the central policy issue of concern here, described certain labor market trends in all industralized countries, and de-

TABLE 1.6

Crude Birth Rates per 1,000 Population for All Countries

	GDR	*Hungary*	*Sweden*	*France*	*FRG*	*U.S.*
1968	14.3	–	14.3	16.7	16.1	17.6
1974	10.6	17.7	13.5	15.2	10.1	14.9
1975	10.6	18.4	12.6	14.1	9.7	14.7
1976	11.6	17.5	13.8	13.6	9.8	14.7
1977	13.3 (est.)	16.7	11.9	14.	9.5	15.3

TABLE 1.7
Under-3 Cohort Size, 1965, 1970, 1975

	1965	1970	1975
GDR	820,413	706,933	532,048
Hungary	381,583	444,100	518,728
Sweden	335,560	330,799	323,463
France	2,560,000[a]	2,509,800	2,529,000
FRG	3,100,000	3,600,000	1,800,000
		(2.5 million German)	(1.5 million German)
U.S.	11,600,000	10,600,000	9,400,000

[a]1968

scribed the societal context in each of the six countries whose child care policies we intend to analyze. Tables 1.6 and 1.7 present comparative demographic statistics.

We turn now toward one component of a child care policy: the social benefits—cash and in-kind—with which these countries provide families to support the care of very young children.

NOTES

1. Although we have no question about the importance and value of "home work," the term "work" is used here to mean market work.

Recent scholarship has revealed that this dichotomy between work and family did not occur at the same time for all families (or all family members) in all industries, or in all places. Over time, however, this has become the dominant pattern. The literature on this subject is far too extensive to be reviewed here. For illustrative purposes see Tamara K. Hareven, "Modernization and Family History: Perspectives on Social Change," *Signs* (Autumn 1976), 2:190–206; Peter Laslett, "Characteristics of the Western Family Considered Over Time," *Journal of Family History* (Summer 1977), 2:89–115; Rosabeth Moss Kanter, *Work and Family in the United States: A Critical Review and Agenda for Research and Policy* (New York: Russell Sage Foundation, 1977).

2. For the consequences for children, see Urie Bronfenbrenner, "The Origins of Alienation," *Scientific American* (1974), 231:53–61, and "Who Cares for America's Children?" in Victor C. Vaughan, III and T. Berry

Brazelton, eds., *The Family – Can It Be Saved?* (Chicago: Yearbook Medical Publishers, 1976), pp. 3–32.

For the consequences for women, see George Brown and Tirrell Harris, *Social Origins of Depression* (New York: Free Press, 1978); Ann Oakley, *Housewife* (London: Allen Lane, 1974); and Nickie Fonda and Peter Moss, eds., *Mothers in Employment* (Uxbridge, U.K.: Brunel University, 1976).

For a very different perspective – the negative consequences on family life when the separation of work and home occur in a country undergoing modernization, where women historically have always been in the labor force – see Christina Oppong, "Modernization and Family Change in Ghana – With Special Reference to Work" (unpublished paper prepared for Aspen Institute–Iran Workshop, Iran, May 25–June 2, 1978).

3. Kanter, *Work and Family in the United States*; Rhona and Robert Rapoport, "Work and Family in Contemporary Society," *American Sociological Review* (June 1965), 30:381–94; and R. and R. Rapoport, *Dual Career Families Re-examined* (New York: Harper & Row, 1976).

4. Bronfenbrenner, "The Origins of Alienation" and "Who Cares for America's Children?"

5. Both popular literature and scholarly studies are full of such material. See, for example, Selma Fraiberg, *Every Child's Birthright: In Defense of Mothering* (New York: Basic Books, 1977).

6. For some discussion of this development, see Alfred J. Kahn and Sheila B. Kamerman, "Child Care," in *Social Services in International Perspective* (Washington, D.C.: U.S. Government Printing Office, 1977), pp. 146–90.

7. These two developments paralleled one another in Europe during the 1960s. That they could be viewed as alternate sources of labor seems dramatically clear if one compares the FRG and the GDR, for example. For some discussion of this point, see Anne H. Nelson, *The One World of Working Women* (Washington, D.C.: U.S. Department of Labor, Bureau of International Labor Affairs, Monograph 1, August 1978).

8. For some discussion of this in the United States, see Ralph Smith, *Women in the Labor Force in 1990* (Washington, D.C.: The Urban Institute, 1979). For European trends, see "Current Labor Force Participation Rates in OECD Countries," in *Equal Opportunities for Women* (Paris: OECD, 1979), pp. 16–27.

9. Charles F. Westoff, "Marriage and Fertility in the Developed Countries," *Scientific American* (December 1978), 239:51–57.

10. Ibid.

11. OECD, *Equal Opportunities for Women*, pp. 19–26.

12. Robert W. Bednarzik and Deborah P. Klein, "Labor Force Trends: A Synthesis and Analysis," *Monthly Labor Review* (October 1977), pp. 3–12; Howard Hayghe, "Marital and Family Characteristics of Workers,

March 1977," *Monthly Labor Review* (February 1978), pp. 51-54, table 3. For 1978, see chapter 6 below. For further discussion, see Elizabeth Waldman et al., "Working Mothers in the 1970's: A Look at the Statistics," *Monthly Labor Review* (October 1979), pp. 39-49, and Beverly L. Johnson, "Marital and Family Characteristics of the Labor Force, March 1979," *Monthly Labor Review* (April 1980), pp. 48-52.

Two

CHILD CARE POLICY:
THE FAMILY BENEFITS

The word "benefit" is derived from the Latin words meaning "to do good" or "to do well." Webster defines "benefit" as meaning "an act of kindness," or a "gift," or "whatever promotes welfare." "Service" is defined as "the performance of labor for the benefit of another." The distinction between a social "benefit" and a social "service," although far from clear-cut, is that between (a benefit) a *unilateral transfer* (cash or in-kind) made by the society at large, through government actions, directly or indirectly, *to certain individual or family recipients*; and (a service) *a payment* made directly or indirectly *to the provider of help, or direct provision of such help under public auspices*. Illustrations of the most important benefits are: social insurance benefits; public (social) assistance benefits; tax benefits. Illustrations of services are: meals services (meals-on-wheels, school meals); homemaker–home help services; well-baby clinics; nursing homes; public schools.

In this chapter, our concern is with those social *benefits* (cash and in-kind) and those legal rights provided to all (or some) parents, contingent on the presence of dependent children in the family and household. We are especially interested in those benefits which may in some way be construed to facilitate child rearing and care of very young children. In contrast, in the two subsequent chapters our focus will be on *services* and programs providing care for the very young child. Following this, we will turn to the question of the relationship between the benefits and the services offered to families with children under the age of three.

SOCIAL BENEFITS FOR PARENTING

Our primary concern in this chapter is with benefits affecting the parenting roles and responsibilities of adults. Although our major focus is on benefits designed to support the fulfillment of these roles by the parents themselves, we recognize that some benefits *may be used*, also, to purchase child care services from others, while still other benefits *can be used only* for such purchase.

We begin by exploring the concept of social benefits for parenting, the types of benefits available, and the questions to be addressed in analyzing the benefits provided in each country.

THE NATURE OF THE BENEFITS

Benefits to support or supplement parenting include both cash benefits, provided directly or indirectly to parents, and in-kind benefits provided similarly. Although the distinction between a cash and an in-kind benefit is fairly straightforward, the purpose of instituting—or selecting—one or the other policy instrument may be more complex.

Thus, a cash benefit usually involves the transfer of money by the government directly to the individual recipient. The beneficiary can use this income in any way he or she sees fit. Family allowances and paid maternity leaves are examples of cash benefits. Such a cash transfer can also be made indirectly, through the tax system as, for example, a tax allowance (deduction or exemption) or tax credit contingent on the presence of a child in the family.

An in-kind benefit also involves direct or indirect income transfer, except that in this case the transfer is limited in its use to a particular good, commodity, or service. Thus food stamps, housing allowances, entitlement to payment of prenatal health care are all illustrations of in-kind benefits provided directly to the recipient.

An inventory of the range of social benefits and rights relevant to our concern here would include the following:

1. cash or in-kind maternity or childbirth benefits;
2. paid maternity or parental leaves for employed women or parents following childbirth;

3. paid maternity or parental leaves for employed parents if no place is available in child care programs;

4. unpaid but job-protected maternity or parental leaves for employed parents;

5. cash allowance (children's allowance, family allowance) provided to a parent because of the presence of a child in a household;

6. cash allowance provided to an employed parent to purchase child care by someone other than the parent;

7. cash allowance for employed women who withdraw from the labor force and remain at home to care for a child until the child reaches a specified age;

8. cash allowance for mothers, regardless of prior labor force status, who remain at home to care for a child until a specified age (mother's wage);

9. cash allowances for families in which there is only one wage-earner (single wage-earner allowances);

10. special credits for social security entitlements for mothers who stay home to care for their children (a calculated benefit in social security, not dependent upon payment of the the usual contribution);

11. tax credits or tax deductions for costs of child care;

12. special housing allowances or priorities for families with children;

13. special benefits for single-parent families;

14. special benefits or allowances covering the use of a relative as a child care person (or permission to include relative under regular benefit);

15. nursing mothers' benefit;

16. special clothing allowances or food subsidy grants for families with children;

17. leave from work or an insurance benefit at home to care for a sick child;

18. allowances to pay for child health services (special maternal and child health programs for all children); and

19. any other special benefits intended to facilitate child care or child rearing by mother or other, for example, statutory provisions for flextime or part-time employment, for flexible workplace arrangements, etc.

THE FUNCTION(S) OF THE BENEFIT

Our primary focus is on statutory benefits for normal, average families, intended to facilitate child care or child rearing by a parent (or parents) or some other specifically designated person or persons, although we are also interested in nonstatutory benefits, provided by employers as fringe benefits. Given this array of benefits, many of which can be found in at least five of the six countries under discussion, one question raised is whether or not there is consensus regarding the function or purpose in providing the benefits.

Clearly, one can use the manifest functions of childbearing, child rearing, and child caring as the bases for classifying these benefits, but obviously there is overlap, there are other manifest purposes, and even more important, there are significant latent functions of these benefits.

To illustrate: Special lump sum cash maternity benefits provided at the time of childbirth, layettes, or other birth "packages" consisting of clothing, diapers, a crib, and so forth, payment of hospitalization at the time of childbirth and immediately after, all constitute examples of benefits related to childbearing. Child care allowances and child care tax credits to permit the purchase of child care services, and child care grants to subsidize an at-home role for a mother are illustrations of child care benefits, while family or child allowances, single wage-earner allowances, housing allowances, flextime would be viewed as benefits facilitating child rearing. On the other hand, a paid maternity leave could be viewed as a benefit related to childbearing (it eliminates some of the stress at the time of childbirth), child rearing (it assures mother's presence at home at a critical stage of the child's development) and/or child care (it facilitates mother's care of the child).

Furthermore, all these benefits are, in essence, income transfers, and as such can be described as income maintenance policies to assure some kind of economic security for families with children. Under this general rubric, however, we can distinguish benefits designed to protect against different conditions of income inadequacy. Thus, for example, benefits may be provided:

To supplement normal individual income in recognition of the fact that the standard of living of families declines with the advent of children, that it declines further with each additional child, and that children represent a "public good" and thus the costs of child rearing should be borne, in part, by the society at large, including those who have no children.

To replace earnings lost temporarily as a consequence of maternity, in recognition of the fact that as more and more women enter the labor force and the two-earner family emerges as the dominant family form, temporary absence from employment (and income loss) at the time of childbirth is as much a normal risk in an industrialized society as the loss of income as a consequence of unemployment, disability, or retirement may be; the risk being even more severe for the growing numbers of single parent, sole wage-earner families.

To substitute for earnings in recognition of the value of the woman's at-home role when children are very young, by providing a cash grant unrelated to previous earnings but representing some form of payment for the mother at home, on condition that she substitutes home "work" for market work.

Although a primary function of these benefits (or of several of the most significant) may be to socialize the costs of child rearing or to attenuate the financial burdens of child rearing—by some form of redistribution from those without children to those with children—at least one other implicit function, purpose, or goal is to assure that the children continue to be borne and reared, and—insofar as we are concerned ultimately with the kind of adults they turn out to be—to be well cared for. Thus there is a strong likelihood that in countries approaching or at zero population growth some attention will be paid to making it easier for adults to bear, rear, and care for children.

At the same time, labor market concerns, either manifest or latent, may underlie benefit choice. Fear of growing unemployment or anxiety about a tight labor market may lead to the development of incentives for women to withdraw from or to enter the labor market.

A still more comprehensive listing of possible functions, manifest or latent, could include any or all of the following:

- to assure the physical and emotional health of children
- to compensate for familial deprivation
- to compensate for the costs of working
- to compensate for the loss of benefits related to the presence of an at-home wife
- to support the family unit rather than individual family members
- to facilitate equality between men and women
- to facilitate closer relationships between work and family life
- to contribute to pluralism in the society.

Reviewing the planning objectives as discussed in different countries, our conclusion is that the family income support, labor market, and population policy objectives are the most significant. All these may converge, however, around the larger objective of assuring that there will be a certain number of children born into the society, and that those children will be given good care.

Given our particular concern with how societies are responding to the growing trend for most adults in the childbearing/rearing ages to be in the labor force and, therefore, needing to manage home and family responsibilities while also fulfilling work and labor market roles, our primary focus will be on the extent to which the benefits in a country are designed to support one of the following policy objectives:

1. An at-home role for women—or a parent—with very young children, without income loss to the family.
2. A wage-earning role for women—or parents—with very young children, without negative consequences for children.
3. Either or both options, depending on the preference of the woman, parent, or family involved.

Whether these purposes are manifest or latent, mutually consistent or potentially in conflict, rhetorical or realizable, remains to be seen. Even more important may be the question of whether provision of the benefits has resulted in the achievement of any of these purposes—and whether other unanticipated consequences have also occurred (and what, if known, the effects of these have been).

WHO BENEFITS? THE ELIGIBILITY QUESTION

In order to assess the validity of declaring one or another purpose as primary, it becomes essential to know which benefits exist in each country, who is entitled to receive them, by what criteria, and with what consequences. We turn now to the individual countries and to the specific benefits provided in each.

The order in which the countries are described below proceeds from those countries with the most extensive relevant benefit coverage in relation to the under-threes (Hungary, then Sweden) to those with the fewest benefits (the FRG and the United States). Provisions in France and the GDR can be assessed differently, depending on whether attention is limited exclusively to families with children under age three or is directed to families with minor children generally.

HUNGARY

Hungary is the country that provides the most extensive statutory social benefits supporting an at-home role for women with young children. A few nonstatutory benefits are also provided by work enterprises, unions, and voluntary agencies, but these are relatively unimportant.

The most significant social benefits are directed primarily at supporting childbearing, early child care, and child rearing for children up to age three. Three benefits represent the heart of Hungary's early child care policy: a maternity benefit; a maternity leave; a child care allowance. The last two are the most important and the third, the child care allowance or grant, represents a significant social invention in the family policy of the last fifteen years, creating something of a stir in international family policy discussion and influencing the debate in several countries. Czechoslovakia has copied the policy in a modified form, and support for a similar policy in their respective countries has come from sources as diverse as Swedish conservatives and French leftists.

In the discussion that follows, it is important to keep in mind that comparing wages internationally is very difficult, particularly where the socialist countries are concerned. Many basic items are heavily subsidized (housing, food, children's clothing) or provided free (health, medical, dental care), thus offsetting some of the wage differential. While we provide an approximation of foreign currencies in U.S. dollar equivalents, readers are reminded that personal disposable income buys different proportions of one's living requirements in each country. Currency equivalents are here cited for the spring of 1977.

The *maternity benefit* is a lump sum cash benefit of 2,500 forints, equal to about 25 percent more than the average monthly wage of a Hungarian female worker. (One forint = $.05.) The benefit level has been increased over the years, and, in effect, is adjusted as if it were indexed. The benefit is given to a woman immediately following childbirth. The amount is larger if there are multiple births and smaller (1,000 forints) if certain eligibility criteria are not met. The benefit was first provided in 1949; however, from then until 1974, the award was made partly in cash and partly in kind (diapers, clothing, and so forth). Only since 1974 has it been an all-cash benefit.

The major purpose of the benefit is to assure the health of infant and mother, as well as to mitigate the extra costs of childbearing.

TABLE 2.1

A Six-Country Inventory of Statutory Benefits: What Is Available (1976)

Benefit	Hungary	France	Sweden	GDR	FRG	U.S.
1) Cash or in-kind maternity or childbirth benefits	Yes	Yes		Yes	Yes	Nonstatutory (N.S.) only
2) Paid maternity or parental leaves for employed women or parents	Yes*	Yes*	Yes*	Yes*	Yes*	N. S. only
3) Paid maternity or parental leaves for employed parents if no place is available in child care program				Yes*		
4) Unpaid but job-protected leaves for employed mothers or parents	Yes	Yes	Yes	Yes	Yes	
5) Cash allowance (children's allowance, family allowance) provided a parent because of the presence of a child in a household	Yes*	Yes*	Yes	Yes	Yes	
6) Cash allowance provided an employed parent to purchase child care by someone other than the parent		Yes**				
7) Cash allowance for employed women who withdraw from the labor force and remain at home to care for a child until the child reaches a specified age	Yes*					
8) Cash allowance for mothers (or a parent) regardless of prior labor force status, who remain at home to care for a child until a specified age			Yes***		Yes****	Yes
9) Single wage-earner allowance		Yes**				
10) Special credits for social security entitlements for mothers who stay home to care for their children (a calculated benefit in social security, without paying the usual contribution)		Yes			Yes	
11) Tax credits or tax deductions for costs of child care		Yes	Yes*	Yes	Yes	Yes
12) Special housing allowances or priorities for families with children		Yes	Yes	Yes	Yes	Yes
13) Special benefits for single-parent families		Yes	Yes		Yes	Yes
14) Special benefits or allowances covering the use of a relative as a child care person (or permission to include relative under regular benefit)						
15) Nursing mothers' benefit	Yes	Yes		Yes	Yes	
16) Special clothing allowances or food subsidy grants for families with children	Yes	Yes		Yes		Yes
17) Leave from work or an insurance benefit at home to care for a sick child	Yes		Yes*	Yes	Yes	
18) Entitlement to child health services (special maternal and child health programs for all children)	Yes	Yes	Yes	Yes	Yes	
19) Any other special benefits intended to facilitate child care or child rearing by mother or other	1		2	3		

1 = extra holidays for mothers of children under 14; shorter workday for mothers of children under age 1
2 = statutory provision for part-time employment as part of parent insurance
3 = extra personal holidays (3 per month) for mothers after specified number of years at work (or after 4 years, for a single parent)

Yes* = of special importance
Yes** = now replaced by a new family allowance called the *complément familial* or family allowance supplement
Yes*** = a minimum daily payment is available to all women covered by health insurance, following childbirth while they are at home, for a specified period of time
Yes**** = a much more extensive program has been proposed and is now being debated

The benefit is universal, granted to all women following childbirth, *but contingent on their receipt of prenatal medical care*. To qualify for the full benefit, women must have had four prenatal medical visits (unless precluded from doing so for medical reasons), at least one within the first 140 days after conception. If less than four visits are made, the benefit level is reduced. A minimum benefit is available as long as at least one visit is made.

Over 97 percent of all births in 1975 were covered by this benefit. The overwhelming majority of women received the full benefit; 16 percent received a reduced benefit.

The benefit is financed out of general revenue and administered by the social security agency in the central government. The average benefit in 1975 was 2,258 forints per recipient. The relative value of the benefit is as follows: full benefit = 116.4 percent of average monthly disposable income; average benefit = 105 percent of average monthly disposable income; and reduced benefit = 46.6 percent of average monthly disposable income. The total cost for 1975 was 431 million forints.

The benefit is viewed as effective in increasing prenatal care and thus as contributing to a decline in infant mortality. There is no debate about it, nor any plans to modify it.

The Hungarian *maternity leave* is of much greater significance. It is a wage-related cash benefit for employed women, covering five months around the time of childbirth. A woman is entitled to take up to four weeks before expected parturition, but neither this leave nor the postchildbirth leave is mandated. The benefit level is equal to 100 percent of average earnings over the last nine months worked in the previous two years. If the woman worked less than nine months but at least six months, her benefit would equal 65 percent of her average earnings.

The benefit was instituted in 1948 when it covered only six weeks after childbirth. In 1953 it was expanded to twelve weeks and by 1963 to the present level, twenty weeks.

The functions of this benefit are 1) to provide a replacement for earnings lost on account of childbirth; and 2) to ensure maternal and child health by alleviating the economic pressures on a new mother to return to work very quickly.

The benefit is universal. Following childbirth, all women are eligible for the full benefit as long as they have worked at least nine months in the previous two years, or for the partial benefit as long as they have worked at least six months in that period. Coverage has been almost complete since the late 1960s, as has participation. In 1975, 53,000 women, representing 1.3 percent of the total labor force, received the benefit. The average benefit is worth about 80 forints per day, or about 11,150 forints for twenty weeks.

The benefit is financed out of the government budget, and the total expenditure for 1975 was 1.276 million forints. It is administered by the social insurance agency.

The *child care allowance* or grant is Hungary's family policy "invention." It has emerged as an important policy alternative in international discussions of child and family policy, and is, of course, of great significance within Hungary. It is a flat-rate cash grant (the benefit level is the same for all recipients), plus an unpaid leave from work (with full job protection, pension entitlement, and seniority) available to women at the expiration of their maternity leave. The grant is available for a period covering up to thirty-one months or the time when the child reaches its third birthday, at which time children enter the preschool program. The grant was first introduced in 1967, following the provision in 1963 of an unpaid maternity leave available to women until their child was three. In 1974, the benefit levels were changed somewhat (see below). In 1976, the policy was modified further, to permit interruption of the leave once a year for a return to work, and to permit beneficiaries to work as family day care mothers (see below). The benefit can be used serially, if additional children are born.

As of 1975, the benefit level was 910 forints a month for the first child, 1,010 for a second, and 1,110 for a third child. The benefit provided to a woman with one child was equal to about 40 percent of the average wage of a young, unskilled worker.

The functions of the benefit are multiple. It was originally instituted for labor market reasons—to provide an incentive for unskilled women to withdraw from the labor force at a time when the economy was not growing and there was increasing concern about finding employment for the "baby boom" population of young people then entering the labor market. It was also expected to serve an important child care objective, at a time when there was clearly an inadequate supply of good day care centers for very young children. The importance of high-quality care for very young children, and the high costs of such care, were of growing concern, and there was a desire to give priority to increasing the quantity and quality of preschool programs for children aged three to six. Thus an implicit function of this benefit was to encourage parents to take their children out of day care centers (or not even enter them in these programs) and care for them at home, although this was not explicit government policy.

In 1974, a distinctly pronatalist component was added, when for the first time benefit levels were adjusted so that a higher grant was provided for second and third children. Another modification occurred in 1976, in response to an increasingly tight labor market, especially in certain fields highly dependent on female labor. This modification, permitting interruption of the child care leave once each year to return to work and also permitting recipients to work as family day care mothers, clearly reflected a changed labor market situation in the country at large.

Throughout its history, however, the benefit has had one other labor market function: to provide an incentive for young women to enter the labor market in order to qualify for this benefit, and thus to introduce them to the labor market at an early age.

The benefit is universal. Women are eligible if they have worked for at least twelve months before childbirth, or, if they were full-time students, if they worked at least ninety days after completing their studies.

Coverage is very extensive, as is participation: 89 percent of the women with one child use the benefit; 82 percent of twenty to twenty-four year olds are home on child care leave at a given time. Of all eligible women, 72 percent used the benefit in 1967, 66 percent in 1969, 86 percent in 1974, and 80 percent in 1976.

There is some difference in participation in relation to level of education. Thus, 81 percent of the women who completed only primary school use the benefit, 76 percent of those who completed only secondary school, and 56 percent of those who completed higher education.

The amount of time taken for child care leave varies. Full leave (until the child is age three) is used by one-third of the recipients, and twenty-four months (median amount taken) is used by half. Eighteen months is the modal amount of time taken by educated women.

The benefit is financed from the government budget and administered by the social insurance fund. The total costs in 1976 were 3,476,000 forints.

Among the consequences of this policy are the following:

Young women have entered the labor force early.

Take-up has increased steadily. The percentage of women using the benefit has increased over time, as has the duration of benefit use. Indeed, since use of the child care leave is defined as labor force participation, it is worth noting that labor force participation rates are higher for women with children under three than for those with older children—a pattern that would be unique if not for the characteristics of this benefit.

If one excludes those women at home on child care leave, the labor force participation rate for women with children under age three is 33 percent, the same as the rate in the FRG and lower than that of all other participating countries. Thus, clearly, the policy is effective in getting women away from the workplace and back into the home. On the other hand, although almost all women use some portion of the benefit, highly trained and educated women tend to use it for a much briefer time—until their child is one or one-and-one-half. Either they cannot afford the income loss or the career interruption, or both, or they have other preferences. Thus, the benefit appears to encourage labor force withdrawal more among the low-skilled and unskilled women, who find a greater advantage in receipt of a grant equaling almost half their normal wage. However, since the benefit guarantees job protection to users and implicitly requires a return to work after two-and-one-half years home on child care leave (unless there is a second child) it has also been effective in maintaining a labor market attachment among even the low-skilled beneficiaries.

TABLE 2.2

Hungary: Mothers Classified by Duration of the Period on Child Care Leave

Time at Home on Child Care Leave	Total	Type of Work	
		Blue Collar	White Collar
Less than 6 months	11.9%	7.8%	18.1%
7–12 months	15.2	12.4	19.5
13–18 months	12.2	10.8	14.5
19–24 months	11.6	11.2	12.2
25–30 months	13.5	13.9	13.0
31 months or more	35.6	43.9	22.7
Total	100.0	100.0	100.0

NOTE: Data on mothers returning to work from child care leave between July 1, 1973 and June 30, 1974.

SOURCE: *Main Data on Child Care Grant, 1967-1974* (Central Statistical Office, 1975).

Several other pronatalist measures were instituted in Hungary in 1974 and 1975, including housing priorities and increased allowances. It is hard to pinpoint any fertility effects that could be ascribed to these measures. Thus far, the only certain effect is a calendar effect: first children are born sooner after marriage, and second children are born closer to the first. There has been no increase in the birth of third children, and it is too soon to ascertain whether any long-term increase in the total number of births has occurred. There is some concern regarding the negative consequence for maternal and child health of the decrease in child spacing.

There has also been some concern that the child care grant can have a regressive effect on male-female equality in that it fosters a return to traditional intrafamily roles, which become harder to modify as couples live together longer.

The child care allowance continues to be the most important family policy benefit in Hungary for families with children under the age of three, and as such remains at the center of the family policy debate there. Among the proposals suggested for modifying the benefit, the following are the most important:[1]

To make the benefit a parental entitlement rather than a right for mothers alone.

To expand eligibility to include grandmothers, so that they could, if they wished, withdraw from the labor force and remain at home to care for a grandchild while their daughter (or daughter-in-law) worked.

To make the benefit wage-related in order to provide real income protection for families.

To index the benefit, if it remains a flat grant, to reflect increases in the cost of living.

To lower the entry age of preschool to age two or two-and-one-half to permit women more options in deciding how long to use the benefit.

To decrease the value of the benefit over time, with the highest level the first year (this proposal is being made now, particularly with the growing need for women in the labor force).

To provide job training opportunities for women while at home receiving the benefit to attenuate the social isolation of the at-home role, and to make long-term occupational advancement easier for women who still suffer from the consequences of occupational segregation.

TABLE 2.3
Hungary: Share of Deciles of Population in Various Types of Income and Benefits

Deciles of Population	Income Gained by Any Type of Work	Family Allowance	Child Care Grant	Benefit Covering the 20 Weeks of Maternity Leave	Maternity Benefit	Benefits in Cash Together	Total Disposable Income
Lowest decile = 1.	3%	16%	4%	2%	9%	13%	4%
2.	5	16	12	3	8	12	6
3.	6	15	16	8	11	11	7
4.	8	13	16	11	12	10	8
5.	9	11	13	15	14	9	9
6.	10	9	11	12	11	9	10
7.	10	7	9	15	12	9	11
8.	13	6	9	13	10	9	12
9.	15	4	6	12	8	9	14
Highest decile = 10.	21	3	4	9	5	9	19
Total	100	100	100	100	100	100	100

Among the other benefits available in Hungary that facilitate child care and child rearing are:

A *paid sick leave* available to employed women or employed sole parents so they may remain at home to care for a sick child. The leave is unlimited for a working mother with a child under one. It is available for up to sixty days for the mother (or sole parent) of a child age one to three, and for thirty days for the mother of a child aged three to six (and sixty days for a sole parent). Participation has almost quadrupled since 1971. The average use of the benefit is nine to ten days per year. Average daily cost is 55.4 forints. The benefit level is 75 percent of average wage for those who have worked two or more years, and 65 percent for those who have worked less. Use of this benefit to care for sick children constitutes 6 percent of all sick leave for employees.

A *family allowance*, a universal, flat-rate cash grant designed to supplement income for families with children. The benefit is 360 forints per month per child and is provided to 1) a sole employed parent with at least one child; 2) a two-parent family with at least one employed parent (who worked full time for the prior month) with at least two children; 3) a one- or two-parent family with a handicapped child. Most beneficiaries are two-parent, two-children families.

Housing priorities are available to families with three or more children.

A specified number of *paid personal holidays* are also permitted employed parents of children under age fourteen: two days for those with one child, five days for those with two, and nine days for parents of three or more children. The daily benefit level is equal to average earnings.

Summary

Hungary provides for almost all women:

1. A uniform, cash benefit on childbirth, contingent on receipt of prenatal care, equal to more than a one-month wage for an average young female worker.
2. A paid leave from employment at full wage, lasting five months, at or following childbirth.
3. A flat-rate cash grant equal to about 40 percent of a woman's average wage in addition to an unpaid but protected leave from work, until a child is age three.

4. A uniform cash benefit for each child in a family, equal to more than one-third the average wage for families with two children.
5. A specified number of paid sick days to care for a sick child at home as well as several paid personal days each year, all at close to full wage.
6. Several special benefits in kind, including housing allowances, food and clothing grants (and subsidies), scholarships.

The combined value of all these benefits, those for all children and those for the under-threes, represents 36 percent of the average total costs of child rearing. Sixty-four percent of child rearing costs are covered by the earned income of parents. Two-thirds of the benefits are in the form of in-kind benefits. Of the remaining third, half are delivered as family allowances and half as other cash benefits plus educational allowances. These combined benefits do function to redistribute income, albeit very modestly, to those families in greater economic need (see table 2.3.)

However, *a much higher proportion of costs—and of income replacement—is achieved for the mothers of very young children under the age of three. Here, social benefits do offer a viable alternative source of income for low-skilled and unskilled women, if not for the more highly trained.*

SWEDEN

The unique characteristic of the extensive Swedish social benefits directed at child caring and child rearing is that they are family-focused, child and *parent entitlements.* That is, the parenting benefits are for either parent, unlike those in other countries which are largely maternity-related, or for the mother—be she a mother at home or a working mother. Moreover, unlike Hungary, where policy is designed to support an economically viable at-home role for women with very young children, or France, where policy is directed at assuring low-income women a choice of roles, *Swedish social benefit policy for families is designed to facilitate management of both roles*—home and family work on the one hand, and market work on the other—*by both men and women,* at the time in their lives when the tension between the two is greatest.

As in France, the Swedish social benefits must be assessed within the larger context of Swedish family policy. Child care benefits are only one component of this policy domain. The overall family policy has as its primary concerns:

1) supplementing family income for families with children;
2) redistributing income, not only from those with no children to those with children, but also from those with more resources to those with less; and
3) assuring equality in the society, between the sexes as well as between the different groups and classes.

The major components of the Swedish benefit package include, therefore, those benefits specific to families with very young children, as well as those available on the basis of other criteria to families with children regardless of their age. Among the most significant in both categories are:

- parent insurance
- parent allowance for the temporary care of children
- child allowance
- housing allowance
- unpaid but job-protected leave until a child is eighteen months old, for either parent
- right to part-time employment (a six-hour day) for either or both parents until a child is eight years old.

Of lesser importance, but also available are: social assistance to single parents; advance payment of maintenance allowances by the court (child support) for single parents; and several tax benefits for families with children, including a tax reduction for married couples with only one earner, regardless of the presence of children, or for single parents with a minor child in the household, and a tax deduction for two-earner families with children.

The Swedish *parent insurance* benefit is a taxable, wage-related cash benefit provided under social insurance, carrying with it an entitlement to pension rights, and contingent on childbirth or adoption. The benefit was established in 1974, replacing the earlier maternity leave benefit. The minimum benefit of 32 Swedish kronor per diem (one Swedish krona = $.24 [spring 1977]) is provided for 270 days to those women who are not in the labor force as well as to those whose wages would not entitle them to more. Otherwise the benefit level is equal to 90 percent of wages up to the maximum wage covered by social insurance.

In addition to a cash payment and entitlement to pension rights, the benefit also gives employed parents (either parent can assign this right to the other) the right to take the first 180 days following childbirth (before

the child is 270 days old and including up to 60 days before expected parturition) as either full days leave from employment or half days, and an
additional 90 days as full, half, or quarter days leave at any time before
the child's eighth birthday. (The operational rules for this entitlement to
part-time work, which began in 1979, vary among the industries and occupations.) The benefit is a replacement for the earlier more traditional
maternity benefit and maternity leave, which were initially established for
health rather than economic reasons.

Its primary purposes are to protect families against temporary loss of
income as a result of childbirth, to protect women against carrying the sole
burden of child care at this time, and to protect the health and well-being
of both mother and child.

The benefit is universal. Eligibility is open to either parent, as long as
that parent does not work for the period of entitlement, regardless of prior
labor force participation. It is contingent only on the birth or adoption of
a child, following at least 180 days health insurance coverage. Housewives
can be covered by health insurance in Sweden. The supplementary benefit
beyond the minimum payment of 32 kronor per day is available solely to
wage earners whose wages entitle them to a higher benefit level. A sixty-
day notice of intent to take up the benefit must be given employers before
commencing or concluding the leave, and parents can use no more than
the specific leave for each period (180 days; 90 days).

Almost all eligible women use the benefit, and many begin before childbirth. Among men, the average use is forty days, and participation has
increased steadily:

Percent of Eligible Fathers Who
Take Up Parent Insurance

1974	2
1975	5-6
1976	8
1977	10
1978	12-14

Two-thirds of those who use the benefit are in private employment.
However, public sector workers make greater use of the benefit (over 11%
in 1977).

The benefit is financed by employer and central government contributions (85% = employer; 15% = general revenue). It is administered by the local social insurance office under the supervision of the National Social Insurance Board. The direct costs of the benefit in 1975 were 1.350 million S.Kr. and, in 1979, 2.540 million S.Kr. (including allowance for the temporary care of children).

Among the consequences of this policy are the following:

1. There has been no measurable dislocation in the job market as a result of this benefit.
2. Eighty percent of the women using the benefit return to work within one year of childbirth.
3. Male eligibility for the benefit is said to have mitigated possible employment discrimination against young women.
4. Men are more likely to share in child care and child rearing during the first year, especially men married to more highly paid women.

It is still too soon to assess the consequences of mandating an entitlement to part-time work.

Some of the issues currently being debated are: mandating a compulsory minimum period for men; extending the insurance to cover a six-hour workday (with the benefit filling in the wage gap) for two-and-one-half or three years, instead of the current nine months; shortening the workday to six hours for all workers in addition to shortening the hours in day care centers for young children.

The parent allowance for the temporary care of children, first established in 1974, is a wage-related cash benefit equal to 90 percent of wages, up to the specified covered amount, paid like a personal sick leave benefit, for an employed parent to remain away from work in order to care for a child under the age of ten. The benefit can be used to take care of a sick child, to substitute for the usual caregiver, who is ill, to take a child for medical treatment, or to visit a preschool program—a specific incentive designed to encourage parents to visit their child's preschool program, limited to two half-days or one whole day per year per parent.

The benefit entitlement is now equal to sixty days per year per child. (In 1978, the benefit was more restrictive: twelve days per year for one child, fifteen for two children, and eighteen for three or more.) The entitlement can be shared between parents. Fathers may use the benefit, too, to remain home and care for a child while the wife is unable to because of childbirth. It is a universal benefit for all families with employed parents with at least one child under the age of ten.

The purpose of the benefit is to facilitate fulfillment of both work and family responsibilities without undue stress for the family, without negative consequences for children, and without placing a special burden on women.

The benefit is financed the same way as the parent insurance, that is, 85 percent from general revenue and 15 percent from employer contributions. The direct costs of the benefit in 1975 were 250 million S.Kr. The costs for 1979 have been integrated with those of the parent insurance.

Forty percent of the families with working mothers used the benefit in 1976 for an average of four days (4.6 for single mothers). In one-third of the families, fathers used the benefit, too, for at least one day. Sixty-four percent of the fathers in families with more than one child used the benefit for an average of seven-and-one-half days on the birth of a new child. The major use of the benefit is made by families with children between the ages of one and seven, when compulsory school begins.

The benefit has received widespread support and there is no debate regarding it.

The Swedish *child allowance* was established in 1948, superceding an earlier tax deduction for children. It is a flat-rate, tax-free, cash benefit equal to 2,800 S.Kr. per child per year, as of January 1980. The benefit is the equivalent of 4 percent of average male earnings and 5.5 percent of female earnings. It is designed as an income supplement serving to equalize the expenses of families by redistributing income from those with no children to those with children.

It is a universal benefit. All children under the age of sixteen are entitled to the benefit, even non-Swedish children after a six months residence in Sweden. It is financed out of general revenue and cost 3,240,000 S.Kr. in 1976 and 4,420,000 S.Kr. in 1979.

This benefit, too has widespread support. The only issue raised currently is whether the benefit should be indexed.

The Swedish *housing allowance,* instituted in 1969, is a two-part, in-kind benefit; one part is specifically for families with children. The full benefit in 1980 is equal to 1,500 S.Kr. per year per child plus 80 percent of the housing costs (rental) up to a specified maximum. It is designed as an income supplement for housing for the families with the greatest need—the low-income families.

The benefit is income tested, for families with at least one child under age seventeen. (Under certain conditions individuals and couples without children are also eligible for a housing allowance.) Families with incomes up to 35,000 S.Kr. per year are entitled to a full benefit. The benefit is reduced by 15 percent for families with incomes between 35,000 and 54,000 S.Kr. and by 24 percent for families with incomes above this level.

In 1975, 50 percent of all families with minor children were beneficiaries of the housing allowance.

It is financed out of general revenue and administered by the local municipalities. The total direct costs in 1975 were 1.530 million S.Kr. and in 1979, 2.390 million.

This is a significant benefit in particular for families with only one wage-earner, single-parent families, and large families. Even though limited specifically to housing, it has understandably been described as a child rearing allowance for low-income families with minor children. It seems to represent something of a disincentive for low-skilled, married women to work.

In addition, two other benefits went into effect January 1, 1979. These are specifically designed to address the interface of work and family life. The first is an entitlement to an unpaid leave with full job protection for either parent until a child is eighteen months of age. The second is an entitlement for one or both parents to work a six-hour day (in effect, a guaranteed right to part-time work) until a child is eight years old. It is still too early for any assessment of the impact of these benefits.

Summary

Sweden classifies its social benefits for child rearing as part of several separate systems: parent insurance, child allowance, housing allowance (and other special, income-tested benefits for families with children), tax benefits, and employment-related, unpaid benefits.

Swedish parental benefits assure the longest period of income replacement among all countries. In addition, Sweden provides several types of income supplement for all families and others specially designed to assist low-income families. That there has been some redistribution of income to families with children seems clear—this, it must be remembered, is part of Swedish overall family policy.

Sweden provides no benefit equivalent to a wage substitute. At the core of Swedish policy is an assumption that women—including single mothers—will be in the labor market. Indeed, the Swedes are convinced that it is beneficial for women, their husbands, and their children if women work, and Swedish policies are designed to encourage this.

Perhaps of greatest significance in the development of social benefits in Śweden is the emergence of a new objective in the provision of such benefits. Thus far we have identified income replacement, income substitution, and income supplement as the goals of these social benefits. Now we add a fourth goal: that of easing the integration of work and family life.

Sweden has clearly begun to move in this direction, but it reports that it has a long way to go. Most men work full time while most women work part time. Parent insurance and the temporary care allowance continue to be used largely by women. But a very high percentage of women do work, even if only part time, and now a guarantee of the right to modify work time on a job and to work a six-hour day is also available to either parent, as is the right to an unpaid but job-protected leave for a limited period of time. An increasing number of men are using at least some portion of their newest benefits, thus sharing home and working roles. Finally, we are told, the very fact of male entitlement helps prevent discrimination against women in the labor market (at least in part) and works toward the long-term goal of full sexual equality, at home and at work.

FRANCE

In Hungary, social benefits are viewed as an alternative child care policy, helping to support mothers to care for their own children for a significant period at home. In Sweden, they are seen as a means for facilitating both labor market and family roles for both parents. In France, these benefits are described as advancing a parallel policy, to assure women the option of alternative roles. In other words, social benefits in support of an at-home role exist alongside child care services, so that women may choose—at least in theory—either the at-home role (without too severe an income loss), or a labor market role (without foregoing good child care at reasonable cost). Whether existing social benefits actually support these options, and with what consequences, is the question we must address.

The very extensive French social benefits must be understood within the context of a long history of multiple, diverse, and categorical cash benefits for families with children, designed explicitly to subsidize and socialize the costs of childbearing and child rearing. Developed first in the

1930s, the family allowance was first established as a wage supplement paid to the head of household (almost always male) in lieu of across-the-board wage increases. It was viewed as such for many years and was completely contingent on labor force attachment (except for those considered to be unemployable). In recent years, the nature and purpose of this benefit have changed, and there has been a proliferation of other special-purpose cash benefits for families. At the same time, the link with labor force attachment has been eliminated. In effect what has now emerged in France is a special *family benefit* system, designed to support and supplement family income needs, just as the social insurance system and social assistance system address specialized *individual* income needs and problems.

Indeed, if we were to single out the most important social benefits supporting childbearing, child rearing, and child care in France, we would identify as first and foremost the French *family benefit system.* Second would be the French *family tax* benefits, and third, of much less significance except for families with very young children, the *paid maternity leaves,* provided as a social insurance benefit.

The French family benefit system includes a large and diverse group of cash and in-kind benefits. Among these are:

- a *family allowance* (to be described in greater detail below)
- a *prenatal allowance* (contingent on receipt of four medical examinations during pregnancy)
- a *postnatal allowance* (contingent on a specified number of maternal and child health examinations following childbirth)
- a three-day, *paid birth leave* for fathers following childbirth
- *a single-parent allowance* (to be described in greater detail below)
- *a housing allowance*
- *a school entering allowance* for children at the beginning of a new school year
- *a special education allowance* for handicapped children
- an *orphan's allowance*
- an *inclusive family allowance supplement (complément familial)* to be described in greater detail below. The *complément familial* or family allowance supplement replaces certain previous benefits— a single wage-earner allowance, a mother-at-home allowance, and a child care allowance to purchase child care services. However, beneficiaries who would have suffered a benefit loss when this new benefit went into effect will continue to receive the former benefits as long

as they remain eligible. Also, all recipients of these former benefits and of the *complément familial* are entitled to credit for their old age insurance as if they had been in the labor force.

The most important of these allowances for families with very young children are the basic family allowance and the family allowance supplement.[2]

The basic *family allowance* is a flat-rate, tax-free cash benefit provided when there are two or more children in a family. The benefit is equal to a fixed percentage of an index number determined by government decision and called a "basic monthly salary." For 1978, this number was 850 FF, less than half of the minimum legal wage and about one-quarter of the average wage (one French franc = $.20 [spring, 1977]). Only with four children does the family allowance equal this index sum. More specifically, the percentage is 23 percent for two children, 61 percent for three (increased to 69 percent in 1979), 98 percent for four, and 35 percent for each additional child. As can be seen, it is the third and subsequent children for whom the benefit has any real value. Even then it is low in relation to wages, although it can be, obviously, a significant supplement to a low wage. The benefit level also varies by the age of the child, and is increased for second and subsequent children at age ten, and again at age fifteen.

As mentioned earlier, this basic family allowance was initially viewed as a supplement to the earnings of male heads of household. Over the years this concept has been modified in a variety of ways. In part, the concept of the "social wage" (the per capita allocation of all statutory insurance and family benefits) has superceded the function of the original family allowance. By January 1, 1978, when the most recent amendment went into effect, eliminating labor force participation as an eligibility requirement for receipt of the family allowance, it had become clear that the family allowance had changed from a wage supplement for an employed parent or parents (usually fathers) to a *child benefit.* Thus, the benefit is now seen primarily as a form of income support or supplement for families with children regardless of the existence of any labor force attachment. In addition, of course, there continues to be an explicit pronatalist objective.

The family allowance is a universal benefit. Any parent, residing in France, with at least two minor children (up to age twenty if attending school) is entitled to the benefit. Its explicit objective now is to provide an income supplement directed at lessening the financial burdens of child rearing by sharing the costs with those who have no children.

The benefit is financed and is administered by the National Family Allowance Fund. Expenditures for the basic family allowance totaled 17.3 billion FF in 1975 and 25.6 billion in 1978. The expenditure for this benefit represented 51 percent of the total family allowance expenditures. Eighty-five percent of the children received family allowances in 1975.

Adding to this benefit, for large families (with three or more children) or very young families (with at least one child under age three), is the newest of the family benefits, the *family allowance supplement,* replacing the single wage-earner allowance (for one- and two-parent families with only one wage-earner), the mother-at-home allowance (for non-wage-earning mothers), and the child care allowance (for the purchase of child care services by employed mothers).

This benefit, which went into effect January 1, 1978, is a flat-rate, tax-free cash benefit available to those with incomes under a specified amount. The benefit level is based on the same basic monthly salary index number as is the family allowance. It is also expected to follow the increases in this basic salary. It was designed to consolidate the existing special cash benefits for mothers with very young children and to establish a uniform benefit level and uniform eligibility criteria. Single-parent families are entitled to a 50 percent increase on the benefit. The basic benefit amounted to 395 FF per month in 1979. Although the benefit amount does not vary, the income ceiling for eligibility does vary depending on the number of parents in a family, the number of wage-earners in a two-parent family, and the number of children in the family. For example, the ceiling is raised by 15 percent when there are two wage-earners or a sole parent. Receipt is contingent only upon the presence of at least one child under three (or three or more children), regardless of whether or not the mother works (see table 2.4.)

TABLE 2.4
Complément familial–Income Ceiling for Eligibility, July 1, 1979

	Income Ceiling	
Size of Family	*Two-parent Family Single Wage-earner*	*Single Parent or Two Wage-earners*
1 child	39,900 FF	46,910 FF
2 children	47,880	54,890
3 children	55,860	62,870
each additional child	7,980	7,980

The benefit is designed especially to supplement the income of low-income families with very young children so that married women with employed husbands can elect not to enter the labor force if they so wish without suffering economic hardship. At the same time, the benefit is still available to families where both parents work, or perhaps more important, where the sole parent, usually the mother, works. (Female-headed, single-parent families constitute 5.6 percent of all families in France.) In 1978, 70 percent of the beneficiaries were two-parent, one wage-earner families; 7 percent were single-parent families, 23 percent were two-parent, two wage-earner families. Almost half of those already receiving family allowances receive this benefit. In addition, about 15 percent more beneficiaries were added to the total as a consequence of this new benefit.

The benefit is financed through and administered by the National Family Allowance Fund. Expenditure for the benefit in 1978 was 11 billion FF, representing a little more than 20 percent of the total family allowance expenditure.

Although there may be an implicit pronatalist objective to this benefit and the earlier special family allowances, we would note that there has been no noticeable effect on the birth rate in France. Indeed, France, like the United States and all other European countries, has had a steady decline in birth rate since early in the twentieth century, except for the brief "baby boom" experienced by all these countries following World War II.

However, family allowances have been successful in redistributing money from those with no children to families with children, and the aid has been especially helpful to low-income families. But family income supplements have maintained neither their proportionate value among social expenditures nor their proportionate role in family income. The family allowance benefit level has not paralleled increases in wages (which have more than quadrupled since 1960), in prices (which have more than doubled since then), or in the purchasing power of direct incomes (which have almost doubled during those years).

Thus, among the issues now discussed are: making the first child eligible for the basic benefit, indexing the benefit, increasing the benefit, making the benefit taxable—all in the interest of targeting it more on families in need while at the same time supporting its role in the family income picture. There is also some discussion of financing the benefit through general revenue rather than through contributions.

Obviously, it is too soon to assess the effects of the family allowance supplement itself. The two allowances combined are estimated to offer the equivalent of about 20 percent of average wages for low-income and working-class families in which there are two parents but only one wage-earner. (In 1977, median wages for women were about 2,000 FF per year, while median wages for men were 2,800 FF.) This is not a negligible amount, and it can be supplemented further by the income-tested housing allowance for families, which varies by the level of rent and the number of children in the family. There are certain other types of housing allowances also. Overall, housing allowances constitute 13 percent of the total family allowance expenditure. The benefit package may be more significant for one-parent, female-headed families. We would conjecture, however, that although these benefits do not provide a real wage substitute, they could offer an incentive to labor force withdrawal of low-skilled married women and a return to traditional gender roles. Given the income ceiling, and a 100 percent benefit reduction above that, such women will find little incentive for working if they can receive a tax-free benefit equal to a significant proportion of the minimum legal wage. Or they may turn toward the underground economy and "black market" work.

The French also provide a *single-parent allowance* under certain conditions. This is a flat-rate, tax-free, means-tested cash benefit, provided to an unmarried, separated, divorced, or widowed parent (usually female) or to a pregnant woman. Eligibility is limited to those single parents 1) whose income is less than 150 percent of the basic monthly salary index number (for the parent) and under 50 percent of it for each child in care; and 2) whose liquid assets are less than a specified amount. In 1978, the benefit level was 1,275 FF per month for the parent and 425 FF per month for each child. Benefit entitlement covers a maximum of one year for those with a child under age sixteen, or until the child's third birthday for those with a child under age three. The average length of benefit receipt in 1978 was six months to one year. In 1977, 35,000 women received the benefit. Sixty percent were unmarried mothers, often teenagers still living at home. The next largest group were separated women. Divorcées and widows constituted the smallest group. Expenditure for the benefit was less than 1 percent of the total expended on all family allowances.

The *family tax benefit (quotient familial)*, a form of tax splitting based on the numbers of family members including children, provides an important benefit for families with earned income, also, and is especially valuable to high-income families. In addition, there is a tax deduction available to cover the cost of child care for children under the age of three, for families with income up to a specified amount.

Finally, of importance to families with very young children is the maternity insurance, which includes medical and hospital coverage for childbirth as well as a *paid maternity leave,* covering at least two and at most six weeks before expected parturition and ten to fourteen weeks after childbirth, for a total of sixteen weeks. The benefit level is equal to 90 percent of wages (up to the maximum covered salary under social security) and there is some additional supplementation available as a fringe benefit in some industries.

The maternity leave was initially viewed as a form of health protection and a component of health policy, along with the prenatal and postnatal family allowances. Over time, however, the primary function of the benefit has changed, and it is now viewed at least equally as an income replacement benefit designed to protect families against income loss at the time of childbirth and to facilitate some reconciliation between family and employment responsibilities.

Eligibility, by definition, is restricted to employed women and contingent on childbirth or adoption. It is a universal, tax-free cash benefit. Between 70 and 80 percent of the working women are covered by this benefit at childbirth. All women entitled to the benefit use it and almost all return to work at its end. The benefit is financed on a contributory basis as a separate social security benefit and administered by that ministry.

Recent legislation has instituted the additional option of an unpaid but fully job-protected leave for up to two years. Either parent is eligible to remain at home on such a leave if he or she has worked one year or more before the birth of a child and is employed in a firm with 200 or more employees (a large firm for France).

Legislation passed in late 1979 provided a special supplementary benefit for a third child and increased the paid maternity leave to six months on the birth of such children.

Summary

The French social benefits supporting childbearing, child rearing, and child care are directed primarily at supplementing the income of those rearing

TABLE 2.5

Family Benefits in French Francs, July 1, 1978 to July 1, 1979

Monthly Basis for Calculating Family Allowances: 850

<table>
<tr><td rowspan="6">Family
Allowance</td><td colspan="2">*Number of Children*</td><td colspan="2">*Increases for Age*</td></tr>
<tr><td>2</td><td>195.50</td><td>Children</td><td>Children</td></tr>
<tr><td>3</td><td>518.50</td><td>aged 10–15:</td><td>over 15:</td></tr>
<tr><td>4</td><td>833.00</td><td rowspan="2">76.50</td><td rowspan="2">136</td></tr>
<tr><td>5</td><td>1,130.50</td></tr>
<tr><td>6</td><td>1,428.00</td><td></td><td></td></tr>
<tr><td></td><td>per add'l. child</td><td>297.50</td><td></td><td></td></tr>
</table>

<table>
<tr><td rowspan="3">Prenatal
Allowance</td><td>*One*
Month</td><td>*1st Pmt.*
(2 Months)</td><td>*2nd Pmt.*
(4 Months)</td><td>*3rd Pmt.*
(3 Months)</td><td>*Total*</td></tr>
<tr><td>187</td><td>374</td><td>748</td><td>561</td><td>1,683.00</td></tr>
</table>

<table>
<tr><td rowspan="2">Postnatal
Allowance</td><td>*1st Pmt.*</td><td>*2nd Pmt.*</td><td>*3rd Pmt.*</td><td>*Total*</td></tr>
<tr><td>1105.00</td><td>552.00</td><td>552.00</td><td>2,210.00</td></tr>
</table>

<table>
<tr><td rowspan="2">Allowance for
Children
Returning to
School</td><td>*Amount Applicable on Return 1977–78 for Child*</td></tr>
<tr><td>170</td></tr>
</table>

<table>
<tr><td rowspan="2">Single
Parent
Allowance</td><td colspan="2">*Maximum Amount*</td></tr>
<tr><td></td><td>*Pregnant Women or Mothers*</td><td>*Per Child*</td></tr>
<tr><td></td><td>1,275.00</td><td>425.00</td></tr>
</table>

<table>
<tr><td rowspan="2">Family
Allowance
Supplement</td><td>*Amount per Family*</td></tr>
<tr><td>354</td></tr>
</table>

children. Special attention is paid low-income families with very young children—or with many children.

The range of benefits provided can be divided into those that are child-birth-related (e.g., pre- and postnatal allowances, childbirth leaves, paid and unpaid maternity leaves) and those contingent on the presence and age or number of children (family allowance, family allowance supplement). Benefits may also be classified by whether or not they are income-tested (e.g., universal benefits include family allowances and maternity leaves; income-tested benefits include the family allowance supplement and the housing allowance). Except for the paid maternity leave and the unpaid parental leave, none of the statutory benefits are labor-force related. There are also some additional special benefits which are part of collective bargaining agreements, but these are of much less significance.

Perhaps the most significant aspect of the French social benefit picture is the emergence of a distinctive, separate family benefit system, unrelated to labor force status, including both income-tested and non-income-tested benefits, and having a primary goal of supplementing the income of families with minor children, especially low-income families with very young children, regardless of family structure.

Although the evidence is quite limited, it would seem that the French benefits might support an economically viable at-home role for low-income, unskilled women with children under the age of three—if they are single, or if they are married and have husbands who are in the labor force. Since they could lose almost as much as they could earn (family allowance supplement; housing allowance), it would seem there is little incentive for such women to work when they have very young children if they have husbands who are earning somewhat above average wages. The fact that the French tax system taxes families as such also means that the wife's added earnings would be taxed at a high marginal tax rate. However, it is clear that the family allowance supplement certainly offers no viable alternative for women who can earn an average wage or higher. Furthermore, there may even be an incentive for low-skilled, low-wage-earning women to enter the labor force, if they are married to similarly low-wage-earning men.

In conclusion, the French picture with regard to labor market incentives or disincentives for women is inconsistent and unclear. Certainly, there is no policy of providing a full wage substitute for women to remain at home—neither for married women, nor even for single mothers—except for a very brief period of time for low-income single women. Moreover, the French benefit providing short-term wage replacement is among the briefest in Europe. Whether those French benefits providing income supplementation can provide a real choice for women—even low-income women—

seems questionable except possibly for a very limited group of women, namely low-skilled women married to slightly higher-than-average earning men. The real impact of the French benefit seems to be to supplement the income of low wage-earners with children, compensating them at least in part for the economic costs of bearing and rearing children. Certainly this is a worthwhile accomplishment, even though it does not make an at-home role for women economically viable and thus cannot assure women a real choice in deciding whether or not to work.

GERMAN DEMOCRATIC REPUBLIC

The primary assumption about adult women in the GDR is that they, like men, will be in the labor force. There is no interest in, or attention to, the development of an alternative role for women. The special focus of GDR social benefits is to permit women to cope with maternity and childbirth while they continue to be employed.

In addition, as in the other countries, there are the family income supplement benefits, which are aimed at mitigating the overall costs of child rearing. Since 1976, these benefits have been increased and extended in response to growing demographic concerns. By the mid-1970s, the GDR had the lowest birth rate of any country in the world and had reached the stage of negative population growth (more deaths than births per year).

The GDR social benefit package includes, first, a cluster of maternity-related benefits:

- a maternity benefit equal to 1,000 DME per child (one DME = $.29 [est.]) and contingent on receipt of pre- and postnatal medical care
- a paid maternity leave (to be discussed in more detail below)
- a supplementary paid maternity leave (to be discussed in more detail below)
- an unpaid, but job-protected, maternity leave (to be discussed in more detail below)
- a cash allowance to remain home if there is no place in a child care program (to be discussed in more detail below)
- a special interest-free loan for those who marry early (the loan is reduced on the birth of each child and eliminated after the birth of a third child).

In addition are several other benefits directed at family income supple-

mentation and child rearing responsibilities over a longer time span. These
include:

- family allowance, equal to 20 DME per month per child (the benefit
  level is the equivalent of 5 percent of a minimum wage, 3.3 percent
  of average wage, and less than 1 percent of a high wage)
- paid sick leave to care for a child under the age of fourteen at home
  (two days per year per child at 90 percent of wages; if a longer leave
  is needed it is paid for at the rate of sick pay, or a somewhat lower
  rate)
- as of January 1, 1979, three paid personal days per month for mothers
  with a child under sixteen or for single parents regardless of the age
  of the child or for mothers over forty, also at 90 percent of wages
- housing allowances for low-income families with children.

The most significant benefits for our purposes are the maternity-related
benefits, especially the maternity leaves and the benefit available if there is
no place available for a child in a day care center.

The basic paid maternity leave is a wage-related cash benefit covering
twenty-six weeks leave from work, including up to six weeks before expected
parturition and twenty weeks after. This statutory paid maternity leave, as
all we have described, guarantees full job protection, seniority, pension entitlements, and so forth. The benefit level is equal to 90 percent of wage.
(The minimum wage in the GDR is 400 DME monthly. Average wage is 600
DME and high wages are between 1,000 and 1,500 DME.)

The benefit is viewed primarily as part of maternal and child health policy. It is universal and used by almost all women who give birth. It is financed out of the government budget.

Recently, a *supplementary maternity leave* was established, covering an
additional twenty-six weeks at 50 percent of wages, for second and subsequent children (or a minimum of 300 DME monthly for a second child and
350 DME for a third and subsequent child). The obvious purpose here is
to provide an incentive for women to have a second child.

Women are also entitled to take an unpaid maternity leave, until the
child is one year old. Such an unpaid leave may be claimed by another family member (father, grandmother) if that individual rather than the mother
assumes primary child care responsibility.

Finally, *if there is no place for a child in a day care center* single mothers
are entitled to receipt of a *flat cash grant* of 300 DME monthly as a sick-

ness insurance benefit. This benefit may be supplemented by as much as 200 DME more per month, if sickness insurance benefits are higher (that is, if the beneficiary makes a supplementary contribution to the sickness insurance fund, as most higher wage earners do). Mothers in two-earner families are entitled to an unpaid but job-protected leave, if there is no child care space.

It is reported that maternity leave take-up for twenty weeks after childbirth is almost universal. Other data on participation in benefits have not been made available.

The GDR has the highest labor force participation rate for women in any industrialized country. Clearly, those women with children are integrating their maternal and labor market roles. We would, however, note two significant consequences of the recent modifications in the social benefits: an increase in the birth rate in 1977, in particular in the birth of second children, and a decline in the absolute numbers of children under age one in day care centers.

Summary

The GDR social benefits have been directed primarily at supporting childbearing and at the early months of maternal care. Families are protected against income loss when women give birth; and work and family tensions are relieved for the first year following childbirth.

In recent years a distinctly pronatalist component has supplemented the basic policy package. The primary concern seems to be in assuring that women can manage both family role and work role without detriment to either. The conclusion has been that thus far women have managed employment at the expense of family—leading to a steady decline in the birth rate as women (or families) seemed convinced that child care and child rearing were too difficult in the existing environment. The recent modification in GDR social benefits appears to be directed at redressing this imbalance. It does not seem to indicate any change, however, from the major goal: to help women manage maternity while they are employed.

FEDERAL REPUBLIC OF GERMANY

The FRG directs a variety of social benefits at all families with children, but eligibility levels and provisions are such that the benefits have significance mainly for low-income families. The most significant benefits are a universal child allowance, a cluster of income-tested, cash, and in-kind benefits to supplement family income, and a paid maternity leave.

The *child allowance* is a flat-rate, tax-free cash benefit which, since 1975, replaces income tax exemptions for children. The benefit was 50 DM monthly for a first child, 80 DM for a second, and 150 DM for each subsequent child in 1975, but as of July 1, 1979, the benefit was increased to 100 DM for the second and 200 DM for the third child. (One DM = $.45 [spring, 1977]). Previously, the child benefit was income-tested and for second and subsequent children only. The tax exemption for children benefited high-income families more than low-income families. The child allowance now replaces both of these.

It was estimated in 1973 by the Federal Census Bureau that the actual per-child expenditure per month to rear a child was 468 DM. A 1974 survey of working mothers with children under age three reported earnings by the mother of 969.5 DM monthly. Average family income for families with working mothers and at least one child under age three was 2,307 DM monthly.

The child allowance is designed to ease the financial burden of families with children, in particular low-income families, and represents a significant proportion of family income for such families. It is a universal benefit and all children residing in the FRG are entitled to it, although the benefit level is reduced to take account of receipt of certain other benefits.

It is financed out of general revenue and administered by the Federal Labor office. The costs for 1978 were approximately 15 billion DM.

There are also several cash and in-kind *income-tested benefits* supplementing family income provided in the FRG (several involving elements of discretion), including:

- benefits for pregnant women
- housing benefits
- social assistance

The primary function of these benefits is to supplement the income of low-income families. They are not contingent on either labor force attachment or withdrawal. Nor are they contingent on any particular family structure. However, since they are all income-tested, participation is highest for single mothers and then, for large families. These benefits vary slightly in amount, eligibility requirements, and so forth among the different states.

The FRG provides a universal, flat-rate cash *maternity benefit* of 100 DM or 150 DM for multiple births, on childbirth.

The major maternity-related benefit, however, is a flat-rate, tax-free, cash benefit covering seven-and-one-half months for employed women (up to six weeks available before expected parturition and twenty-four weeks after childbirth). The statutory benefit level is 750 DM per month, equal to 77 percent of the average female wage in 1978. (Women whose wages are higher than this amount are entitled to an additional supplement up to their full net wage, for the first fourteen weeks, paid by their employer.)

The function of the benefit is primarily to protect maternal and child health, and then to protect against income loss, and loss of employment, as a consequence of childbirth.

The benefit is universal for all women working in covered employment (all jobs subject to social security coverage, thus almost all jobs) for at least eighteen weeks prior to childbirth. Women currently receiving unemployment insurance are also able to interrupt that entitlement and take up the maternity leave for the period of entitlement, returning to the unemployment insurance system when their maternity leave is exhausted.

Almost all eligible mothers receive the basic health insurance benefit. There are no data available on those receiving supplementation from their employers.

Health expenditure data are not disaggregated in such a way as to reveal the costs for this benefit and no data are available regarding the costs to industry.

There are no data on the effects of this benefit other than that it is fully utilized. There is some impression that the burden on employers has resulted in some discrimination against young female entrants into the labor force, but there is no hard evidence to support this. Since there is now some concern regarding growing unemployment anyway, it might be hard to ascertain how much of the female unemployment problem is attributable specifically to this factor.

In addition to the benefits described above, employed parents are entitled to a *paid leave* of up to five days per year, at 80 percent of wages, *to care for an ill child* under the age of eight at home, and a tax deduction of 600 DM for the cost of child care by nonfamily members. Finally, there is a means-tested social assistance benefit which, although somewhat stigmatized, does permit an at-home role for a limited group of women. About

10 percent of the single-mother, single-parent families—which constitute 7 percent of all families with minor children—receive this benefit. Among the issues currently discussed in the FRG are the following:

- assuring parents of children under age six the right to modify their work schedule, so as to work only part time and still receive proportionate fringe benefits and full pension entitlements
- extending the paid sick leave to cover children up to age twelve
- providing a time-limited, unpaid leave for single parents
- providing an income-tested, flat-rate cash benefit (*Erziehungsgeld*) of 300 DM monthly until their child is age one (or age three, according to some proposals) to single mothers who do not work.

Summary

The social benefit provision in the FRG is focused primarily on supplementing the income of low-income families with children, regardless of age of child, family structure, or labor force attachment of parent(s). There is one universal cash child benefit, two universal cash maternity benefits (the more important are limited to employed women), and several income-tested family income supplement benefits. Because these last are income-tested, they are most likely to benefit female-headed families.

Except for some small experiments and the limited coverage under social assistance, the FRG has no social benefits designed to make an at-home role economically viable. Nor, except for its maternity leaves, does it provide much in the way of help to facilitate a labor market role for women.

UNITED STATES

The United States is the only country in the group here studied with no statutory maternity-related benefits, no universal child rearing benefits, and no universal maternal and child health service benefits. Moreover, the United States is the only country in which the basic income support program 1) assures no uniform minimum cash benefit, 2) is restricted almost completely to single-parent, female-headed families (although 28 states provide this benefit on a very limited basis to families with unemployed fathers), and 3) is designed primarily to support mothers who are not in the labor force.

There are no social benefits specific to childbearing, child rearing, or child care in families with young children. Instead, the most significant benefits are limited to two types, one of which is a child rearing income benefit and the other a benefit covering some portion of purchase of child care. Both of these entitlements are for families with dependent children regardless of the age of the child but contingent on other eligibility criteria.

The most significant of these benefits is *AFDC–Aid to Families with Dependent Children*. This is a cash benefit primarily for low-income single mothers with at least one minor child. The benefit level is set by the individual states and therefore varies among them. For the most part it is set well below the officially defined poverty threshold, although it is above that level in a few states. Its function is to substitute for earned income in families with children.

It is an income-tested benefit specifically restricted to one-parent, female-headed families in almost half the states, and is predicated, for the most part, on the absence of sufficient earned or other income. The benefit is the gateway to the only free medical entitlement for nondisabled children, who are eligible until age eighteen, or age twenty if in school. It is not available to two-parent families in which the male works full time, regardless of income or family size. However, a number of AFDC mothers work and receive income supplementation (16%). The income ceiling is such that it is nonetheless largely unavailable to most single, employed mothers.

In 1978, there were 10.33 million beneficiaries, including over 3 million adults, mostly women, and over 7.2 million children. Single-parent families represented 15 percent of all families in the United States in 1978. Almost all these were female-headed. Forty-two percent of the single-parent, female-headed families had incomes under the poverty level in 1977. Thirty-eight percent of the single-parent families received public assistance in that year (and 40% in 1978).

Some 15.8 percent of the 8 million children receiving AFDC in 1975 were under three; almost one-quarter of the AFDC families had children in this age group.

AFDC is financed out of general revenue by the federal government and the state (and sometimes the localities also). It is administered at the state or local level. The total expenditure for 1977 was $10.6 billion.

Although coverage is extensive, as is take-up (it is estimated that a high proportion of eligible women use the benefit), recipients are still stigmatized. Moreover, the benefit still does not provide a uniform, adequate entitlement that would assure by itself a decent living standard. Excluded from any benefit are at least 5 million children who live in two-parent families with income under the poverty level. Finally, since AFDC eligibility also opens food stamps, Medicaid, and (often) public housing eligibility, the total of means-tested benefits could create a significant work disincentive for low-skilled women.

Although there have been several efforts at modifying this benefit to make it more uniform, more adequate, and available to two-parent families, thus far the effort has not been successful.

The United States also provides a series of tax benefits for families with children.

First is a *tax exemption* for children, which benefits high-income families more than others.

Second is the *earned income tax credit*, which provides a small tax benefit to one- or two-parent families with at least one wage-earner and a child under nineteen (or who is a full-time student or disabled). In 1979 the maximum credit was $500. The benefit is a refundable tax credit to families with gross income up to $10,000 (1979).

The benefit has been described as partially offsetting social security contributions of low-income workers with children (or as partially relieving low-income families from increases in food and fuel prices). In 1978, the 10 percent credit offset nearly 85 percent of the social security contributions for eligible beneficiaries. The total expenditure for 1978 was $1.230 billion.

A third tax benefit is a nonrefundable tax credit to cover some portion of child care expenses for working parents. The allowable tax credit is 20 percent of expenses up to $2,000 (for a maximum credit of $400) annually for one child under the age of fourteen (or a disabled dependent or spouse) and up to $4,000 (for a maximum credit of $800) annually for two or more children. The credit is permitted for payments to anyone, including relatives, as long as they are treated as employees. This tax credit replaced an earlier tax deduction which provided proportionately more benefit to higher income families.

The function of the credit is to compensate for the cost to wage-earners of obtaining certain essential services. It is also supposed to provide incentives for in-home care of aged or handicapped dependents as well as children, and offer some support for obtaining child care services for employed middle-class parents.

It is a universal benefit for taxpayers who are employed full time, or married couples where one spouse or both work part time, or where one is a student and the other is employed.

The child care credit was claimed by 2.7 million taxpayers for 4 million children in 1978, at an approximate cost (in estimated lost tax revenues) of about $565 million.

At present, there are no data regarding how this benefit is used. It is, of course, of no value to families with incomes below the tax threshold.

There is a work-expense allowance for child care costs available to recipients of AFDC, which permits them to deduct the cost of child care services as a necessary work expenditure when their income is assessed for entitlements to benefits.

There are also income-tested, in-kind food benefits (food stamps, breakfast and lunch at child care centers) which supplement income for families with young children—not only those under three. A maternal and child nutrition program for pregnant mothers and for infants offers an expanding source of food supplementation for those "at risk." While important in the U.S. context, such programs are mentioned only in passing elsewhere. The Special Supplemental Food Program for Women, Infants, and Children (WIC) began in 1972 but has only just begun to assume quantitative significance. Children are eligible up to age five. Child dependents of retired, deceased, and disabled workers also receive monthly grants. There were 67,000 recipients under age three in 1975. Such dependents allowances, not related to the labor force status of their mothers, exist everywhere in some form.

Finally, there are fairly extensive nonstatutory benefits covering maternity in the United States. In 1978 about 40 percent of the employed women had such coverage, which could include both medical care and hospitalization as well as paid leave from employment. There are neither uniform benefit levels nor uniform amounts of leave. Maternity leaves rarely involve full wage replacement and tend to be very brief (six weeks on average).

Summary

Neither childbearing, child care, nor child rearing has been viewed as an appropriate arena for government attention in the United States. There has been no interest in facilitating female labor force participation. Indeed, only recently has the fact that many married women with children work been acknowledged by the society at large. Similarly, there is no announced interest in supporting an economically viable at-home role for women with very young children. Despite this, U.S. policy serves to support this role for some women and the results are reflected in the society. Existing policy explicitly supports an at-home role (at minimal or less than adequate income levels) for single mothers with minor children well beyond the age of children in families so protected in many other countries. Furthermore, this policy implicitly discourages labor force attachment for these women for a significant portion of their lives. While not immediately relevant here, the picture is even more complicated, since AFDC mothers are stigmatized and told they should be working; and some legislation attempts to reduce work disincentive. There is also a work-and-training incentive program, WIN, which is small-scale and not very effective. Nonetheless, except to a very small extent in the FRG, no other country in this group supports nonwork for needy mothers of children into adolescence.

Thus, U.S. social benefits, like Hungary's child care allowance and the FRG's social assistance, provide a substitute for earned income. In contrast to the Hungarian benefit, however, the benefit is means-tested, inconsistent, and generally at a very low level; it is provided only to a very restricted family type, regardless of prior labor force attachment, but for a more extensive period of time. In effect, this group is defined as unemployable and given an incentive to remain so.

Finally, unlike every other country in the study, the United States has no policy of family income supplementation, except in a very minor way through food subsidies and the earned income tax credit. There is no acknowledgment in U.S. policy of child rearing as contributing to the continuity and betterment of society generally, and therefore, no interest in subsidizing in any way the costs of child rearing.

WHAT DO THE BENEFITS ACHIEVE?

A SIX-COUNTRY OVERVIEW

We have reviewed in some detail the social benefits provided in each of the countries to support child bearing, child care, and child rearing. Our conclusions are:

Child bearing—the health aspects as well as the income loss attendant on childbirth—receives attention in all countries except the United States, through a variety of maternity benefits and maternity and parent leaves.

Child rearing (within the family) also receives substantial attention in all countries but the United States, in the form of cash and in-kind family income supports.

Child care benefits are the most limited, and exist in different forms for different purposes in Hungary, France, and the United States. In Hungary, the relevant benefit supports almost all mothers in their child care role until a child is three years old. In France, the benefit is one of several theoretically making it possible for some women to choose roles, either a labor force role, by purchasing child care, or an at-home role. In practice, the benefit is too low to allow a real choice, and thus becomes a supplement to low income instead. In the United States, two benefits are available for different types of beneficiaries, to support opposite functions. One benefit supports some low-income, single mothers in an at-home child care role for an extended period of time. Another benefit permits higher wage-earning mothers some compensation for the costs of purchasing child care, thus making it easier for them to continue in their labor market role.

Despite the U.S., French, and FRG tax benefits for purchase of child care, the main purpose of the most extensive social benefits supporting child care is to support parents as primary care givers, rather than to subsidize other care. In other words, these benefits are designed to support an at-home role for women with children. Has this been accomplished?

We have assessed the extent to which these social benefits replace lost earnings when employed women leave work because of pregnancy, childbirth, or child care, or provide a substitute for earned income while mothers remain out of the labor force to bear and rear a child. We have analyzed the extent to which governments transfer income (in cash or in kind) to families with children so that an at-home role for mothers becomes economically viable regardless of family income or husband's earnings.

Our analysis suggests the following:

All countries except the United States provide a benefit that assures *income replacement* (in toto or in large part) for the loss of earnings by women at the time of childbirth and for some time immediately thereafter. The benefit is wage-related in all countries and covers about 90 percent of wages. (In Hungary it is equal to full wage replacement. In the FRG the extended portion is provided at a significantly lower level, with a fixed, relatively low maximum.) Moreover, except for a portion of the benefit in the FRG, financing is such that the direct costs do not fall on industry but rather are shared by the society at large. Although the amount of time covered by this insurance benefit ranges from three-and-one-half to nine months, the trend seems to be toward a modal pattern of six months. The Swedish benefit covers a longer time period and is an entitlement to both parents; the GDR offers a basic six-month benefit as well as a more limited supplementary benefit for women with second and third children; the FRG has just extended its benefit to cover six months. Several countries also assure an unpaid but job-protected leave. *Regardless, there does not seem to be any discussion of such a paid benefit as anything other than a form of short-term insurance, covering at the very most, one year.* Quite clearly, the costs of extending such a benefit for much longer would be prohibitive. Moreover, the standards for short-term income replacement benefits regardless of the type of benefit suggest about one year as the norm.

A true *income substitute*, conditional on the mother remaining out of the labor force and not working, is provided in Hungary, the GDR, the FRG, and the United States. (The FRG is proposing a benefit to cover one year, for low-income single mothers, at a higher level than provided under social assistance.) However, these are very different benefits, with very different amounts of coverage. In Hungary, the entitlement is universal, covers two-and-one-half years (until the child is age three), is contingent on prior labor force attachment, and equals about 40 percent of average female wages. In the GDR the benefit is equal to about 50 percent of wages, is contingent on there being no child care program space available, or on the birth of a second child, and covers only about six months, or at most a year, until a child is one or perhaps one-and-one-half. In the FRG, the benefit is available to a very small number of single mothers, and certainly is not yet an expression of explicit policy in supporting an at-home role for women. AFDC, in the United States, provides a benefit covering a larger period of time, but at very inconsistent and often inadequate levels, to a very specific group of women (single, low-income mothers). The French family allowance supplement is still too new for assessment of its impact, but it seems far too low to provide a real alternative for *many* women (although it may for some), even for the three years that it covers.

Thus, at present, except for Hungary, and the United States for a limited group of women, no country supports an at-home role for women beyond the time a child is about one year old.[3] If women choose such a role, it seems clear that the direct economic costs are largely their own, although the indirect costs may be borne by the society as well as by the women themselves.

WHAT THEN DO THESE BENEFITS PROVIDE?

The most significant contribution these benefits make is in support of the economic aspects of child rearing. Indeed, every country but the United States provides a cluster of cash and in-kind benefits assuring a significant *income supplement* to families with children.

These family income supplements may be income-tested or non-income-tested. Eligibility as well as benefit levels may reflect the age of the child, the ordinal position of children, or the number of children in a family. Despite these variations, what is most significant is that *they are available regardless of labor force attachment and regardless of family structure* even though single parents are entitled to special supplementations in every country.

Even though France may be the only country in this group to provide a special income supplement to families with very young children, the extensiveness and pervasiveness of these family income supplements for families with dependent children, regardless of age, appears to be one of the most significant findings in our analysis.

Indeed, we would note here, for further study, the seeming emergence of a "family benefit system" in several countries, parallel to the larger and older social insurance systems, and to the smaller and more disparate social assistance programs. This family benefit system is distinguishable from social insurance primarily in that it is unrelated to labor force attachment, and in that it serves to supplement rather than replace income. It is distinguishable from social assistance, similarly, in that by disregarding labor force attachment it does not mandate labor force withdrawal. In addition, its stress on income supplementation rather than income substitution, and its greater uniformity and consistency in provision, is also in contrast to the more disparate, discretionary, and stigmatized social assistance.

Indeed, from a broader perspective, one could view this emerging system as including, also, such "family" specific benefits as the various maternity and/or parental leaves—both paid and unpaid. The extensiveness and variety of such benefits—and their very recent history—suggest the beginning of a very significant and distinctive development which we can only begin to touch on here. We will turn to this again in our concluding chapter.

Finally, we would note four other consequences of these benefits.

Assessing the effectiveness of any of these benefits as fertility incentives or labor market determinants is a complicated endeavor. Specific benefits may be viewed as effective in individual countries in achieving desired aims. However, no measure is established in a vacuum. Both the country-specific context and the additional supporting policies would have to be assessed more rigorously, with data not available to us here (and often not available at all) in order to go beyond what we stated in discussing each country. Of greater importance is the fact that a benefit which is viewed as having one goal and one result in one country may be viewed very differently in another. Moreover, many of these concerns overlap and converge, making cause and effect very difficult to disentangle.

Thus, sometimes the benefits follow growth in female labor force participation, sometimes they precede it, and sometimes they are followed by still greater growth. No industrialized country has successfully influenced fertility behavior over any extended period of time. Nor are the variables that influence such behavior fully understood. All that we can conclude is that some countries seem convinced that multiple incentives can influence fertility and labor market behavior, but most of the countries discussed would agree that the benefits described here have not had such an effect, or have not been in effect long enough to reveal one, or are inconsistent in their effects and therefore, as we said above, must be assessed within a larger context.

Similarly, because the same benefit may be employed in different countries to achieve different objectives, comparing costs and benefits is a complicated and questionable endeavor, too. Moreover, it is further complicated by the different approaches used in disaggregating costs in each country, as well as in identifying benefits and assessing their value. Assessing the cash costs of a benefit involves not only assigning a monetary value to the benefit and the administrative costs of providing it, but also acknowledging the different value placed on who bears the costs (or portion of the costs)—government, industry, wage-earner, taxpayer, beneficiary—and often which level of government. Similarly, the question of opportunity costs (the costs of alternative choices foregone) for the individual as well as the society at large must be addressed. All of this is not only beyond the available data and technology, but also may be beyond what is truly fruitful, given our initial conclusions that the costs and benefits by definition are assessed differently in each country.

Assessing the extent to which these benefits do or do not facilitate equality—equality between men and women, equality within the society generally—is even more complicated. Most analysts would agree that any parental benefits in which eligibility is restricted to women functions almost by definition to reinforce traditional roles for women and therefore keeps women in an inferior position in the society at large. The debate over whether or not protective legislation for women results in excluding women from high-wage jobs is part of this. The same is true for maternity leaves or child care leaves limited only to women. Such benefits, while offering some kind of protection, continue to assign to women the primary responsibility for home and family tasks and as a result leave them overburdened generally and also at a significant disadvantage in the work world. It seems clear that until these "benefits" are available to men as well as women—to either parent— and men are expected to use them, women will remain disadvantaged even though they may be better off than they would be if no such benefits existed.

A related issue, however, has to do with whether flat-rate or wage-related benefits are more likely to promote equality, regardless of whether entitlement is open to either parent or only to the mother. Two opposing arguments are offered here. The traditional argument is that a flat-rate benefit assures the same treatment for all, while a wage-related benefit gives more to high-wage-earning, high-income families, thus further reinforcing existing social inequities. The counterargument is that if a benefit is contingent on prior labor force attachment and current labor force withdrawal for eligibility, a flat-rate benefit, unless it is very high, would appeal only to low-wage-earners, the great majority of whom are women. As a consequence, low-skilled, low-wage-earning women would be the major benefit users, and once again would find themselves in traditional roles, suffering the usual occupational and economic disadvantages.

We would argue that any benefit which is designed to replace—or substitute for—earned income, must be earnings-related if women are not to be penalized since, at present, women earn far less than men do in all the study

TABLE 2.6
The Major Statutory Benefits by Benefit Function and Country (1978)

Benefit Function[a]	Hungary	France	GDR	Sweden	FRG	USA
Income Replacement (Benefits provided to protect against loss of earned income due to the existence of a socially defined risk, e.g., unemployment, disability, retirement)	Maternity Leave Non-income-tested Social insurance Cash benefit Wage-related Covering full wage For 5 months For employed women following childbirth	Maternity Leave Non-income-tested Social insurance, tax free Cash benefit Wage-related Covering 90% of wage For 16 weeks For employed women following childbirth	Maternity Leave Non-income-tested Social insurance Cash benefit Wage-related Covering 90% of wage For 26 weeks For employed women following childbirth	Parental Leave Non-income-tested Social insurance Cash benefit Taxable Wage-related Covering 90% of wage For 9 months For employed parents (one or the other) following childbirth Can be prorated and used to cover part-time work	Maternity Leave Non-income-tested Tax free Cash benefit Wage-related (Minimum provided as social insurance benefit; supplementation to full wage by employer for first $3\frac{1}{2}$ months) For $7\frac{1}{2}$ mos. For employed women following childbirth	—[b]

Supplementary Maternity Leave
Same as above for an additional 26 weeks, *But* covering 50% of wage
For employed women following birth of 2nd and subsequent children

Paid leave to care for an ill child at home
For employed women at 90% for first 2 days, then at sickness insurance rate

Paid leave to care for an ill child at home
For employed parent at 90% of wages

Paid leave to care for an ill child at home
For employed men and women
Five days at full covered wage minus contributions

Paid leave to care for an ill child at home
For employed women at 75% of wages

TABLE 2.6 *(Continued)*

Benefit Function[a]	Hungary	France	GDR	Sweden	FRG	USA
Income Substitution (Benefits made available on the assumption that there is no or little earned income available to the family)	*Child Care Allowance* Non-income-tested Cash benefit Flat grant (equal to 40% of average female wage) For a maximum of 31 months (until a child is age 3) For employed women following the end of the maternity leave, contingent on labor force withdrawal	*Social Assistance* Discretionary, nonuniform cash benefit of limited duration for individuals	—	*Social Assistance* Means-tested nonuniform cash benefit of limited duration for individuals with or without children	*Social Assistance* Means-tested cash benefit for individuals with or without children	*Public Assistance* (AFDC) Means-tested nonuniform cash grant to women with one or more children (in some states, under some circumstances, to families with an unemployed father)

Income Supplementation (Benefits predicated on the assumption that earned income may not be adequate to meet family needs)	Family Allowance	Family Allowance Supplement	Family Allowance	Child Care Benefit	Family Allowance	Child Allowance	Child Allowance
	Non-income-tested	Income-tested	Non-income-tested		Non-income-tested	Non-income-tested	Non-income-tested
	Cash benefit	Flat rate	Cash benefit	Cash benefit	Cash benefit	Cash benefit	Cash benefit
	Flat rate	Cash benefit	Tax-free	Flat grant	Tax-free	Tax-free	Flat rate
	For: (a) a sole employed parent with at least 1 child; (b) two parents, at least one employed, with 2 or more children; (c) any family with a handicapped child	Tax-free	Flat rate	For a single woman who cannot obtain a place for her child in a child care center	Flat rate	Flat rate	For any parent with one or more children
		For families with one child under 3 or 3 or more children	For any parent with two or more children		For any parent with one or more children	For any parent with one or more children	

TABLE 2.6 (*Continued*)

Benefit Function[a]	Hungary	France	GDR	Sweden	FRG	USA
		Single Parent Allowance Income-tested Flat rate Tax-free Cash benefit				*Housing Allowance* Income-tested (Covers very few even among those eligible)
		Miscellaneous Small Income-tested Cash benefits related to presence of child in family				
	Housing Allowance Income-tested for families with a minor child	*Housing Allowance* Income-tested		*Housing Allowance* Income-tested (Covers 50% of all families with a minor child in Sweden)	*Housing Allowance* Income-tested	Food Stamps Income-tested Subsidy for food and WIC food supplementation for women and children at "nutritional risk"
	Special food subsidies	Various and special in-kind benefits, some of which are income-tested	Special food subsidies			

Family-based Tax System (Quotient familial)

Tax Allowance For dependents

Child Care Tax Credit

Tax Allowance For dependents

Earned Income Tax Credit For low income families with at least one minor child

Child Care Tax Credit Non-income-tested For families with a sole employed parent and parents (or one employed and one fulltime student)

[a] In addition to the benefits described above, all countries except the USA provide:

- a maternity benefit (cash or in kind) at childbirth (a lump sum or a "layette")—Not available in Sweden
- full medical and hospital coverage at childbirth
- comprehensive, free maternal and child health care services
- unpaid, but job-protected, leave for all (or some) workers following the end of the paid maternity (or parental) leave.

Sweden now guarantees parents with young children the right to work a six-hour day but without additional compensation. Other special benefits are provided in several countries; however, they are of less significance than those described above.

[b] Although there are maternity leaves provided some employed women through private disability insurance, less than 40% of the working women are so covered and benefit levels are low, not uniform, and last only about six weeks on the average. In addition, both France and the FRG have supplementary maternity leave coverage as part of trade union contracts or special arrangements in certain industries.

countries except Sweden. Only with an earnings-related benefit (albeit to a maximum, perhaps the social insurance coverage maximum) is there any hope of assuring male participation and some attenuation of traditional role expectations for women. Furthermore, if these benefits are included in taxable income, the consequences for societal inequities could be significantly reduced.

Where benefits are designed to supplement income—and are added to earned income whether one or two parents are in the labor market—the issue is different. As can be seen in several countries, but perhaps most clearly in France, flat-rate benefits can make a significant contribution to family income. Here, too, if they are included in taxable income their value may be proportionately higher to low-income families.

The key issue in deciding between flat-rate and wage-related benefits would seem to be whether the purpose is to replace earnings, substitute for earnings, or supplement earnings. It is critical for women's equality that benefits designed to replace or substitute for earnings be wage-related. Apart from this, including benefits in taxable income may have significant implications for decreasing income inequities among families generally. This is a development which has only begun to emerge in a few countries.

Finally and of special importance, we would note the emergence of an additional function of the benefits described here, and that is to facilitate a closer relationship between work and family life. More specifically, in some countries some social benefits are being viewed as part of a policy strategy to make it possible for adults to manage both roles simultaneously, without negative consequences in either domain. Thus far, only in the GDR, for women, and in Sweden, for men and women, is there any clear and deliberate attention to developing benefits which will make it easier for adults to fulfill home and labor market roles. This is a recent development and one which should be monitored closely in these and other countries for what it may suggest about future trends. We will return to this subject in the concluding chapter.

Given our conclusion regarding the limited societal support for an at-home role for women beyond the first year after childbirth, we turn, in the next chapter, to exploring the provision of child care services in these countries. Does child care policy in any of these countries facilitate a labor market role for women, by providing services to care for children during the day when both parents or the sole parent are away from home, at work?

NOTES

1. For further discussion of this benefit, its rationale and consequences, see Zsuzsa Ferge, "The Relation Between Paid and Unpaid Work of Women, a Source of Inequality—With Special Reference to Hungary," *Labour and Society* (April 1976), 1:37–52.

2. Full discussion of family allowances as part of family policy in France can be found in Nicole Questiaux and Jacques Fournier, "Family Policy in France," in Sheila B. Kamerman and Alfred J. Kahn, eds., *Family Policy: Government and Families in Fourteen Countries* (New York: Columbia University Press, 1978), pp. 117–82.

3. Outside the countries studied here, Czechoslovakia provides a benefit similar to the Hungarian benefit for second and subsequent children for two years. England provides a cash assistance program for single mothers which in many ways resembles AFDC. England also provides an income-tested supplement for one- and two-parent working families.

Three

CHILD CARE POLICY: SERVICES AND PROGRAMS

One response by government to changes affecting the family is to offer cash and related benefits that permit or require at-home care of very young children by a parent. These benefits were described in the previous chapter. An alternative is to facilitate, support, or provide out-of-home care of infants and toddlers, in order to encourage—or at least make possible—labor market participation by parents without damage to children. This chapter explores the latter alternative.

Again, the countries differ substantially. Any categorization misses some nuances. The following is basically correct, however; caveats will be presented as the discussion proceeds:

Out-of-home care is dominant in the explicit societal response to the under-threes in the *German Democratic Republic* (GDR) and in *Sweden*. However, the GDR has implemented its position, whereas Sweden offers only a modest amount of service thus far.

Out-of-home care is formally a *coequal* part of a deliberate policy response in *France*, along with diverse benefits. However, in fact, France has insufficient coverage (as experienced by parents) despite the most extensive provision of care in the West, the second most extensive among these six countries, and the most varied among all the countries.

Unattributed quotations in chapters 3 and 4 are from the country reports.

The following terms are used interchangeably in this chapter (with some distinctions introduced by country): day nursery, preschool, *crèche*, *Krippe*, center care. Similarly, we treat the following terms as synonymous: family day care, childminding.

Out-of-home care is not provided as an explicit policy response for *most* families in *Hungary*. However, it is growing, especially for children aged one-and-one-half to three; this is a pragmatic response to demand, despite modest coverage at present, and despite official preference for the benefits approach.

Out-of-home care for the under-threes is unacceptable in the *United States* and in the *Federal Republic of Germany* (FRG) as an explicit policy to be applied to *most* families. However, resources have been created, albeit on a modest scale, by parents whose children require care and by caretakers willing to respond. In addition, U.S. policy does support some provision for low-income families, as does, to a lesser extent, policy in the FRG.

Data are not complete or fully comparable, and there is no consensus as to what to count and compare among countries. Publicly provided or subsidized care only? Publicly licensed and supervised care, no matter by whom operated? On the one hand, there is special interest in efforts made by government to offer service, or to subsidize it. On the other hand, market systems are complex: the lack of direct or explicit positive involvement does not necessarily mean a truly neutral position. Licensing or regulation to protect children who are in care may be a fuller measure (or at the least a minimal measure) of a positive public stance in favor of out-of-home care. But even this is a shaky inference: perhaps licensing and inspection is only a reluctant act of child protection, deemed necessary but not meant to encourage anything!

The assessment of intent and attitude is thus deferred until we describe the individual countries. We begin here by reporting whatever numbers are available, whether from "consumer" surveys or supply censuses.

Our special focus is the under-three cohort, infants and toddlers, but provision for the preschoolers (under age six, generally, but under age seven in Sweden) is included for useful context and contrast.

In looking at the under-threes, we separate *center care* (*Krippen, crèches*, day nurseries, preschools) and *family day care* (childminders). The center programs are all day or part day, large centers and small. Most are publicly operated, regulated, or licensed; many are subsidized by public treasuries. There is also publicly operated, regulated, licensed, subsidized, accurately counted family day care. However, because several countries have large

TABLE 3.1
Where the Young Children Are: Center and Family Day Care in Six Countries (1975)

Country	Size of Under-3 Cohort	Under-3 In Care	Type of Care		Children 3-6 in Preschool	Comments
			Centers	Family Day Care		
Sweden	323,463	23%	7%	16%	28%	By 1978 the Swedish under-3 coverage was 30 percent and the 3-6 coverage was 32 percent (to age 7).
France	2.5 million	31	11	20	95+	
German Democratic Republic	532,048	50	50	—	85	If one does not consider children under 20 weeks of age (not eligible for centers), the 1977 under-3 coverage was 60+ percent (or 48 percent of the *whole* cohort), and the preschool coverage was 89 percent of the cohort. GDR centers overenroll by 10 percent to achieve this rate.
Hungary	519,000	12	12	—	78	
Federal Republic of Germany	1.8 million	3	4 (Children of Working	5 Mothers Only)	75+	1975: 9% of children of working mothers in care. Kindergarten not included. By 1977 it was known that 3.1 percent of the total cohort was in *Kindergarten*, and 1.5 percent in *Krippen*. Total under-3 coverage approximated 6-7 percent of the cohort, probably 15 percent of children of working mothers. Clearly 1975 count an underestimate.
U.S.A.	9.4 million	10-11	3-4	7	64	The 3-6 coverage includes preschool, kindergarten and day care, much of it part-day.

amounts of "market" and "black market" family day care as well, these counts are not precise. Some analysts argue that such care should not be counted at all in any assessment of positive policy within a country.

With these caveats in mind, we note in table 3.1 the following percentage rates for out-of-home, nonfamily, nonrelative care of children under age three in these six countries as of 1975:

FRG: 3
USA: 10-11
Hungary: 12
Sweden: 23
France: 31
GDR: 50

The 1977-78 updates which we report for several countries in the table and text suggest a continued growth in coverage, but not a change in the rank order. The FRG data probably should be corrected to show close to 1 percent of the cohort in kindergarten, too. (See table 3.10.)

We note both relatively high and relatively low coverage countries in Western Europe-United States and in Eastern Europe. East European coverage clearly features centers; while grandmothers and relatives have not disappeared as informal caretakers anywhere, there is no longer a significant labor force for more formal family day care in Eastern countries.

Within Western Europe and the United States family day care offers significantly more coverage than does center care, but centers are not insignificant. Sweden and France, it will be seen, define centers as coequal in policy, even though not yet in coverage.

The coverage rates—and perhaps they are indices of national policy commitment—read differently if we remove unlicensed-unregulated family day care from the country coverage totals. The relative rankings do not change, however. The following is an approximation:

FRG: 2
USA: 7(?)
Hungary: 12
Sweden: 14
France: 21
GDR: 50

(There are no reliable estimates for the United States as to the portion of family day care for under-threes which is unregulated. We have here made the overoptimistic assumption that half of infant-toddler day care is in some sense licensed-regulated or agency-operated.)

The data should be read against the backdrop of a tradition in most of these countries involving elements in the religious and secular culture, reinforced in modern time by psychoanalytic theory, and holding—in various formulations and to differing degrees—that responsible or "good" mothers take care of their children themselves (or, if prosperous, employ nurses for the role and supervise them); that children are deprived by out-of-home care and show the consequences in their later development; that group care of young children inflicts permanent developmental damage on many young children (and may even lead to mental retardation, mental illness, speech defects, delinquency, psychopathy, etc.); that widely sanctioned out-of-home care arrangements, certainly group care of the very young and perhaps even family day care, may be seen as part of a malignant process by which government disciplines the family and usurps its functions. Various motivations are assigned for the latter.

These and related views are still held by many people. Yet, some people in all countries, and a majority in some, clearly have rejected such conclusions. New rationales or rationalizations have been formulated as part of the process in which social provision develops.

In the first instance, formal arrangements for out-of-home care would seem to be a more drastic policy than one offering resources and benefits to sustain at-home care. Is "cash" not the most parsimonious and family-supportive response? The contrary may be true, however. In the poor law history of Europe and North America, parents were condemned morally if unable to meet their own needs; if public aid was required, "indoor" (institutional) provision was preferred because cash might "demoralize" and create disincentives for those managing on their own. Whether or not it is applicable in the present instance, we note this cultural precedent only to remark that in some places out-of-home care may be culturally as acceptable as, or even more acceptable than, cash and related social benefits—at least for the poor and the troubled. Or perhaps the cultural tradition is irrelevant, and the important questions are costs and the specific labor market situation.

On the level of professional and political debate, as will be seen, there are many positive arguments now offered for family day care and/or center care for infants and toddlers—arguments referring to the advantages for a child's socialization, development, and learning.

GERMAN DEMOCRATIC REPUBLIC

Group care of children—even overnight or week-long group care, if necessary—was adopted after World War II as the automatic solution to the problem of the very young children of working mothers. The early results were not satisfactory: frequent contagion, inadequate development of speech, other developmental problems, were common and were acknowledged. At this point, in theory at least, there was the choice to be made between making it financially possible for the mothers to remain at home for some years, and making group care better. For the GDR the reality, dictated by the particular industrial and labor force circumstances, left only the second choice. The GDR embarked on a remarkable and obviously successful effort to improve the center care (*Krippe*) for young children. The question of the appropriateness of group care for the three to five group was never seriously questioned; like the rest of the continent, the GDR provides a preschool program which is practically universal.

Center care coverage has been achieved in the GDR at a rate unmatched elsewhere in Europe: 48 percent of the 591,470 children under three as of 1977. GDR reports tend to compute rates by defining as "not eligible" for care all children under twenty weeks of age, since mothers are covered by maternity leaves. In this sense the overall 1977 coverage rate is given as 60 percent. The actual rate of center registration is about 40 percent for those under one and some 80 percent for the one- and two-year olds.The 260,000 *Krippe* places are distributed as follows:

Age	Percentage
0-1 years	16
1-2 years	41
2-3 years	41
3+	2
Total	100

Of the available *Krippe* places, it should be noted that in 1978 some 8.7 percent still were used for all-week care and 89.3 percent for the usual daytime care. GDR experts note that when the development began the all-

TABLE 3.2

GDR: Growth of Krippe and Kindergarten Coverage (1955-77)

Year	Facilities (Krippen)	Capacity (Krippen)	Coverage (Krippen)	Kindergarten Coverage Rate for 3-6 Age Group
1955	2,341	67,106	—	34.5%
1960	3,691	104,781	14.3%	46.1
1965	4,798	142,242	18.7	52.8
1970	5,278	183,412	29.1	64.5
1975	5,867	242,553	50.8 (50)[a]	84.5
1976	5,970	250,499	57.0	87.4
1977	6,062	257,990	60.1 (48)[a]	89.2

SOURCE: Margot Krecher, Gerda Niebsch, Walter Günther, "Gesellschaftliche Kinder-einrichtungen" in *Zur Gesellschaftlichen Stellung der Frau in der DDR* (Leipzig: Verlag für die Frau, 1978), tables on pp. 263, 278.

[a]The rates in parentheses are our calculations. This is the coverage rate, comparable to our rates for other countries, the ratio of "places" to the total cohort. The official tables now follow GDR practice of not counting children under 20 weeks of age because they are not eligible to attend centers. However, for 1977, we have included the reported 10 percent overenrollment to take account of absences.

week *Krippen* provided half of all capacity. The recommended policy in all of Eastern Europe now is to phase out child care that keeps children from their own homes and parents for the whole week.

There is no significant amount of family day care in the GDR. The only alternative resources sometimes available to mothers when they return to work are grandmothers already out of the labor force.

The *Krippe* is an established, permanent institution. When housing blocks are constructed, there is automatic construction of buildings for center care of the under-threes, as there is of kindergarten and elementary school space. Currently, joint construction of *Krippen-Kindergärten* is favored. (Each unit has its own director, but the kindergarten head tends to be in charge of the overall facility as well.) The training of personnel is built into national labor force planning. A national institute conducts research on the effects of the experience on children and produces the guidelines and norms that are implemented at the local level. An intermediary system of institutions guides the operating staffs and conducts ongoing training. There is a widely understood and implemented "curriculum," perhaps better described as a programing guide, derived from research and experience.

In short, the GDR has an extensive, relatively centralized program offering a high rate of coverage. Attendance at a center is the typical experience of a one- or two-year-old in this country. The goals are commensurate with the effort: not to provide mere custodial care that avoids damaging the child's development or assures normal physical growth, but focused and specific efforts to assure that there is optimum cognitive, social, and physical development of children in programs in which the curriculum is based on empirically formulated norms. The related ideology rejects the notion of takeover from the parents: parents are to remain responsible; the *Krippe* role is to "help the parents in education and health care while the parent works." Leaders in the field cite the continuing research findings to the effect that, in the GDR, "the family is the most important variable" affecting the child's development; especially critical is the education level of the mother.

As is the case in most countries, *Krippe* programs originate in a health ministry. Personnel caring for the children are often referred to as nurses, although they are more broadly trained. Doctors are dominant in the leadership. Despite this tradition and many medical survivals still visible in program operations, the programs have by now achieved a broader educational-socialization-developmental perspective.

FRANCE

Out-of-home care of young children has a very long history in France which is not accounted for by labor market conditions alone. "Wet nurses," the predecessors and namesakes of the present family day care mothers (*nourrices*), were important by the eighteenth century and used by all social classes. Group care in centers, the predecessor of both center day care and public nursery schools, started early in the nineteenth century in care houses (*salles d'asiles*) linked to poorhouses and workshops. The *école maternelle*, which now enrolls practically all three-to-five-year-olds in a public, free, universal nursery school, was regarded as a "given" in France by the 1950s. This development clearly was independent of labor force participation for mothers.[1] In short, out-of-home care is acceptable, familiar—and there are no strong publicly offered disincentives for most women, except perhaps for those at rather low income levels. Moreover, public involvement and regulation have been long established and increasingly important.

TABLE 3.3
*France: Child Care Arrangements for Children
Under 3 (1975)*

		Percent
Own mother		49.2%
Relative (in relative home)		18.0
Foster home or institution		0.6
Own home (by domestic)		1.5
"Supervised" out-of-home care		20.7
Center care	2.0	
Agency-operated		
family day care	1.0	
Licensed family		
day care	8.5	
École maternelle	9.2	
Unlicensed family day care		10.0
		100.0

NOTE: Calculated from official sources.

The pattern of provision is both more diverse and more comprehensive than that in the GDR. For one thing, there is specific provision for the children of families in which the mother is not in the labor force. For another, both center care and family day care are well developed and each has strong proponents.

About half of the under-threes experience out-of-home care. Almost 21 percent of the under-threes take part in publicly sponsored, licensed, supervised, nonrelative, out-of-home care. The current trend is toward increased public regulation of all out-of-home child care (private and public).

A more detailed overview for one area is provided in table 3.4 for the region that includes Paris. The data are derived from a survey conducted by the *Observatoire Regional de Santé*, Île de France. The licensed coverage percentage is a bit higher than for the country, but the demand also is greater given the higher labor force participation by mothers of children under three in this area.

More specifically, looking at the *école maternelle*, the single most important "supervised" resource in France, we find that infants and toddlers of mothers who do not work also have access, if there is space. This public nursery school, which serves practically all the three-to-fives, is also open

TABLE 3.4
Île de France: Child Care Arrangements for Children Under 3 (1975)

		Number	Percent
Total children under age 3		460,000	100%
In at-home care		220,000	48
Children of working mothers in care		240,000	52
In unlicensed, unsupervised care		130,000	28
In supervised out-of-home care		110,000	24
Nourrices—licensed family			
day care	45,000		9
Crèches familiales—municipal			
agency-operated family day care	9,231		2
Écoles maternelles	30,000		7
Crèches	25,400		6

to the twos. The development is limited only by the lack of capacity. As a consequence, 27 percent of the age two cohort attended in 1975 and 32 percent by 1977; as a practical matter, this means the two-and-one-half year olds primarily. Of these 69 percent had working mothers in 1975. (Under the French Seventh Plan, and before recent economic difficulties, there was a target goal of 45 percent coverage for the two-year-old cohort by 1980. Many of these would be children approaching their third birthday.)

Unlike the crèche, the école maternelle is free. It is open for a six-hour day for its regular program, four-and-one-half days per week (closed Wednesday and half-day Saturday) from either 8:30 or 9:00 A.M. to 11:30 A.M. or later, and then again from 1:00 or 1:30 P.M. to 4:00 or 4:30 P.M. Working parents pay for meals and supplementary care in the garderies, before and after regular school hours and Wednesday, to ensure coverage that coincides with working hours. Groups are large in this public nursery school: officially thirty-five or more children per class, even though actual attendance and effective group size are somewhat lower. The FRG and Hungary have a small amount of such usage—as space has become available. France, it will be noted, is the only country that offers two-year-olds access to a public nursery school as a matter of deliberate policy.

Also available to the children of nonworking mothers, but not entering into our "coverage" statistics, is the haltes-garderie, a part-time, center-type program which is used (by appointment) only a limited number of times per week for part of the day. When écoles maternelles are closed on Wednesday, the *haltes-garderie* may offer coverage for children of working mothers, too. One typical facility, which serves 20 children at a time, is used by 200 during the week.

As noted (table 3.3), care resources for children are more extensive than this. First, there are the *crèches*, serving under-threes whose mothers work and open to children aged two-and-one-half months to three years. The major form of *crèche*, *crèche collective*, had 47,063 places in 939 centers in 1975. The staffing ratios in the *crèche collective* are dramatically different from the *école maternelle*: the "preferred" norm is one adult to five children who cannot walk and one adult to eight "walkers." Groups range in size from six to fifteen, depending on child age. (The topic of standards receives more systematic attention in chapter 4.) The *crèche* operates on a twelve-hour, five-day week, 7 A.M. to 7 P.M. and is closed Saturday, Sundays, and holidays. There is a regrouping in a few centers for August holiday coverage, as needed.

There are also a small number of *mini-crèches*, an experimental form in which groups of a dozen children are cared for in renovated apartments or private houses, staffed by publicly employed personnel.

In addition, and far more important statistically, there are two types of family day care. First is the private *nourrice*, now officially known as the *assistante maternelle*, the "mother's helper," or "childminder," or, as she is known increasingly in the United States, the family day care mother. This is a woman who cares for children of others in her own home and collects fees directly from the child's parents. While, as noted, there were more unlicensed than licensed *nourrices* in 1975, new legislation (1978) is expected to change the ratio. Second is the *crèche familiale* (a misleading name), known elsewhere as "municipal family day care" or "agency-operated family day care." This form of family day care is publicly subsidized. The family day care mother in this relatively small-scale program is on the staff of a social agency which collects parental fees (and public subsidies) and pays her. A directress, at the head of each *crèche familiale*, supervises all the *nourrices* (usually thirty to forty) and controls admissions. The average *nourrice* in the *crèche familiale* cares for 1.56 children. The more typical private *nourrice* cares for an average of two.

French out-of-home child care provision in 1975 may be summed up from the "supply" side, relying on program reports, except in the instance of unregulated family day care (*nourrices*):

Écoles maternelles:	almost 233,000 under-threes attended
Nourrices (licensed):	approximately 100,000 cared for about 215,000 children
Nourrices (unlicensed):	approximately 100,000 cared for about 250,000 children
Crèches familiales:	14,402 *nourrices*, organized in 343 units, cared for 21,856 children
Crèches collectives:	939 had a capacity 47,063
Mini-crèches:	coverage insignificant
Haltes-garderies:	858 caring part time for different children, many of them with nonworking mothers

In 1975, 7,357 of 47,063 *crèche* "places" were located in hospitals, public institutions, and private firms. All other center care was publicly operated. Counting "facilities," 756 centers were publicly operated, 13 were semipublic, and 170 were in private firms or voluntary institutions. Family day care, as noted, also is public (*crèche familiale*) or private, licensed and unlicensed.

Except for the private *nourrice*, each of the care forms is subsidized directly and quite substantially, since public provision leads inexorably to higher standards and salaries and to a convergence of costs. For the user-

Figure 3.1

French Child Care Facilities and Their Clientele

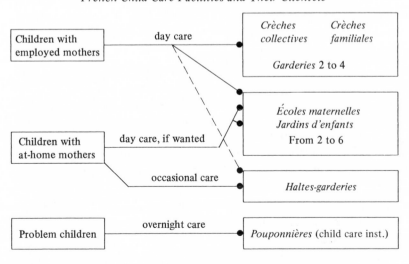

parent the *nourrice* has been the most expensive care form until recently; currently centers are more expensive for upper-income parents because of the graduated fees. The *crèche collective* and the *crèche familiale* are free or very low cost for low-income parents, but for others, are quite expensive. The *école maternelle* is the least expensive for almost all, although the charge for meals and supplementary before- and after-school programs makes it more expensive than the *crèche* for those very low-income families for whom the *crèche* is completely free.

There is no strong challenge to the idea of having out-of-home care arrangements for infants and toddlers, although some participants in the current debate prefer an emphasis on a "mother's wage" or other cash benefit alternative. The French maternity leave is of relatively short duration; thus the assumption is that such care may be needed. However, there is a lively debate about the relative superiority of the *nourrice*, especially the *nourrice* in the *crèche familiale* and the *crèches*. Until recent years, it was assumed that the motherlike *nourrice* was preferable for the very young. This system was known to be cheaper if operated in an unregulated way under limited standards. Now, as the picture of care becomes better known, the balance is shifting. More and more people apparently recognize that the *nourrice's* care is not truly comparable to care within the family. If well done it is not cheap. Instead, these represent two alternative forms of care: the *crèche* is more visible, offers staff diversity and the possibility of a consciously directed program, the *nourrice* is more flexible in hours and location, and often more familiar to "lower-class" parents. Clearly, the middle class now makes more use of *crèches collectives* than does the working class, and the *école maternelle* is popular with both. Once a "welfare program," the *crèche* is now established and generally accepted by parents.

Half of all *crèches collectives* are in the Paris region; nine counties have none as yet. There are waiting lists everywhere. The regions outside Paris employ the *école maternelle* somewhat more than does Paris for under-threes, in part, it is assumed, for lack of alternatives.

Given an enormous variation in quality, however, proponents of each form can produce well-documented cases against the alternatives. Professionals debate about program specifics and modes of parent participation. Many political groups urge *crèche* expansion while others reject such expansion, in particular because of the high capital expenditure. Parents argue about philosophy, convenience, and what, in their view, is truly best for children. *École maternelle* is free and does not require that the mother work—both influential factors. The French Seventh Plan (1976-80) took a middle position: under the heading "harmonization of parenting, work, and education of children," the plan calls for 25,000 more places in family day care, 25,000 in *crèches*, and more *école maternelle* space for the under-threes to bring coverage to 45 percent.

Numerous problems of discontinuity, competition, and confusion arise out of the fact that *crèches* and *nourrices* are in the health administrative system and *école maternelle* is in education. Reform efforts and policy clarification must deal as much with "turf" and professional bureaucracies in their competitions as with substance.

HUNGARY

Hungary, it will be recalled, provides strong financial support for at-home care by parents on leave from work for the first three years of a child's life. The support then ends abruptly, but preschool provision is becoming universal: some 78 percent of the three to five cohort attend preschool (76%) or child care center (2%). Even more complete coverage is expected.

It has been noted, however, that a significant number of women return to work before the child's third birthday. This is particularly the case with better-educated women in the higher occupational categories. Their children thus are especially likely to need out-of-home care. It is provided in approximately equal amounts by *crèches* and by grandmothers. The child care picture is summarized in table 3.5.

We note the similarity of the Hungarian coverage rate for out-of-home nonrelative care to the U.S. rates (and, for that matter, to rates in a number of other countries in the north and west of Europe). Coverage rates vary widely between urban and rural areas, as in many countries. In Budapest the coverage rate is almost 25 percent, while it is lower in small towns and rural areas and totals 12 percent for the country as a whole.

As in the case of the GDR, Hungary's formal provision is *center* care. Nonetheless, a small amount of nonrelative, out-of-home care (that would elsewhere be unlicensed family day care) exists.

Waiting lists and relatively high ratios of registration to *crèche* places have led to general agreement that some expansion is needed. The 1985 target is coverage for 15 percent of the cohort.

The center, then, is the one real out-of-home care model. However, as noted, there is a small amount of preschool (kindergarten) use for children

TABLE 3.5
Hungary: Care for All Children Under 3 (1975)

	Number	Percent
At home with mother who is on child care leave	295,000[a]	57%
At home with mother (who was not in labor force before childbirth)	89,000[a]	17
Crèches	55,000	11
Preschool (kindergarten)	6,000	1
Resident nurseries, infant homes	4,000	1
Other (mostly grandmothers; also includes newborns whose mothers are still on maternity leave; also some paid care in own home and by nonrelative)	70,000	13
	519,000	100

[a]Informed estimate.

under three (1% of the cohort), in particular for those children aged two years and nine months or older. Currently there is some discussion of possible extension of the preschool to include even more of the two-year-olds. As will be seen, this development has also begun in the Federal Republic of Germany. France, we have noted, has had a policy that opens the public nursery school to twos for some time, and coverage is very significant already.

One sees in Hungary, in relatively sharp focus, a phenomenon which we believe is developing everywhere; the tendency to concentrate under-three group care in the older two-thirds of the cohort as maternity or parental benefits, plus other entitlements, permit mothers (or fathers) to remain at home with the child of six, eight, or even twelve months or more.

The Hungarian *crèche* age distribution as of December 1975 was as follows:

Age	Percentage
0–11 months	6.6
12–17 months	22.0
18–35 months	61.2
over 36 months	10.2
Total	100.0

Of the 1,132 *crèches* with 49,356 places at that time, 39,573 places were in *crèches* directly operated by public authorities (80%) and 9,783 (20%) in centers operated by enterprises (largely factories). The typical center has forty-four "places," registers forty-nine children, and has an average daily attendance of thirty-nine.

Since both *crèche* and preschool (kindergarten) open for a twelve-hour day, there is no special program required to meet the after-school needs of children in these age groups.

There is, however, some possibility that more extensive provision of family day care may evolve, more out of governmental permission than extensive initiative. New regulations for the child care grant permit a mother, home on child care leave, to take one to three other children in care and still receive her grant. This should, perhaps, be interpreted as a response to a tight labor market situation for relatively unskilled workers and a willingness to have more back at work sooner (and thus the need for more rapid expansion of care resources). There is also discussion of a possible cash grant to purchase child care in the marketplace if center space does not meet all needs.

Despite the possible expansion of informal care, however, Hungary has relatively few variations in its out-of-home resources. The discussion of centers is consistent with the policy: acceptance but not enthusiastic promotion. The most common viewpoint is that one should postpone use of center care as long as possible even if it is unavoidable. The argument is a familiar one. More specifically: "The child builds up the first and decisive patterns of emotional life and the whole of his personality in the first year of his life. The precondition of a well-grounded pattern is the opportunity to establish a *constant* and *close* relationship with a person who concentrates love and attention on the child. The chances for the realization of a stable connection with one person are higher in a family than even in the best group care."

Given such a rationale, it is not surprising that the *crèche* "program does not offer education for the child." However, in stating as the central goal the establishment of "a situation as close to [the] home situation as possible," the additional point is made that it is the goal of the *crèche* to "assist the child in developing many-sided abilities." Clearly a curriculum is not absent. In reaction to the notion that formal teaching at this age stifles creativity, the Hungarian center places major emphasis on autonomous activity and *peer* interaction. A leading Hungarian pediatrician, Dr. Emmi Pikler, is known world-wide for innovative theory and practice in this area.

The argument for at-home care, buttressed by the child care grant, is weaker in the case of deprived families, neglected children, large families generally. For these the *crèche* is seen in a more positive light. One notes a similar viewpoint in the Federal Republic of Germany, and its historical continuity: *crèches* were originally invented as a social service for the deprived. In Hungary, however, the practice does not reflect such viewpoints: the percentage of children in the eligible age cohort who actually are in the *crèche* is closely related to social class; from 30 percent of children of upper white-collar workers (two-parent households) the percentage declines to lower white-collar, skilled nonagricultural labor, to manual work in agriculture. Exactly the same progression holds for one-parent families.

The Ministry of Health supervises the *crèche* system. Facilities, staff, and practices reflect health system origins. However, in daily operation and in their increasingly close linkages with kindergartens, the *crèches* are focusing on child socialization and development and are responsive to relevant research and theory. A district pediatrician supervises the health aspects of the program but children are cared for in the general neighborhood-based child health system.

SWEDEN

When both parents (or the sole parent) of young children are employed outside the home, the Swedish policy preference is to provide out-of-home care. Because such provision is built on the foundation of the parental insurance, however, it means care from six to nine months of age onward, in most instances—or this would be the case were there sufficient facilities. In reality, care coverage has not begun to approximate what is implied in the policy and is not likely to do so in the near future.

There is some preference in the more articulate leadership groups in the field for centers over family day care arrangements. After a long predominance of family day care, near parity has been established between the two modes of official municipal care, center and family care. However, there is also substantial private family day care, which tips the overall balance away from center care, for the youngest children in particular. Furthermore, there is currently more public acceptance of a combined system involving both

TABLE 3.6

Sweden: Care for Children Under Age 3, 1975 and 1977

Care Arrangements	Number		Percent	
	1975	*1978*	*1975*	*1978*
Centers (public)	20,000	30,000	6%	10%
Family day care (public)	24,000	30,000	7	10
Family day care (private)	30,000	30,000	9	10
Total	74,000	90,000		
Under-3 cohort	323,000	300,000		
Percent in care			23	30

centers and family day care than there was several years ago. Most expansion plans, nonetheless, deal with preschool centers; increasing discussion of a possible child caring cash allowance (perhaps along the lines of the Hungarian model) does not seem to affect the determination to provide sufficient care facilities as soon as feasible and affordable.

Also integral to the policy—again somewhat more related to centers than to family day care—is substantial stress on quality. Both the physical environment and the curricula are carefully dealt with, and standards for both are as high as, or higher than, those of any other country here represented. The relatively modest coverage is in sharp contrast with the striving for standards, however—an implicit interim trade-off of quantity for quality.

Swedish data from the consumer end for the care arrangements of the total under-three cohort are not completely firm. It is possible to approximate the picture, however, from the supply side. The total under-three cohort in 1975 consisted of 323,363 children. By 1978 it was about 300,000. Government experts provide the estimates for table 3.6; the data are more firm for programs involving public expenditures—whose participants can be counted—than for unofficial and often unrecorded family day care.

Sweden has made the indicated rapid progress in under-three coverage while concentrating on the need for preschool space for its three to six group. While elementary school begins at seven, most of the six-year-olds are now in preschool.

Since Swedish program plans do not in fact separate out the under-threes, we note the following 1978 coverage (with part-time care either included or excluded):

Without part-time care:

Total 0–6 in care	250,000
Total cohort	800,000
Coverage rate	32 percent

With part-time care:

Total 0–6 in care	365,000
Total cohort	800,000
Coverage rate	47 percent

The relatively low Swedish census of center care space, given the general approval of such provision, is best understood in historical perspective. Sweden lacks the long tradition of preschool education found in France and in Germany. Indeed, even elementary school has been delayed until age seven. In 1966 when the new policy emerged there were only 10,000 center care places. The current statistics—including full provision for the six-year-olds—is thus a significant achievement in a dozen years.

Despite financial constraints, expansion of preschool centers continues in Sweden. It is expected that the additional 100,000 places originally planned for 1976–80 will be achieved only one year behind schedule.

The basic *municipal preschool center* model calls for an infant department with ten to twelve children ages six months to three years and a sibling group of fifteen children in the ages three to seven. Recommended staffing ratios are two adults to five children under age three. The actuality is close to a one to five coverage. Of the 277 municipalities in Sweden, some 70 have

TABLE 3.7
Sweden: Coverage Rates, Children 3–6

	No.	*Full Time*	*Part-time Included*
Centers (public)	85,000	17%	17%
Family day care (public)	45,000	9	9
Family day care (private)	30,000	6	6
Part-time center care (public)	115,000	—	23
Total, full time	160,000	—	—
Total, full time and part-time	275,000	—	—
Cohort size	500,000	—	—
Total percent		32	55

no infant departments at all. There are many such departments in Stockholm, however.

Municipal family day care, the other major official care model, serves the preschool group and also school-age children in the after-school hours before parents have returned from work. This childminder program recalls the French *crèche familiale*: childminders are employed by the municipality. The childminder may care for a maximum of four children including her own. Childminders are supervised/coordinated by a municipal social service staff member on a middle-management level. Fees are identical with those for center care.

The third model, the *private childminder*, is clearly quite significant numerically, although little detail is available. Along with relative care, the unregulated family day care homes help to make up the deficit in places in the preferred programs and help working families to cope. As in other countries, they become part of an underground economy, often paying no taxes and conferring no social security entitlements upon their workers.

Leisure centers, the final form, are the after-school provisions, a group program for those over seven. Centers often share buildings with sibling groups and infant-care programs, thus permitting children to return after school to places where they attended day nursery. Apart from their own special, informal group programs, many interact with both the sibling and infant groups in the preschool center.

There are a small number of experimental group programs in centers which include infant and sibling groups in one unit. There are other experiments in which childminders and their charges share center care experiences part of the day, whether daily or once a week.

The Swedish program does not identify different objectives for under-threes' programs from those formulated for the three to five group. On one level these objectives are to care for children whose parents are working or attending school, or for children requiring "special care and stimulation." Given the shortage of places and the center priority system, care for these groups is clearly the manifest and real objectives. However, a series of commissions and related official reports in Sweden have gone well beyond this in stating the goal for those children admitted to the center programs. Highlighted among the latter aspirations, which set the guidelines for staffing, buildings, and programing, are such overriding aims as "to cooperate with parents in giving each child the best possible chance of comprehensive personal development" and to "encourage children to seek and use knowledge." There are more specific goals related to self-image, ability to communicate, and concept formation as well.

In the context of Swedish discussion, there is another implicit objective: to share child rearing with parents or to provide support for parents in their child rearing in such a way as to permit them to redefine their respective roles as spouses and citizens.

Government does not try to recover full costs of care, perhaps because the objectives are societal, as well as parental. The national government subsidizes a substantial portion of the capital costs of group facilities. Parental fees to the municipality are geared to their incomes and the number of children, with a recommended total maximum of two-thirds of operating costs.

There are practically no industrial or proprietary (profit-making) child care centers in Sweden.

A full and objective picture of public preference in this field is not available, but in 1975 the trade union confederation, LO, completed a large survey among its members. Large unmet demand for municipal day nurseries and municipal family day care was reported, particularly for the former. Significant numbers wanted to give up private childminders. As was found in a U.S. study (see below), parents tend to prefer whatever care they use (center or family day care); however, when they are dissatisfied, the preference is almost always for center care, not for family day care.

Not all surveys show the same results, but there is a consistent preference of more-educated parents for group care as contrasted with family day care. In some surveys, staff members oppose center care for the very young, especially for children under age one.

There are widespread waiting lists, especially for center care in the large cities and the suburbs, so that municipalities all have priority rating systems favoring single mothers, those with various problems, immigrants, and the less affluent.

It is expected that center care for infants and toddlers will increase, and a commission is considering suitable form and content for such expansion.

Sweden places these programs in a social welfare administrative context rather than under health or education, and the programs do display ease in giving dominance to child development concerns. At the same time, the responsible unit under the National Social Board, which supervises, inspires, and leads local initiatives, avoids identification either with social work or with early childhood education. The child care centers (preschool) serve all children from infancy to compulsory school age (7) and attempt to integrate early childhood education, social service, and health. The atmosphere is certainly not medical. Localities do attempt to integrate child care center health services with the regular child health system.

UNITED STATES

The United States and the Federal Republic of Germany, the final two countries in the group, are federal republics, and the national government neither operates programs directly nor normally subsidizes or aids providers directly. Much in service delivery depends on state (*Land*) initiative.

In the case of the United States, while federal funding patterns and regulations could create irresistible incentives for states in a field such as this, the initiative has not been forthcoming. There is no explicit policy at the federal level or in the states as to the place of care arrangements out of the home for most children under three. Nor is there firm policy or direction as to the form of that care, where it is developed.

In general, mothers on AFDC (public social assistance, mostly for single mothers and their children) with very young children are not expected to take training or to accept jobs, so there is no serious effort to develop care arrangements for their children on a large scale in publicly operated or funded day care—with exceptions in some states or communities. Mothers who want or need to work, therefore, enter the market and find service in regulated or unregulated family day care homes or in social agencies and church center facilities, or in centers operated by the profit sector, and may be able to choose from different centers catering to their areas.

This, at least, would appear to be the situation. Because of lack of systematic programing, or policy debate, or a leadership agency for the under-threes specifically, there has been no basis for systematic data collection. In fact, this may be said about the entire under-five cohort and its care needs. Federal day care regulations (really guides, not widely endorsed) were adopted in 1968 and made no special reference to the under-threes. In 1974, in amending legislation for social service funding, the Congress for the first time differentiated this group, perhaps signaling some recognition of the infants (under-two) and toddlers (2-3) as a special group. A flurry of survey work during the 1975-78 period has sought to clarify the program and care picture of the birth to age five group in the United States, and large, expensive surveys as well as comparative studies were undertaken. Symbolic of the only partial recognition of the under-three group thus far is the limited analysis and tabulation of coverage and programs relevant to the present discussion.

Nonetheless, the outlines of the picture begin to emerge, even though the results reported are probably inexact, and important questions are unanswered.[2] As indicated, provision in this field is a result of a combined social and economic market. The former is a nonprofit response in the social service tradition to "need" and "problems" of problem families"; the latter operates in response to both low-income and upper-income groups.

For context, we note first the generally unrecognized coverage rates for the three-to-five-year-olds. In 1976, of 9.7 million in this age group in the United States, 49 percent attended private nursery, public prekindergarten (three- and four-year-olds), and public kindergarten classes. This total included 31 percent of the threes and fours and 81 percent of the fives. In addition, 11 percent of the five-year-olds were in elementary school. Some 1 million day care children were not simultaneously in these prechool arrangements, yielding an estimated unduplicated 6.2 million three-to-five-year-olds in a day program or 64 percent of the cohort (the comparable figure for 1978 is about 68 percent). The preschool day is short, but parents may arrange overlapping shifts and may package preschool and day care, especially family day care—along with own care, relative care, and sharing with neighbors. A half-million of the children in preschool also attended center day care or family day care. There are other after-school programs not adequately reported.[3]

Only the United States, of the countries here discussed, employs day care centers for the over-threes, views day care and preschool as two separate if parallel systems serving the same age cohort, and is not committed formally to a coverage goal through one standard system. Nonetheless, the day care plus preschool totals begin to approximate European totals, if short day center care and unregulated family day care are counted. The same is apparently the case with the under-three picture, despite its dependence on an unorganized amalgam of a social and economic market.

The much publicized Head Start, a compensatory program for deprived, poor children, was originally more often part day than all day and not geared to the schedules of working parents. In 1970, some one-third to one-fourth of the participation was all day. Depending on the local auspice of the particular facility and definitions adopted by different surveys, Head Start data may be tabulated as preschool or as day care. By 1979, Head Start had capacity for 387,500, most over age three, and the all-day proportion may have grown.

No complete data are available, but it is known that a majority of current Head Start children have single mothers who are black and often very young. It is believed that as many as two-thirds of the mothers may be employed. Initially most Head Start mothers did not work. A Head Start variant for working parents is under discussion.

Data from a 1975 sample survey of consumers show that only a minority of the parents of children under three use a significant amount (over 10 hours) of substitute care each week. There is, of course, much "baby sitting" connected with parental recreation. Of those who turn to out-of-home care arrangements, the larger proportion, by far, seek or find family day care. (By using the consumer survey, we are able to distinguish relative and nonrelative family day care—as do the French.) In the "substantial care" category, over thirty hours per week, 2 percent of the under-threes are in center care and 4 percent in family day care. The ten to twenty-nine hour totals are not to be ignored, however, since many parents have shift or part-time work arrangements which are compatible with such service. Another 1–2 percent are in center care and 3 percent in family day care in this subgroup, for a grand total of 10–11 percent of the cohort (see tables 3.8 and 3.9). Unfortunately, totals are not available for subgroups within the ten to twenty-nine hour totals.

The best, if somewhat inaccurate, absolute numerical counts, based on the consumer survey, thus add up as follows for children under three in the United States (1975):

- 650,000 (7 percent of cohort) in *nonrelative family day care*
  (286,000 for 10–29 hours weekly)
  (364,000 for over 30 hours weekly)
- 286,000 (4 percent of cohort in group care (*center care*)
  (106,000 for 10–29 hours weekly)
  (180,000 for over 30 hours weekly)

There are few details about licensed or unlicensed *family day care* for the under-threes, but a survey is under way.

A sample study,[4] based on extensive data collection in 3,167 day care

TABLE 3.8

U.S. Care Modes: A Consumer Survey

	Number and Percentages of Children under Age 3 in Care	
Type of Care	*Percent*	*Number*
In Own Home by Relative		
10–29 hours per week	3	245,900
30+ hours per week	3	239,900
In Own Home by Nonrelative		
20–29 hours per week	3	238,500
30+ hours per week	1	130,500
Relative's Home		
10–29 hours per week	4	402,500
30+ hours per week	3	287,300
Nonrelative's Home		
(Family Day Care)		
10–29 hours per week	3	286,000
30+ hours per week	4	364,600
Nursery and Day Care Center		
10–29 hours per week	<2	106,300
30+ hours per week	2	179,700

SOURCES: *National Consumer Day Care Study*, vol. 2, table 6; also, Mary Jo Bane rate calculations from *National Consumer Day Care Study* as presented in Mary Jo Bane et al., "Child Care Arrangements of Working Parents," *Monthly Labor Review* (October 1979), 102:51.

centers out of 183,000 centers identified in fifty states, showed that of the 900,000 children enrolled in *center care*, some 121,800 were age two or younger (see table 3.9). Almost 15 percent of enrollees were infants and toddlers, whereas half were three to four, and 21 percent were five. Fifteen percent were school age, an age representation not found in other countries. Of the under-threes, 39,849 were under two and 81,974 were age two to three. The survey report recognizes that the count is probably incomplete. We assume that the consumer survey comes closer to an accurate count.

Thus, if one looks at the supply end, only a little over 1 percent of children under three were in center care. But if one looks at the consumer study and includes less-than-full-day care, this figure reaches 3 to 4 percent.

The supply study (whose totals are admittedly low) disclosed that of all

TABLE 3.9
United States: Children under 3 in Center Care

Age of Child	Private Funding		Public Funding		All Centers
	Profit	*Nonprofit*	*Profit*	*Nonprofit*	*Total (Percent)*
Under Two Years (Birth to 23 months)	15,400	11,200	4,000	9,300	39,900 (4.5)
Two Years (24 to 35 months)	27,300	22,500	9,900	22,300	82,000 (9.1)
Three Years (36 to 47 months)	51,900	57,600	22,200	72,400	204,100 (22.7)
Four Years (48 to 59 months)	62,300	74,800	25,300	95,200	257,600 (28.7)
Five and Older (60 months and older)	81,600	85,600	30,000	116,900	314,100 (34.9)
All Children	238,500	251,700	91,400	316,100	897,700

SOURCE: Abt Associates, *Children at the Center* (Cambridge, Mass.: *National Day Care Study*, 1979), 1: 262.

U.S. day care centers, 72.4 percent had no children under age two, and 80 percent had fewer than five such children; in fact, 50 percent of all centers had fewer than five children under age three. Only 1 percent of some 2,500 centers served infants (under two) exclusively, and 18 percent served five or more children under age two along with older children. Most of the infant-toddler center care was for over forty hours weekly.

The infant-toddler center programs were apparently relatively new and geographically concentrated. Of the under-threes in center care, 61.2 percent were in the southeast and the southwest. In fact, 80 percent of the under-twos were in the southern regions. The care picture was dominated by 10 southeastern and four southwestern states. The age distribution was: under eight months of age, 0.9 percent; 8 months to two years, 3.6 percent; and two to three years, 9.1 percent.

Here, too, whatever the causal factors, the U.S. picture is not unlike that in Europe, despite the lack of a public maternity benefit program. Only 250 children under six weeks of age are known to be in center care at any time, and the age concentration is at the upper end of the cohort.

Average capacity of day care centers nationally is 57, and average enrollment is 51. Centers that include under-twos enroll 69 and have a capacity of 77. There is generally little age mixing in infant-toddler centers. If anything, children under and over two are joined more often than they are combined with those aged three and four. Nonetheless, as noted, virtually all centers with infants and toddlers also serve older children. Centers that accommodate under-twos seem to be growing more rapidly than others (a tentative conclusion).

While a high adult-to-child ratio has been sought (one adult to four children under age three) the goal is not attained in many places. The norm is being reexamined and group size standards considered (see chapter 4).

The public-private ratio of centers caring for children under age three is one to three. Direct public operation is by state and local government, schools, and other agencies. More than half the private centers are proprietary—organized to make a profit. Of these, some are franchised by national chains, but the majority are independent. The nonprofit centers are often affiliated with churches and religious organizations or with private social service agencies. In southern states, over 75 percent of children under age three attend privately funded centers; this is the situation for 45 percent of the under-threes in the north and west. In general, users of these centers tend to have low incomes; 29 percent are black.

Between 50 and 60 percent of couples in two-parent families using under-three center care or family day care for under-threes are at work. Even higher proportions of the single mothers are. When asked about why care is used, the vast majority cite work or training. However, there is clear interest in more than custodial care. Parents of children in centers feel that a wide range of cognitive and social skills should be taught these children and often say that it is the educational program that makes them choose the center over baby-sitting or family day care.

Two preference surveys among care users are of interest.[5] The majority of parents of children of all ages, questioned in a consumer sample, interchanged the terms "day care" and "nursery school" and were pleased with the programs. Many with children under two would prefer such care to the in-home and other-home (relative and nonrelative care) arrangements now used. And when a sample of parents of under-threes in centers were asked about preferences, they said they would like to continue their patterns or be given cash instead—and remain at home (25%). Few would turn to family day care.

Unlike all countries in this group except Sweden, the United States places its public day care in a social service (social welfare) context. (However, this is not the case for private nursery schools.) Facility inspection may be a local health-fire department responsibility and standard setting at the state and local level is variously distributed among health, education, and social welfare departments. But the social service and public assistance origin of the public programs (and the lack of a separate system for the under-threes) means that the U.S. program does not have the "health" atmosphere or history of most of the others. There may be local health supervision but, with some exceptions, children are individually served by private or public pediatricians, depending upon parental circumstances.

FEDERAL REPUBLIC OF GERMANY

The FRG is the largest of the European countries in the group and its under-three cohort consisted of 1,810,684 children in 1975 (1.5 million projected for January 1978), down from 3 million in 1965. While there is no specific policy for children under three, the FRG has a distinct family policy: a preference for buttressing the family via child allowances, health services, and housing supports, and for encouraging the mother to ramain at home in her child caring and homemaker roles. As we have seen, however, female labor force participation is not particularly low—and birth rates are very low. Nonetheless, there is little deliberate public effort to actively expand out-of-home care. As in the United States, the states (*Länder*) are in any case the service delivery initiators, and they have been given little federal encouragement in this regard. The results are low coverage, a scarcity of relevant data, and some tendency not to face what is occurring—and nonetheless some innovation and expansion, as the "social market" responds to need.

For 1975, the base year for our intercountry comparisons, the only data available come from a survey of care modes for children of working mothers only (table 3.10). Even this report presents problems because it does not deal deliberately with multiple use and yields a total of 108 percent. It does confirm the primacy of "in-family" arrangements (over half the chil-

TABLE 3.10
FRG: Care of Children under 3 with Working Mothers (1975)

Caretaking Persons		Persons: Family and Nonfamily		Environments	
Mother	18	Mother	18		
Grandparents	46	Other family members	56	In family environment	81
Other adult relatives	7				
Older siblings	3				
Domestics, child nurses	7				
Neighbors, friends	4	Persons not belonging to the family	34	Outside of family environment	27
Family day care (1 licensed)	5				
Foster families	1				
Krippen	4				
Other (child institutions, homes)	13				
	108		108		108

SOURCE: FRG report, citing Arbeitsgruppe Tagesmütter, "Das Modellprojekt Tagesmütter," DJI aktuell (Munich: Juventa Verlag, 1977), p. 44.

NOTE: Figures given are percent of children under 3; 100 percent is surpassed because of multiple use, as under certain circumstances working mothers take advantage of several care arrangements.

dren of working mothers), the significance of grandmothers in such arrangements (46%) of the children), and the relatively small roles of *Krippen* (4%) and family day care (5%). The catch-all 13 percent "other" is known to include some under-threes in *Kindergärten*.

Since in 1975 in a cohort of 1.8 million children under age three some 541,000 were children of working mothers, this 9 percent coverage rate in formal, nonfamily care (including unlicensed family day care) translates at most into a coverage rate of 3 percent for the total FRG under-three cohort in 1975 (table 3.1), and that could be an overstatement.

This estimation is confirmed on the *Krippen* side at least by the following calculation:

5 percent in "official" and unofficial family   27,050 children
    day care
4 percent in *Krippen*   21,640 children

Since this *Krippen* total coincides with a national count of *Krippen* space, it confirms the virtual limitation of *Krippen* use to children of working mothers. It is not known, however, how much unregulated family day care may exist and may be used by other than working mothers. In any case the available material and any assessment of its error rate suggests less than half the coverage rate of the Unites States, the next lowest country on the list.

A facility survey offers some precision: Some 829 *Krippen* had 24,251 places. (There were, by contrast, 23,310 *Kindergärten* for the three to five group with almost 1.5 million places and 2,376 *Kinderhorten* providing after-school care.) The 24,251 *Krippen* places, related to an under-three cohort of 1,810,684, yields 1.3 percent coverage. Of these places, 8,160 were in Berlin and 3,240 in Hamburg. Munich, with 3,630 places, half of the Bavarian total, has only 10 percent of that state's population. The *Krippen* development is, in short, urban.

A 1977 survey appears to offer a more complete coverage picture and is not limited to children of working mothers. The cohort totaled 1.68 million, of whom 513,000 had working mothers. (Some 31.3 percent of the mothers of under-threes were working, 60 percent of these full time.)

Especially interesting is the information, reported for the first time in 1977, that as birth rates have fallen and space has become available, FRG kindergartens have admitted children under age three. Thus, as in France, there is more coverage by *Kindergärten* than by *Krippen*. While more and

TABLE 3.11
FRG: Child Care Facilities for Children under 3

		Krippen		Kindergärten	
		Number	Percent	Number	Percent
Total under 3	1.6 million	24,719	1.5	52,000	3.1
Children of working mothers only	513,000	24,719	4.8	26,000	5.0

more *Kindergärten* have begun to offer optional all-day care, half are still completely limited to half days.

If one assumes for 1977 the licensed and unlicensed family day care totals (27,050) of 1975, the overall coverage rate for all children under three becomes:

Krippen	1.5 percent
Kindergärten	3.1 percent
Family day care	2.0 percent (approximate)
Total	6.6 percent

For children of working mothers it is:

Krippen	4.8 percent
Kindergärten	5.0 percent
Family day care	5.0 percent (approximate)
Total	14.8 percent

By 1977 there were 830 *Krippen*. The *Krippen* sponsorship is 73 percent public (states, cities, localities), 22 percent by private social agencies, and 5 percent industrial (especially hospitals), according to 1975 data. By contrast, *Kindergärten* are 28 percent publicly sponsored and 68 percent voluntary. There were 23,000 *Kindergärten* in 1977. In effect, *Krippen* are associated with a public aid tradition: the state is seen as stepping in only when the family cannot manage, as in cases of a single mother who works, two parents who work, or child neglect. The heaviest users are low-income, foreign, and single-parent families. (We lack similar data for family day care.)

Regional *Krippen* coverage is quite unbalanced. One-third of all places are in Berlin. Almost all facilities are in big cities in the industrial regions.

TABLE 3.12

FRG: Krippen and Kindergärten
Availability per 1,000 Children (1965-76)

	Kindergärten	Kinderkrippen
1965	327	6
1970	385	7
1975	655	13
1976	705	14

SOURCE: *Die Situation der Kinder in der Bundesrepublik Deutschland* (Wiesbaden: Statistisches Bundesamt, 1979), p. 132.

NOTE: Ages 0–3 for *Krippen*; 3–6 for *Kindergärten*.

There are no data available as yet on the geographic concentration of *Kindergärten* now serving children under age three.

Symbolic of the status of *Krippen* is the fact that whereas a *right* to *Kindergärten* has been established, and a child socialization-development mission stated, no such action has been taken for *Krippen*. The target for *Kindergärten* was coverage for 75 percent of the cohort in 1978. This now has been reached nationally and was exceeded in some places before the target date. The basis for public provision of *Krippen* is the view that government must assure that the mother or a substitute is available to rear each child. And since the issue is substitute *care*, there is no curriculum aimed at specific socialization or learning. Protective and health components are stressed, particularly in the construction guidelines for *Krippen*. Table 3.12 compares the growth of *Kindergärten* and *Krippen* in recent years.

It is perhaps reflective of the basic intent to avoid expansion of *Krippen* and of use by a broader population that when in 1974 the government decided to explore a pattern for more extensive care, it inaugurated a *Tagesmütter* project. In general, this would be similar to the *crèche familiale* or agency-sponsored family day care in other countries. There was emphasis on high-quality caretakers, agency supports, adequate income. However, despite a most impressive and rigorous research design, this project for 250 was planned to restrict eligibility through use of means-testing and, like the *Krippen* and other family day care, was shaped to serve poor and deprived families. Despite evidence that the children developed well, the effort was attacked by prominent pediatricians as unwisely building up out-of-home care and encouraging mothers of young children to work.

On the other hand, a small-scale *Krippe* initiative in one state (Nordrhein-Westfalen) recalls the Swedish integrated model in its attempts to ensure program quality and attractive, suitable premises. The program creates "groups of fifteen," consisting of two infants, four children ages one to three, and nine who are three to six. There is an emphasis on interaction among children, as there is a curriculum which stresses cognitive growth, social-emotional development, and observational capacities. Elsewhere in the FRG there are parent-cooperative *Krippen* and others that share the interests of exemplary programs in all countries in their broad objectives. In a significant number of communities, facilities may be combined in a large entity known as *Kindertagesstätten*, which join in one plase the *Krippe*, *Kindergarten*, and *Kinderhort*. Sweden has similar facilities know as preschool centers, as does France.

Krippen are open for both half-day and all-day care. The modal facility has 36.5 places and qualified staff. The groups range in size as follows: six to ten for the under-ones, seven to twelve for the ones, and eight to fifteen for the twos. The adult-to-child ratio is approximately one to six. Eligibility rules for child admission are locally determined, governed somewhat by supply, but reflect the policy described.

Leadership in the several FRG efforts comes from a Ministry of Youth, Families, and Health, whose family policy mission offers opportunity for a comprehensive and integrated perspective. Operations are largely a matter of state, municipality, and voluntary agency initiative, however.

Parental preferences are not clear. The largest recent survey posed "mother's wage" and "work" as alternatives. While the preference ratings for centers are a bit lower than for family day care, these answers are not analyzed by prior parental experience in use of facilities or exposure to information about all alternatives.

SUMMARY

For coverage of children under three, the countries rank as follows: GDR, France, Sweden, Hungary, USA, FRG. The ranks persist even if one discounts unlicensed-unregulated family day care. Group (center) care predominates in the GDR and Hungary, since there is no substantial labor force for family day care. Hungary may be in the process of creating a small force in the form of mothers at home on child care leave. Where parents are working, grandmothers are important in all countries, but labor force trends suggest a decreasing supply of such caregivers.

While family day care is a preferred or coequal form in the *policies* of the other four countries and dominant in actual fact, there has been relatively recent and significant growth in center care for infants and toddlers and some evidence of parental preference for this in some places. Especially interesting is the importance of kindergartens or *écoles maternelles* for under-threes in France, Hungary, and the FRG—and the prospect of greater growth.

Of the countries here reviewed, France is planning significant expansion in all three care modes: *écoles maternelles*, *crèches*, family day care. Sweden is concentrating on centers but is not discounting family care. Hungary projects center coverage to 15 percent of the cohort. The GDR, with good coverage, has announced plans to expand care to 70 percent of children aged twenty weeks to three years. And, despite slow and steady expansion in group care, the United States especially, and the FRG as well, rely heavily on unlicensed family day care and have no clear policy at all favoring a specific expansion of care for the under-threes.

Except in the FRG and the United States, center care is largely publicly operated. Industry-based facilities are few and are declining. Family day care may be public or proprietary, although there is a clear tendency toward public operation and supervision for licensed or official family day care. Each country has some "market" family day care—with apparently extensive unofficial developments in the FRG, the United States, and Sweden, very little in Hungary and the GDR, and the intent—as yet unimplemented—to bring it all under public surveillance in France.

The effects of available benefits on the use of child care facilities are seen in the following pattern of *crèche* age clustering:

> Hungary: ages eighteen months to three years
> GDR: ages one to three years
> France: ages five months to three years
> Sweden: age six months and over

More must be known and understood about the effects, requirements, costs, and optimal patterns of operation of centers and family day care before they can be weighed as policy instruments. We defer further discussion to the next chapter, which deals with some of these matters.

NOTES

1. See Patricia Walters, "Pre-school Care in France," *SSRC Newsletter* (London) (November 1978), p. 10.

2. The major 1975 U.S. consumer survey analysis is flawed and/or incomplete in its age breaks, length-of-care categories, exclusion of school care in most categories. Unco., Inc., *National Childcare Consumer Study: 1975*, 4 vols. (Washington, D.C.: U.S. Department of Health, Education, and Welfare, 1977.)

3. For a U.S. day care overview, see Sheila B. Kamerman and Alfred J. Kahn, "The Day Care Debate: A Wider View," *The Public Interest* (Winter 1979), 54: 76–93. For a description of how some parents develop a "package" of several types of care arrangements to meet their needs, see Sheila B. Kamerman, *Parenting in an Unresponsive Society: Managing Work and Family Life* (New York: Free Press, 1980).

4. Abt Associates, *Children at the Center*, and *Day Care Centers in the U.S.: A National Profile, 1976-1978*—vols. 1 and 3 of the *Report of the National Day Care Study* (Cambridge, Mass., 1978 and 1979). Published and distributed by the Office of Child Development, U.S. Department of Health, Education, and Welfare, Washington, D.C.

5. Thomas W. Rhodes and John C. Moore, "American Consumer Attitudes and Opinions on Child Care," constituting volume 3 of Unco, Inc., *National Childcare Consumer Study: 1975*. See especially pp. 1–3 and 3–23; also tables 3-10 and 3-11 on pp. 3-12 and 3-13.

Four

CENTERS AND FAMILY DAY CARE AS POLICY INSTRUMENTS

Are child care centers and family day care programs good instruments of societal response to the needs of children under age three? The question has several aspects:

- Is there enough such care?
- Does out-of-home care harm children? Is it good for them?

If out-of-home care is an appropriate response, what choices are made—or should be made—among the programing options which are being debated?

- Is center care or family day care emphasized? What is desirable?
- If under-threes are to be cared for outside the home, when do they enter care? When should they?
- Is the "age three" boundary between center and preschool a useful one?
- What governmental administrative arrangements exist? What if any arrangements are needed to back up an appropriate conception of the roles of family day care, center care for infants and toddlers, and a preschool program?
- Does center care for under-threes have and need a curriculum?
- Is parent participation assured? What does it consist of?
- What participation—if any—is essential? Can it be provided?
- Are there agreed-upon standards that should be enforced for staffing, group size, the physical setting of child care? Have these standards been validated and found practicable?
- What does it all cost? Is it worth the price?

- What are the costs of the status quo, of *not* developing care arrangements?

While a review of these subjects will not satisfy all requirements of a child care debate, it will serve to organize much of what has been learned in six countries about child care services as a policy option.

IS THERE SUFFICIENT CARE?

Centers and family day care do not constitute a realistic policy choice unless they are quantitatively sufficient, well-distributed geographically, and accessible to all population groups. For most of the countries studied, this does not seem to be the situation as yet. We summarize:

Only the *GDR* is without a major problem in this sphere: with very high female labor force participation—women are half the labor force, and over 85 percent of those in the prime years do work, some part time—it has ensured *Krippen* space for 60.1 percent of the cohort under three and over twenty weeks old, i.e., their "eligible" population. Only modest, slow growth is now seen as necessary, given the alternative of care by relatives and part-time work. The GDR is now concentrating on program improvement, closing the all-week *Krippen*, shortening the length of the care day.

If for the moment the GDR provision is an index of adequacy, however rough, *France* notes that even its leading position in the West is not enough. With over 30 percent of the cohort provided for, there is nonetheless a report of average waiting lists of 100 at *crèches* and full utilization of space for two-year-olds as it becomes available in *écoles maternelles*. The precise degree of shortage cannot be calculated from such data, but this information and the political debate suggest that more facilities are needed. Indeed the current French National Plan has projected significant increases for family day care, *crèches*, and *écoles maternelles*.

Hungary has planned modest center expansion, to accommodate 15 percent of the cohort, and some childminding (family day care) by mothers home on child care leave. There is some discussion, too, of the need to subsidize market care for parents unable to find center space. This suggests some shortages, but one cannot be precise here either.

Sweden regards its coverage situation as inadequate given female labor force participation rates and its policy preferences. While extraordinary progress has been made in achieving expansion targets and in quality of care, there is no short-run expectation that demand will be met, and priority systems are imposed everywhere.

If one compares *U.S.* and *FRG* female labor force participation rates and child care coverage with those of the other countries, there is evidence of a gap in child care provision. Some FRG observers argue that grandmothers and mothers meet much of the need, but arguing against this is the evidence of long *Krippen* waiting lists and the use of unlicensed family day care. The United States, with far fewer grandmothers offering care and relatively high female labor force participation, seems to have a larger gap. In any case, neither of these two countries has developed a clear philosophy or program for the care of children under age three, whether in centers or in family day care. Public debate in the FRG often rejects this option; not so in the United States, where the public issue is federal involvement.

One must, then, conclude that if out-of-home care is to be a significant element of the policy response in these or similar countries, expansion of child care facilities must be planned and projected. It is not possible to state exact specifications for such expansion, since the total socioeconomic context and the remainder of the particular country's policy response will affect the scale of need: the employment situation over the next several years, the extent of part-time or full-time work, the existence of benefits offering substitute income which enables a parent to stay home from work after childbirth. Nonetheless, serious commitment to an out-of-home care option will demand some expansion in most places. It thus becomes necessary to ask about the price of such expansion in terms of child and family effects and actual money costs. And what form of such expansion will yield the best child-family results and make the desired policy impact?

DOES OUT-OF-HOME CARE HARM CHILDREN?

The existence of need or demand is not enough—one must deal with the question of consequences for children. Clearly, all these countries care about the quality of the life experiences to which they expose their new generations. There is a tradition of opposition to center care of infants deriving from psychoanalytically oriented research into institutions and a history of difficulty with mass day care in some parts of Eastern Europe in the 1950s. Those who would make policy certainly must pause to ask: what is known about the effects of existing child care services on children under age three?

The six-country investigation yields four conclusions:

- Little is known about the consequences for children of placement in family day care, the major care mode for under-threes in several countries.
- Most attention by researchers (to the extent that there is attention) is paid to the effects of center (group) care.
- There are no known negative consequences of "reasonably decent" group care.
- It is held by some experts, and there is some (if inconclusive) evidence, that some children do benefit from group care.

First, a general note about effects. As first consideration, it might be agreed that the question of effects on children, on parents, and on families should be the point of departure for everything—for the choice between no policy and policy, between programs and benefits, and among program alternatives, especially group care versus day care. It will soon become apparent that, of the countries discussed, only the United States and the GDR have substantial and rigorous "effects" research, from a child development perspective. The GDR research starts with a policy choice made and uses child effects as the vantage point for designing ever more satisfactory programs. And, when the U.S. research is reviewed subsequently, it will be noted that despite its substantial scale and a large monetary involvement, the U.S. research effort as a whole does not begin to offer specific policy guidance. As one studies the other countries as a group, it becomes clear that to a considerable degree the status of "effects" research is not only a matter of the specific preoccupations of a country's behavioral and social scientists and their research capacities. The amount and focus of such research also are related to the questions asked in the public debate and to the presence of or lack of conviction as to the relevance of research to the fundamental policy decisions to be made. There are varied views as to which outcomes are good or poor for child or family, about the time frame for the judgment, and as to whether a country has the choice of abandoning a policy with unsatisfactory effects or must, on the contrary, define negative results as a challenge to improvement. For, like much else in social policy, this domain is governed by complex value hierarchies in which developments are assessed and responded to.

In a sense, the "effects" which are attended to are not only child-development measures of what happens to children. While there are few comprehensive scientific reports as to the quality of the at-home-with-mother alternative, attitudes and opinions about such care may also affect the discussion. Also important are questions as to relative costs of alternatives, of who benefits and who pays, and of who responds more positively to what experience, and who expresses what preferences. Even viewpoints about program requirements, which we shall discuss subsequently (age grouping, presence or absence of *crèche* curriculum, for instance), imply criteria for assessment, too, and if such criteria are met, positive judgments are made. In other words, *process* criteria often substitute for measures of outcome, since outcomes are difficult to establish or difficult to define precisely. Nor is it always clear to what they should be compared. Ability to engage parental participation, to take another example, may be considered as a desired end and success may be defined as a positive indicator for programs—without knowledge of the impact on children.

Nonetheless, we must focus on effects on children as the central issue. As indicated, there is surprisingly little that is firmly known and in only a few places are efforts being made to learn more about effects. Despite much myth and rhetoric, no research offers an argument against either center care or family day care because of proven harm to children or families—and a research case can be made for quite positive results from some center programs.

There is both testimony and research from Eastern Europe (GDR, Hungary, Poland, Czechoslovakia) to the effect that, as it developed in the 1950s and 1960s, large all-week (Monday to Friday, usually) institutional day care of infants was harmful: speech retardation was reported, as were high incidences of emotional difficulty and childhood illness. Undesirable effects for such facilities continue to be reported as their number and importance diminish. (They now account for 8.7 percent of all the GDR day care.) A consensus has developed and has been endorsed by the relevant committee of East European experts: all-week child care arrangements should be phased out. There is little dispute about this conclusion. Currently, in Sweden, there is active discussion about nighttime child care because women as well as men work night shifts, as, for example, in hospitals. However, Swedish policy makers note that the scheduling of center hours to cover nighttme work is not at all the same as week-long care. Children go home each day, even if at unusual hours, and can spend considerable time with their parents. (Several small-scale pilot projects have not yet been evaluated.)

The GDR has a considerable tradition of *Krippen* research, beginning with the concern about results of overnight and week-long care and continuing and intensifying with the recognition that infants and toddlers in *Krippen* did have speech and development problems. Under the leadership of Dr. E. Schmidt-Kolmer and now of her students, researchers have identified the problems, by comparing home-reared and *Krippen* children. Initially, the home setting provided the developmental norms and targets. The negative *Krippen* picture spurred program improvement, since home care was not considered a viable option. A long-term series of comparisons, as *Krippen* were improved, showed a remarkable turn-around. By the time a new series of studies was inaugurated in the mid-1960s, there were some areas of better functioning and development for *Krippen* children, as there were some better areas for the home-reared. The new norms, which currently guide the *Krippen* programing described in a later section, reflect the "possibilities" experienced in both settings. *In general, GDR research establishes that infants and toddlers do not suffer any developmental disadvantages because of the experience.* Indeed, since the experience is now normative, children who are not in center care when age one or two are less self-sufficient, independent, or adjusted to social experience than most of the others in their society. A small group of children for whom "many negatives" come together (physical, familial) do not do well—and are of concern.

Large numbers of *Krippen* infants and toddlers continue to experience high rates of infection, however, Although, by the kindergarten years, there are no differences between the illness rates of *Krippen* and home-reared children, and although no long-term effects of the *Krippen* infections are known, intensive efforts are under way to deal with the problem. The *Institut für Hygiene des Kindes- und Jugendalters* in Berlin is conducting research on the *Krippen* environment and also experimenting with conditioning approaches involving building up the body's thermal regulation capacities—all in an effort to control susceptibility to infection.[1]

"Adaptation problems" are also described by GDR center experts as frequent, but no research reports are available. The solutions devised include

carefully implemented slow transitions into all-day care, with active parental participation, and, if necessary, withdrawal of the child and return at a
later date.

The GDR research begins with the premise that children will be in center
care and then seeks out optimal solutions to identified negative effects. This
is quite different from the U.S. context in which the policy debate is premised on the belief that mother's own care, at home, is best, and that this
care is indeed, always available. The U.S. discussion thus focuses on the
effects of out-of-home care—and then also inspires studies of the differences
between center care and family day care. (We here describe the research
ethos, not the actual impact of studies, which thus far have not been the
critical element in U. S. policy, either!)

The other countries are all similar to the GDR: they decide about care
or noncare, and how much care, on grounds other than proven effects on
children and do not pretend that evaluative research makes the policy. Thus,
in Sweden, the center programs and the "pedagogic dialogue" technique
were framed deductively from existing child development theory, societal
values, and the best judgment of serious people. When asked why they act
before they measure and evaluate, they respond that a test of results in a
controlled experiment would take many years—and by then the program
being studied would have been improved in response to experience in any
case. For many reasons, they know they *want* center and family day care
programs and they can see how children respond—without rigorous studies.

Some experts question the emphasis on *crèche*-generated illness in infants. They say that there is as much illness in family day care. They also
note, as do the French, that *crèche* observation identifies more illness in
crèche attendees than in home-reared children. That more illness is reported
does not necessarily mean that there is more illness. And the sick leave entitlement for a parent to remain at home to care for a sick child may create
a certain amount of inaccurate reporting among some employed parents.

The Hungarians recognize health problems in centers similar to those
identified in the GDR. There also are recent studies that report creativity
endangered by the center, since the teachers follow a "preschool" model
and want to "teach" children how best to play. Children at home are said
to show more initiative and autonomous thinking. Hungary has a National
Methodological Crèche which is at work on improvements and solutions. In
brief, the major research is focused on *how* to do the work, not *whether* the

results justify or negate having center care. Given current needs—mothers who do not take the entire three-year child caring leave—there are plans to expand center care to 15 percent of the cohort, although at-home care remains the officially preferred mode.

The FRG does not have large-scale research on the effects of *Krippen* or family day care, since there is no preferred mode to evaluate. Available studies, while often of high quality and scientifically rigorous, refer to particular settings and are noncumulative. The large investment in *Tagesmütter* research will at most show that well-supported family day care is not harmful—but neither children nor programs are representative, either of children of working mothers or of family day care. Research by Dr. K. Beller on enriched center care also contributes to basic scientific child development knowledge and shows that deprived children may respond to cognitive stimulation. It thus may encourage center expansion initiatives. However, the design of the research and program content do not provide general answers on effects for typical programs and typical families—children facing typical alternatives. Thus the research cannot guide overall policy making.

While there are many ideological debates in France about child care policy and programs (*crèche, crèche familiale,* etc.), there is a tendency to go from goal to policy. There is some controlled research on the relative effects of the several possible approaches. But most program comparisons are not definitive because of the self-selection of families and children involved. A French review of all available comparative research of good quality yields either mixed results or the finding that children do better at home with mother or in a center than they do in family day care. Most important, these studies show a normal developmental pattern for children with day care center experience—the attendant problems have long since been identified and corrected. Some leading French child development researchers also attack available studies of *crèche*-reared and home-reared children by questioning the methodologies; they doubt that available instruments measure the right things.

Only the United States, of these countries, has made a large, long-term investment in child development and child care evaluative research. For some time now there has been a tradition of evaluation, mandated by Congress and policy makers, and often heavily subsidized by the federal government and private foundations. There is a plethora of studies, and the lack of available research answers to questions is not a reflection of under-investment. *It is difficult to obtain definitive evaluations where programs are not standardized and well developed and where objectives are still debated.* There are problems of conceptualization, theory, and methodology in the United States, as in all countries. They are, in fact, more visible in the United States because there is more research, and the results are well publicized.

In late 1977, in a comprehensive and independent review for the present report of all major research available in the field, Louise Silverstein concluded:

The focus of current research on day care, as defined by the stigma of institutionalization, has been narrowly confined to examining the potentially negative effect of day care on maternal attachment and intellectual development. The findings to date suggest that day care has a neutral effect on these aspects of development. However, because of the narrow scope and limitations of the research, the existing data must be considered preliminary and inconclusive. It is still premature to conclude that raising children in day care vs. home care makes little difference.

For the full Silverstein assessment, see Appendix A.

Silverstein's methodological critique is extensive and comprehensive. She notes, with reference to sampling procedures, that much of the available data employed has been collected at centers offering high-quality care rather than in a broad range of settings. Groups are not randomly assigned and samples are often small. Some of the assessment techniques, while imaginative, are debatable, involving generalization from laboratory situations to real-life settings and assuming validity of tests that are not clearly valid. Central concepts like "attachment" are not readily defined and measured, so that results are imprecise.

There are disagreements, too, about the measures employed for cognitive functioning in the major relevant U.S. research, and there are not widely accepted standardized approaches to assessing infant relationships with peers and adults other than the mother. Silverstein concludes that

The general approach to measurement in day care research has limited ecological validity. Dependent variables are not assessed in a longitudinal context. Experimental and laboratory situations rather than real-life settings are relied upon. Constructs are not assessed by multiple measures in several settings to verify impressions provided by one measurement instrument.

Finally, among the methodological limitations of available studies is their tendency to look only at one variable, day care. Much else is of course operating, some of it attended to in some studies: sex, socioeconomic status, father's presence or absence, ethnicity, age of entry, time spent in care, and so on. There are also organismic variables and variations in activity levels among children. With much variance unaccounted for in most research, the statistical power of comparisons undertaken is low. It may thus be methodology (including the general lack of multivariate statistical techniques) that clouds real differences.

Silverstein also defines a series of conceptual limitations affecting most U.S. day care research: the reliance on the confusing and confused Bowlby "maternal attachment" research; the tendency to employ day care as a global variable; the failure to locate most of the research within an adequate developmental framework; overreliance on traditional infant IQ tests; the failure to consider individual differences—or to attend to differences among families who choose center care, family care, and home care. There are of course scholars and researchers who on a small scale have suggested or demonstrated solutions to some of these problems. The research investment and the activity are considerable—but definitive results are not available nor will they be forthcoming in the near future.

Special attention, however, must be given to the New York City Infant Day Care Study, a unique longitudinal study comparing low-income children reared at home, children with center experience, and those in family day care. Final measurements took place at age three. Silverstein's summation of findings and her critique follow:

The New York Infant Day Care Study was a longitudinal, comparative field study of 31 service-oriented group and family infant day care programs, and the effects of these programs on 400 children and their families. The primary contribution of this study is that it provides large-scale empirical data on issues for which research evidence has not previously been available. The major findings are outlined below in the context of popular misconceptions about infant day care which these new data dispel.

Infant day care may adversely affect the psychological development of children.

On all measures of intellectual, social and emotional functioning, children attending infant day care programs for several years did as well or better than equivalent samples of home-reared children.

Infant day care may adversely affect the family as an institution.

The families using infant day care programs did not appear to be greatly affected by these programs. No significant differences in the longitudinal sample, in terms of socioeconomic status, economic resources or family functioning emerged over the several years of the study. At completion of the study, the families who had used infant day care for several years did not differ significantly from families who had recently entered the program.

Age at entry is an important variable interacting with the effect of day care on psychological development.

No relations emerged between age at entry and any of the outcome measures of psychological development at 36 months.

Differences between the group and family day care settings may have serious consequences for psychological development.

The major difference observed between group and family programs related to nutrition and health care, rather than to psychological development. The group programs were found to be superior to family programs in providing higher quality food and health services. This finding was due to the contrasting role which the New York City Health Department assumed in the two types of day care programs, rather than to intrinsic differences in the group vs. family settings. In the group programs, the Health Department closely supervised and, in some cases, directly participated in the provision of these services. In the family programs, in contrast, the responsibility was left to the individual provider mothers and the children's families.

The two types of programs were found to be basically equivalent in their effects on the children's psychological development. There was some evidence to suggest that group programs enhanced intellectual performance, and that family programs positively affected social competence—but the case is not conclusive.

A small but rigorous Swedish study reported in 1978 from the Laboratory for Stress Research at the Karolinska Institute by Aubrey Kagan and colleagues includes psychological measures along with more usual approaches. Comparing only children in day care with one another, but with some at a ratio of five children per adult and some at three per adult, the researchers found some marginal advantages for the children and a better situation for caretakers in the smaller ratios. For present purposes, however, it is also clear that neither group was showing serious adverse effects—and that there was considerable parental and caretaker satisfaction.

Silverstein's final research overview (which would not be contradicted by anything reported out of research in any of the six countries) follows:

1. No empirical evidence exists to indicate that good quality infant day care has adverse consequences on maternal attachment, or intellectual or social development.

2. Facilitative effects have emerged only in terms of attenuating the IQ test score decline usually observed in children from high-risk environments.

3. The only current valid overall conclusion, then, is that good quality day care, as evaluated by existing techniques, appears to have a neutral effect on development.

However, available research is limited in both quantity and depth. Unresearched or poorly researched issues include:

1. The effect of poor quality care.

2. The effect of day care on the neonatal period for both infants and parents.

3. The effects of day care on language development.

4. The effects of day care in a long-range longitudinal context.

5. The differential effect of family vs. center care.

6. The impact of day care on the family as a whole.

7. The differential impact of different types of programs for different types of children and families.

8. The impact of day care on society.

9. Many possible positive effects of day care.

To the extent that effects of day care would be overriding considerations in policy making, one must note the limitations of existing research data and the number of issues which have not yet been investigated. Extensive, high quality research efforts (such as the New York City and Stanford studies), which continue to explore the consequences of different types of childcare, should thus be a policy priority.

The general Silverstein findings have been confirmed by an independent review by a team of U.S. child development experts published after the completion of the Silverstein work and before its general circulation. The core conclusions are stated as follows:

Although research on day care has increased substantially in volume during the last 8 years, our actual knowledge of its effects is exceedingly limited. Generally, investigations have been conducted within high-quality centers which are not representative of most substitute-care environments. More seriously, most studies have been limited to the direct effects of the care experience on the individual child and have consequently ignored important questions concerning the broader impact of day care on parents, the family, and social institutions. Present knowledge about the effects of day care can therefore be summarized in relatively brief compass. Experience in high-quality center-based day care (1) has neither salutary nor deleterious effects upon the intellectual development of the child, (2) is not disruptive of the child's emotional bond with his mother, and (3) increases the degree to which the child interacts, both positively and negatively, with peers.[2]

Neither the Silverstein nor the Belsky and Steinberg review above takes account of the full reports from the comprehensive U.S. *National Day Care Study* (Abt) which subsequently appeared. Also completed is a U.S. government report to the Congress on child care standards, which draws upon the Abt research. This government report utilizes the results of the observation studies, involving large center, caretaker, parent, and child samples to assess the impact of *variations* in major center characteristics (staff-child ratios, staff qualifications, classroom size, etc.) on the development of children and on costs. Eventually there will be a comparable family day care report. U.S. government policy makers have concluded from the evidence that "small groups of children and caregivers best promote competent child development. . . . Small groups are especially important for children under age 3." However, low child-staff ratios and small group size, of course, interact with caretaker competence. These reports summarize impressive, but *only suggestive* evidence about the specifics of desirable caretaker qualifications, educational and developmental services, environmental standards, health services, nutritional services, parent involvement, and social services. While the work is not complete or definitive and does not compare home-reared, center-reared, and family day care children (and while most of the children in the centers are over age three), it is noteworthy that no suggestion appears anywhere that center programs are damaging and should not be continued. The perspective is that they are here to stay and to grow and that standards should be specified to guide future development.[3]

Also not considered by Silverstein and Belsky is a recently reported 1976–77 follow-up of the Head Start children from fourteen different projects. Some 1,200 of 2,000 children served in the projects before 1969 were traced. The programs were hardly typical of child care, since the population was selected for need for compensatory experiences, and the offerings, while diverse in theory and technique, were in all instances enriched. Of interest is the evidence that appears to contradict earlier findings about Head Start, although there are methodological conditions that make the picture less than definitive. In any case, with some exceptions, youngsters exposed to these programs on follow-up seem better able than "controls" to keep pace with their classes, end up less frequently in special classes for failing students, score higher on achievement tests, and show gains not immediately apparent after the Head Start experience.[4]

We have concentrated on the U.S. research because it is by far the most extensive and sophisticated. It remains incomplete and not definitive, but nothing in it can or should deter serious policy making to assure adequate care arrangements.

A final side note should be added to this "effects" discussion. Even progress on the various methodological issues summarized above will not be fully responsive to the question. Dr. Ursula Lehr has pointed out that the issue for the children is not only the *direct* consequences of experiences between birth to age three, as measured during those years or immediately thereafter, but also the implications of their experiences for their later years. For instance, she suggests that adolescent girls may be better off over the life course if they have had working mothers as role models. Similarly, Dr. Lehr urges that policy not ignore the parents even though most of the research is not parent focused. (We describe research on at-home mothers later in this chapter.) Some observers have hypothesized that low-income and poorly educated women are better off if they work. There are some limited studies, also, that would appear to show that elderly women in retirement who have previously had out-of-home work have a much happier old age than do those without a comparable experience.

WHAT PROGRAMING CHOICES NEED TO BE MADE?

There is no research evidence justifying discontinuance of child care programs, and there may be a case to promote expansion. To the extent that problems exist, there is strong inclination to correct them, and to improve programs. It thus becomes useful to turn to our six-country studies and to ask: What is known about how to make out-of-home child care good or better? What programing choices require specific consideration? We focus on the issues in the forefront of policy debates and professional discussion. First, the question of the *type* of care.

CENTER OR FAMILY DAY CARE?

The care question is tied to ideology about the family: If not parental care, can the available care be parentlike? Should it? Thus the discussion of the type of care is a policy question, not limited to technical matters.

TABLE 4.1

Major Care Modes—Children Under 3

Country	Total Coverage	Center Care	Family Day Care
GDR	High	Major	None or little
Hungary	Relatively low	Major[a]	Minor
Sweden	Moderate	Coequal	Coequal (municipal) but higher if private included
FRG	Low	Low—not favored[a]	Low—de facto preferred
USA	Relatively low	Lower—except in some regions	Higher
France	Relatively high	Lower—but status coequal[a]	Higher—but status coequal

[a]Some two-year-olds now in preschool, especially in France, where it is policy to admit them as there is space.

We may sum up briefly (see table 4.1): The *GDR*, stressing coverage and universalism, offers only *Krippen* and has extensive provision. *Hungary*, it will be recalled, officially prefers at-home care by a mother who withdraws from work for up to three years and who is given a cash benefit; but Hungary, too, offers centers as the public care mode and will expand somewhat over the next several years. Neither of these two East European countries, whose economies assume female labor force participation, assigns a labor force to at-home family day care. However, Hungary will now experiment with permitting mothers at home on child care leave to take care of others' children, thus freeing more women to work if they wish to.

The *FRG*, whose family policy prefers that the mother remain at home, provides neither extensive center programs nor family day care, except as a social welfare service for the disadvantaged, but does apparently have fairly extensive unlicensed family day care—a market response to the lack of an active policy. *Sweden* began with a social service day care tradition, too, and its most extensive provision was family day care until the deliberate policy making of the 1960s. Then a series of commission reports and governmental actions placed center care in the forefront of the policy. All growth targets referred to group service expansion, as consistent with ideology and child care theory. However, both internal debate and assessment of cost and staffing realities now lead to a balanced commitment: resources seem equal for both modes of municipal provision, public subsidy is not too dissimilar, and most important, fees by parents are the same. However, private family day care is still extensive in Sweden, since municipal provision is not equal to need.

The *United States*, too, has both components in its care system, and the "causation" dynamics have elements of all the above. There is an expanded program to support work or work-training by public (social) assistance mothers. The majority of under-threes in care are in family day care. However, although there is no explicit policy behind it, federal funding is so administered as to create a de facto preference for center care expansion. The working poor are admitted to publicly supported care on a subsidized basis but meet most of their needs through market-provided care, some of it in regulated centers, much of it in unlicensed family day care. The more prosperous also use both day care centers and nursery school programs, presumably at higher cost levels, as well as in-home care. A growing number of private nursery schools accepts two-year-olds.

France, with the best overall coverage rates of the Western countries, is not unlike the United States in the far heavier emphasis on family than on center day care. However, the ratio of licensed to unlicensed family day care in France is far higher than in the United States and the effort to assure full licensing is becoming more vigorous. There are clear social class preferences between the care modes.

Although family day care is the dominant mode generally in France, there is more emphasis on motherlike care in "lower" classes and occupational groups. Middle- and upper-class parents make more use of the *crèche*. In 1975, the mothers of *crèche* children in Paris were occupationally distributed as follows: top officials in industry and trade, 1.6 percent; executives and professionals, 8 percent; middle-level executives, 23.7 percent; white-collar workers, 44 percent; blue-collar workers, 6.5 percent; service workers, 7 percent; other, 9.2 percent. However, all social classes make use of *écoles maternelles*, which do not require labor force attachment of the mother, and the rate of use is higher in the regions outside of Paris, where *crèches* are in shorter supply.

Beyond these current realities in all the countries there is lively debate that affects policy and perhaps will shape the future care modes. Once the fact of care is accepted, the key formal questions are *effects* (which is better for children, families, and parents?) and *costs* (which is more affordable for the society?). The latent issues are *compatibility of the several modes with family ideology and psychological beliefs in the several countries— and with consumer preferences.*

First, it should be stressed that the debate is about children below the age of three, or between two and two-and-one-half. The assumption is general in Europe among these countries—but not in the United States—that preschool, a *group* program, is to be universal, if voluntary. (The question of the two-to-three-year-olds is later discussed separately.) After-school care is apparently largely group care but there is substantial family day care after school, too, especially in the United States, and the debate is not yet joined.

We may summarize the arguments for and against these modes as follows:

Family Day Care: For

- It is more like the child's family.
- It offers more flexible hours, locations.
- It is more familiar to lower-class users since it is more similar to their home culture and physical settings.
- It is cheaper.
- It offers more individualized attention.

Family Day Care: Against

- Quality control is difficult.
- Staff quality is poorer; training less likely.
- Turnover is higher (family day care mothers in some countries, children in others).
- Settings are less stimulating and interesting since there is little equipment or play material.
- When well done it must be as expensive or more expensive than group care, since there is less economy of scale. The major costs everywhere are for staffing.
- It institutionalizes a female stereotype and perpetuates female inequality; men do not staff family day care.

Day Care Center: For

- Peer interaction is important for child development in the early years.
- Given a multiperson staff, the child is less at the mercy of one adult who may be a poor match for him.
- There is more likely to be proper equipment, materials, a concept, training, supervision, leadership.
- The caretaking role can be professionalized and the facility staffed in a stable fashion.
- Some men are willing to do child care work in centers and others can be employed in maintenance and related roles.

Day Care Center: Against

- Children in centers are ill more frequently and more severely than other children.
- Center care infants and toddlers may be retarded in speech and suffer in their emotional and cognitive development. They may be "lost" in a group.
- It is a "collective" approach to child rearing.

In effect, the salience of the argument seems to depend on the country's specific situation (and none of the above arguments is completely right or wrong empirically). In France, the public debate has long posed the *nourrice* as the "good mother" (substitute) as against the "bad *crèche*." But the current answer is that the children do not need substitute mothers: they *have* mothers who work. A care arrangement is a *supplementary* care arrangement—and a case can be made for a good *crèche* (and is not defensible for a poor *nourrice*). Proponents stress the *crèche* advantages to redress the balance: *nourrice* care has been long acceptable. Thus the values of peer interaction are much discussed.

Historically, as already noted, it has been true that children in very large centers (and especially in large institutionlike overnight and week-long *crèches*) have shown developmental and speech lags. It is also reported that all countries eliminate speech and developmental problems by better staffing and programing. Many studies show *crèche* infants and toddlers ahead on many developmental norms. The New York City Infant Day Care Study, referred to earlier in this chapter, shows that both modes may be successful and each can have advantages, depending on exactly how it is implemented.

The health problem is apparently real. Center-attending infants and toddlers get more infections, earlier, and it is of concern to those who administer the programs. While no long-term effects are apparent, remedial health and physical environment measures have decreased the problem and new efforts are under way. There are some claims that the problem is exaggerated: after all there are no fully comparable data for at-home or family day care children. Centers are organized for effective case-finding, and parents may overreport illness when they want an excuse to stay home from work as they are entitled to do under health insurance (see chapter 2).

There is also agreement in a number of countries that it is possible to improve the quality of child care by improving staff recruitment, training, supervision, the physical setting, the program, the linkages, and parent participation. It is easier to do this with center care than with family day care, which is often unregistered and difficult to locate.

However, it is clear that public response is not uniform. Data available from studies and surveys or from use-pattern analyses in Sweden, Hungary, and France do show a tendency for the middle class and the educated to be more comfortable with the use of the center: it is a mode of operation more familiar to them and likely to reflect the dominant value system of which they are part. The lower-class members, in general, are more ideologically comfortable with familylike care, and accept something more like home, however poor the physical setting and however uneducated the caretaker. A center, like a school, is strange and unfamiliar—after all, even kindergarten and elementary school may be foreign to the experience of such parents. Deprived families, in particular, may find the routines of *crèche* hours, advance registration, and required parental participation to be quite formidable—they do not qualify in these terms.

None of this will surprise. The more prosperous middle class in all these countries, when able to afford it and when able to find people to hire, arrange for care in their own homes. Often they seek a warm and nurturing women, however uneducated, and they settle for a foreign background, possible lack of acquaintance with modern hygiene, and lack of either peer stimulation or curriculum in favor of the motherlike emotional response which is rated very highly. Or they are motivated by the convenience of care arrangements which meet their personal scheduling needs. But they also are eager to have their children attend group programs said to offer early cognitive stimulation, good experience with peers, and opportunity for socialization. The less-educated and the foreign are not so sure of the responsiveness of the system and of their capacity to use it.

The debate often refers to existing care modes as though they reflect carefully considered and unshakable consumer preferences. Woolsey in the United States, for example, has thus argued against any systematic public provisions, center or licensed family day care, because many women work and they manage, often with unlicensed, unregulated, local arrangements. This, Woolsey argues, may be interpreted as preference.[5]

The cross-national comparisons tend to underscore the degree to which even more systematic and articulated preference data reflect the immediate and visible in this field, or the ways in which alternatives are structured by those who conduct surveys. Responses to survey preference questions clearly must be shaped by an amalgam of access, availability, responsiveness—as well as compatibility with a family's value system. Rapid growth of participation in several countries when new programs are introduced also points to quick changes in response once there is experience with a resource.

For example, a French poll in 1972 showed a majority of respondents opposing group care for children under age three; if there was to be care, they said, it should be by a *nourrice*. By 1975 a similar poll showed rather favorable overall response to the *crèche*. In a 1976 sample survey, a significant number of French parents with children cared for by a *nourrice* expressed preference for a *crèche collective*, a center. Low-income families chose a care allowance ("like a salary") over *crèches*, and religious groups preferred cash benefits to care services. Middle- and upper-class groups and trade unionists preferred *crèches*. Asked to rate modes for out-of-home care, lower-class groups preferred the family day care model, while the more affluent and better educated chose group care.

An FRG study (1975) of working mothers with one or more children under three showed that the majority of those mothers using any care mode reported "no difficulty," but there were differences. The ranking of positive reports (leaving out care by relatives) was as follows: first, neighbors; then in-home "baby sitters"; family day care and centers, both little used, were ranked equally. Overall preferences for alternative modes were ranked as follows: *Erziehungsgeld* (cash grant), 33 percent; shift to part-time work, 33 percent; family day care, 28 percent (half-day family day care was apparently the only family day care option offered in the survey); and center care, 20 percent. While those using family day care preferred it, this was also true of those now using center care. There was general satisfaction expressed.

At about the same time, in a representative national U.S. consumer survey, parents with children in care (age not specified) generally preferred the care mode they were using. However, significant numbers of parents reported a preference for changes, and the most common preferred shift was from care in nonrelatives' homes (licensed and unlicensed family day care) to group care or care in own home by nonrelative. Whereas "45 percent of those wishing to change would prefer day care centers or nursery schools over their current arrangements" and almost "one in three would select care in the child's own home. . . only about 3 percent would prefer Family Day Care Homes."[6] Swedish surveys show similar tendencies: if there is a shift, it is from family day care to centers, as center programs develop and become known.

Where does all of this leave the issue of family day care versus center care?

For Hungary and the GDR there is no real policy issue: family day care is not a work role that the economic situation permits on a large scale. For the FRG it was said to be considered for a while as "a care pattern most similar to the family environment": if the *Tagesmütter* experiments were shown to be successful in the child development sense, government would subsidize many such jobs, thus meeting care needs and incidentally helping to deal with unemployment. The problems of finance, as the economic situation changed, and an outcry against active promotion of the entry of more mothers of very young children into labor market, appear to have stalemated these proposals. The United States continues to flirt from time to time with the idea of the public assistance recipient as family day care mother, while at the same time its public social service funding, by de facto policy, favors center care (with far fewer jobs for the uneducated). And there is much more preoccupation in the United States with center care standards than with family day care norms—an approach that would tend to create a two-component system with unequal quality built in.

For countries whose labor force situation encourages both forms of care, centers and family day care, the situation in both Sweden and France may indicate the requirements of each form and possible future interrelationships. Municipal family day care in Sweden is increasingly well paid, has good benefits, is supervised and conducted by professionals, requires training courses. There are also interesting experiments whereby on some days of the week or during some parts of each day, the family day care mother gets relief and her charges get group experience by exposure to the center setting. There are numerous experiments along similar lines in the United States and in several other countries—all concerned with some degree of integration of the two modes. Thus, for various reasons—to give children some group experience, to relieve family day care mothers, to train family day care mothers, to ensure access to central resources—arrangements are made for family day care children to visit centers or even to spend part of each afternoon with center groups. The total of such efforts is small as yet and there are no systematic evaluations.

The French *crèche familiale* is the nucleus of a similar facility. It is a public operation, family day care mothers (*nourrices*) are on staff, there is central supervision and intake. An increase in training and more cooperation with the center system are entirely possible. Currently, many of the staff members leave to operate as private *nourrices* when they are experienced and have their own contacts. However, salary and social benefits reform and enforcement of the licensing rules could change this.

As already noted, the only relatively rigorous comparative research, the systematic U.S. study cited in the previous section (but hardly representative of all U.S. circumstances and certainly limited in its applicability) suggests a "draw" in the debate between centers and family day care. For child, parent, society, each of the major program models maximizes some elements. A policy maker could argue for retaining both components in a system where labor force realities permit.

If the current unemployment rates in Europe and North American reflect only current economic problems (our premise) and not a permanent change (as alleged by some), we would, however, expect a continuing decline in the size of the unskilled labor force that provided domestic and child care help in the past—and an acceleration within this generation of the virtual disappearance of the grandmother as the last "at-home" childminder for large numbers of children of working mothers. Family day care then would no longer expand and would eventually decline, unless countries continued to admit large numbers of uneducated women from poor lands and to assign child care to them. Growing sophistication about child development could inhibit this process.

One might then predict, and rather tentatively at that, that in most places group care, the center, would eventually predominate for typical, average children. Where family day care continues, however, and it clearly will, it should not be permitted to suffer in its level of public support or subsidy; family day care can amd should be implemented through good quality programs. Then, with acceptance accorded both modes, but with a need to use the family day care resource parsimoniously because it would be scarce, there would be incentive to upgrade some family day care for the special roles, chosen on a case-by-case basis. It may also serve the very frail child who finds the group situation too difficult, or the child with other special individualized needs.

Planning for optimum use of both systems is best advanced by uniform administration, increased professionalization of family day care, strict licensing, and *operational integration*. Confident prediction is not possible since preferences will continue to change, as will the labor market. It is difficult to assess the acceptability of the family day care mother assignment, however professionalized, in future labor markets and in relation to the thrust for equality between women and men. This could be an important factor.

AGE CONSIDERATIONS IN THE PROGRAMING OF CARE

If centers and family day care are to be used as part or all of a policy for children under-three, when should a child enter into care? Is three the correct upper age limit for center day care and entry into nursery school or preschool? What about the overlap for two-year-olds who attend either day care centers (*crèches*) or *écoles maternelles* and other preschools?

Are the under-threes one group for programing purposes in centers? What is the significance of age-integrated programing in some countries? Clearly provision for the under-threes requires attention to the age question. The countries offer a diversity of perspectives and experience.

Four countries—the GDR, France, Sweden, and the United States—exemplify four different structural-administrative patterns for center programs. A review of the patterns offers a point of entry to the age discussion and the several issues posed (see figure 4.1):

1. *Separation of the under-threes and over-threes into two systems, Krippen* and *Kindergärten*, administratively relating to the health and education ministries (GDR).
2. *Separation of the under-threes and the over-threes into two systems*, day care centers and preschools, relating to health and education ministries, as above—*but with some overlapping for two-year-olds*. In France as a matter of policy (and on a large scale) and in Hungary and the FRG on a small scale and because there is space, two-year-olds are now in preschool or in centers.
3. *An integrated preschool* encompassing all children under elementary school age (7). The Social Board, not education or health, provides the ministry umbrella. Most centers separate infants for program purposes (Sweden).
4. *Two parallel systems*, one based in social welfare and one in education, offer competing programs for children under the usual public kindergarten age (5) (U.S.).

Figure 4.1

Administrative-Structural Pattern for Out-of-Home Group Care

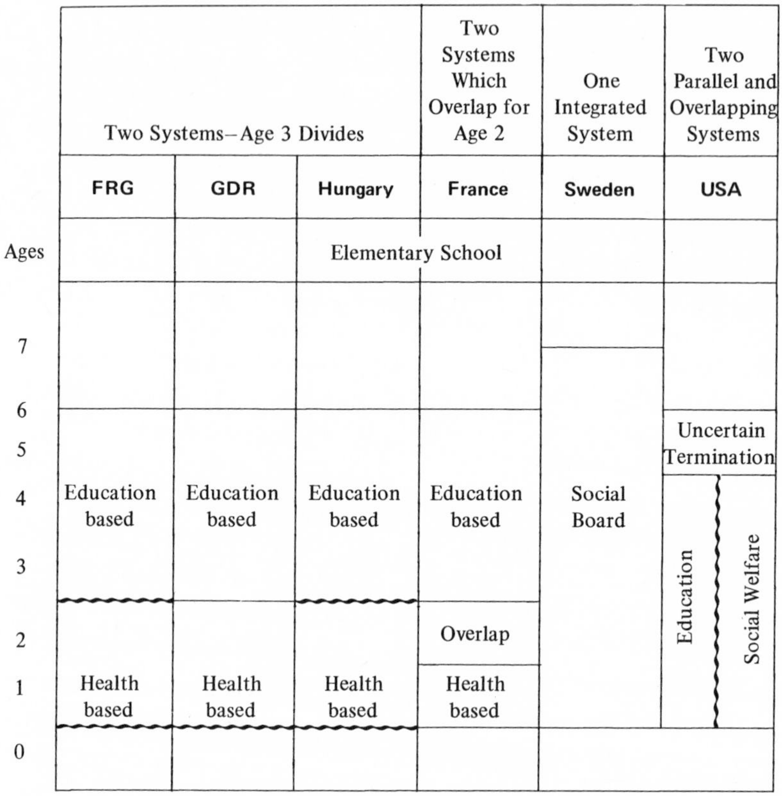

Ages	Two Systems—Age 3 Divides			Two Systems Which Overlap for Age 2	One Integrated System	Two Parallel and Overlapping Systems
	FRG	GDR	Hungary	France	Sweden	USA
			Elementary School			
7						
6						
5						Uncertain Termination
4	Education based	Education based	Education based	Education based	Social Board	Education / Social Welfare
3						
2				Overlap		
1	Health based	Health based	Health based	Health based		
0						

As will be noted below, there are no clear trends—not even good data or a focused discussion—relating to age policy for family day care programs. Because center programs are most debated and are controversial, the age question has been located there. What can be said about age at entry and age-related elements in grouping and programing?

Age Boundaries for Centers and Preschool

When one asks why the center or *crèche* ends at age three, the prevalent answer is, that is when preschool (kindergarten, nursery school) begins. A search through the most widely respected child development literature provides no convincing theoretical or empirical rationale. Some experts testify that the work of Piaget could perhaps make a case for age two as the dividing line.

However, the voluntary but universal *French* public nursery school, *école maternelle*, admits two-year-olds as a matter of policy, restrained somewhat by lack of space. The usual age of admission in practice is two-and-one-half, and 32 percent of the two-year-olds were in the *école maternelle* by 1977. National plans project a significant expansion of capacity for the twos. This is, for the French parent, the most popular and least expensive of the group care options, and is equally attractive to all social classes.

There are no systematic data about how well the two-and-one-half-year-old children adapt to *écoles maternelles*. As one visits various *écoles maternelles* to discuss the subject there are proponents and opponents. Age grouping within the program does permit age-appropriate programing and supervision. Perhaps the issue is, "How mature is the *particular* two-year-old?" "To what extent has the program been adapted for the younger child?"

For observers from outside France the group sizes in *école maternelle* for children aged three to five are a shock. It is an educational setting, and the norm is a class of thirty-five or more, with one teacher. While various administrative devices are invented locally to underenroll, so that the twos in particular have smaller groups, these remain very large groups by any international standard. Even the assignment of attendants and trainees to assist teachers does not basically change the situation.

But this remains a French issue—a question of group size—and does not provide definitive evidence as to whether three or two-and-one-half or two is an acceptable entry age for preschool. Most countries, after all, have much smaller groups. There are many kindergartens and nursery schools in many places whose groups are no larger than those in *crèches*, in center day care. Clearly, the question is one meriting exploration.

We note that *Hungary*, with center waiting lists and some expansion plans, is considering lowering the preschool age to two-and-one-half, also. The rationale given does not refer to child development considerations. Educated women seldom stay home until the child is three. The others are needed in the labor force or may want to return to work despite the child care benefit. Some kindergartens have already admitted children under age three as space has become available—and they now accommodate 1 percent of the cohort (just as child care centers serve 2 percent of the over-threes).

Given a declining birth rate and space in *Kindergärten*, the *FRG* has also developed a de facto acceptance of two-year-olds. The growth of the practice is recent and significant, accounting for the substantial under-three coverage expansion for 1977 noted in tables 3.1 and 3.10. The *Kindergarten* now is more important than the *Krippe* statistically in the FRG group care development for under-threes, even though the public discussion has not yet caught up with the fact. And in the United States, because of the existence of parallel, unrelated center care services (education or social welfare), there also are many under-threes in nurseries, mostly private nursery schools (see table 3.8).

Four countries thus have two-year-olds in preschool, one by design; two as a practical matter: they have space, use it, and thus far see no problem in the practice. The fourth, the United States, has largely developed its nursery schools as a marketplace response. A recent report from CERI, the educational research and innovation arm of the Organization for Economic Cooperation and Development (OECD), makes age two the dividing point between day care center and preschool.[7]

Sweden has been changing gradually from strict age segregation to a more age-integrated approach. The preschool covers all children to age seven, but there are, as noted earlier, two subgroups within most centers: the infant group from a few months to two-and-one-half, the sibling group for all other children. Programing experiences and the recommendations of a 1972 Child Care Commission shaped this pattern. Although both groups are in one building, permitting interaction and exchange, they are separate and different. And there are far fewer infant groups. There are some Swedish experts who state that the very same factors which justify an integrated effort for ages two-and-one-half to seven actually suggest that there should be no separation at all by age within the child care center. There is little relevant research but the anecdotal evidence offered states that a fully age-integrated center is better for infants in that it offers more stimulation and opportunity for interaction. The older children could be deprived by the practice, if it were carried to an extreme, but the realities of age-integrated programing, where it exists, really permit some separate, enriching experiences for six-year-olds, as for others, during the day. Age integration does not imply that there would be no special activities in age groupings at all. Nonetheless, most Swedish preschools still have infant groups and recognize the division at about two-and-one-half.

Because mothers take advantage of maternity leaves and related benefits, *GDR* infants enter into group care relatively late in the first year of life, after the twentieth week. The *Krippe* programs remain age-segregated despite visiting back and forth. *Krippe* personnel report that integrated programs are not good for the infants, since they lose out on rest and suffer from too much overstimulation.

Another *FRG* development in one state is of interest (Nordrhein-Westfalen). In a challenge to the prevalent age segregation, experimental "groups of fifteen" are age-integrated: nine children ages three to six, four ages two to three, and two infants in the one to two-year range. But these groups of fifteen, in turn, are located in *Kindertaggesstätten*, larger administrative units offering most children in most groups a usual pattern of age segregation.

The *United States* does not have a universal preschool, so day care covers all the preschool years, too, usually to age five and entry into public kindergartens. There is no theory or ideology which calls for division at age three. A recent national supply study chose age two as a dividing point for its analysis. Almost three-fourths of all day care centers had no children under two. As we have seen, over half had no more than five under-threes and would be elsewhere (in Europe) classified as kindergarten, not as day care at all. Only some twenty-five U.S. day care centers were exclusively for under-twos, the core of a day care system for infants-toddlers, and they were geographically concentrated in the southeast and southwest.[8]

There are no widely adopted norms about age segregation or integration for *family day care* anywhere, since it apparently is assumed that in this sense at least one can have either familylike situations (age integration) or age similarity (a group), depending on the prevalent family day care theory. Swedish municipal day care practice limits the family day care mother to one child under age one, among the four in her care. In general, in the United States, Sweden, the FRG, and France, more of the under-threes, and especially more of the youngest children in care, are in family day care rather than in center care. Whatever the realities, and they are unknown, the implicit assumption in these countries is that better care and more attention are assured in this way. However, substantial numbers of children in elementary school are also in family day care after school hours, until parents return. Despite the development of centers, after-school programs, and *Hort* facilities (the terms vary), few countries have satisfactory and sufficient after-school provisions for school-aged children.

Age-related Content

As we shall see, while there is some debate as to whether the centers-*crèches* have or should have a *formal* curriculum for infants and toddlers, there is very little debate about the need for an experience that features interaction with adults who speak to them, learning through play, some peer interaction, health and nutrition components, physical activity and stimulation—guided by knowledge of the physical, emotional, and cognitive development of young children. Nor is there much disagreement that the chief caretakers should be especially trained to implement knowledge from early child development theories—while equipment, setting, food, and routines are informed by medical pediatrics. This much said, there is little substantive case for a specific age three cut-off. If any group is to be separated because its routine requires more protection, different food, perhaps higher adult ratios, somewhat different content—it would be those who are under two or two-and-one-half. (Even this, however, does not necessarily argue against the Swedish and FRG experiments with full age integration, covering those who are a few months old and including others up to elementary school.) In short, the evolution of the systems has undermined the case for the rigid age three cut-off and perhaps suggested lowering it by six months or a year. Not that this is the critical issue, given the widespread shortages. It is a large problem only in France where the two-year-olds are in both *crèches* and *écoles maternelles*.

Entry Age

But the age discussion is not complete without consideration of the entry age. Two elements emerge: 1) despite the lack of firm empirical evidence (there is a plethora of psychoanalytic theory and deductive generalization), there is widespread intuitive feeling that mothers or parents should be with children in the very early months; 2) the transition into care is complex and should be undertaken slowly—in the interest of both children and parents.

Much of the frequently cited research deals with gross deprivation: deprived children in large institutions, full time or for all week, most of them dependent, neglected, or abused children. The work of Spitz and Bowlby is known everywhere. There are similar reports in all countries. But it is not firmly known how good programs, adequate adult-child ratios, small groups, affect development *of children living with their parents* if the child enters care at three months, or at four or five, or six or eight, and is served in an

average setting for a country, as contrasted with exemplary facilities. However, the reports of Bowlby, Spitz, and other similar reports, and the direct
observations reported in the GDR and Hungary of unsatisfactory results
with large week-long and overnight institutions for infants, have led to a
counsel of caution. All countries except for the United States, among the
ones here covered, offer some cash assistance in the form of statutory paid
maternity leaves for employed women (parental insurance in Sweden),
which makes too early placement unnecessary.

What is "too early placement" is not clear. The maternity leave (parental
insurance) period among these countries ranges from sixteen weeks to nine
months. Some weeks may be elected or mandated before childbirth. Most
countries also permit some unpaid but job-protected leave after the expiration of the maternity leave (see chapter 2). Several others also make (less
generous) cash benefits available after maternity leaves expire. Several protect jobs for longer periods, after the paid leave. As a result, the once early
crèche entry ages are now six or nine months. One sees very few infants
under such ages in centers. Discussion and observation suggest that the typical *crèche* entry age could become—increasingly—nine months or a year
(again, except for the United States, which has no national policy for universal maternity-parental leave).

Thus the center, if separate from the preschool, may be seen as a child
caring resource for the age period of nine months to two or two-and-one-
half—a briefer period than originally contemplated. This affects the number
of places needed and program content. It may also affect the outcome of
the preschool vs. *crèche* boundary question, and the possibility of full age
integration, with separate infant groups if considered desirable.

It is not that the entry age poses no problems. The child development
theoreticians and practitioners in all these countries report a "difficult"
entry period, located somewhere in the age span beginning at six or eight
months and extending to sixteen or eighteen months. Some believe the
period inherently difficult; others hold that it is difficult if not dealt with
appropriately. Many believe that the child makes the transition to other
than mother's care more readily either before or after this time. The dynamics relate to "bonding," the recognition of the mother and the unique
attachment to her; once the attachment is achieved, the separation is more
threatening until much later.

The phenomenon is not fully evaluated psychologically. Nonetheless, both child development experts and policy makers in all the countries draw the conclusion that entry into care can be planned for the six to twelve months age period, if that is when maternity or parental leave ends. There are various different theories and reported experiences in the several countries about ideal and undesirable times within that period. However, what is urgent, they testify, is careful and gradual, and thus reassuring, initiation into care. The French, Hungarian, GDR, and Swedish centers for infants all have routines and recommendations, but Hungary's is most impressive. Since there is a child care grant, authorities can refuse admission unless there is a slow and effective initiation procedure. Thus there are detailed procedures for implementing the most prevalent pattern, a one-week period during which the moher spends each day in the center with decreasing specified involvement; the seventh day is the child's first "normal" day. Other, less prevalent, patterns involve nonparticipation by the mother, but only gradually lengthening days for the child over a week period; or a two-week cycle including decreasing participation by the mother; or a two-week buildup of child participation, but with the mother not participating at all. In the GDR, similar transition arrangements have been developed.

Administration

The differences as to age groupings have implications beyond programing concerns ("Which grouping gives most children the richest possible experience?") or psychological theories ("What age splits are dictated by developmental needs?"). There are different professions and bureaucracies in control of the under-three and the over-three systems. In the GDR, Hungary, and France the preschool is administered by an education ministry and dominated by educators. The younger children, whether in *crèches* or family day care, remain the responsibility of health ministries. In FRG, preschool is administered largely by voluntary social agencies and church-related institutions, regulated by the Education Ministry and (on the state level) by ministries concerned with health, labor, and social affairs. The *Krippen* are regulated by health ministries. The historical roots for these distributions of responsibilities are self-evident. The only issue today is whether the health-protection emphasis for the younger children, under age two-and-one-half or three, remains so overwhelmingly a consideration as to require separation—and whether the lack of a developmental curriculum for any children is anywhere justifiable. If not, can adequate program content be achieved under the health ministry? Or if the Education Ministry is to deal as well with the younger children, can it protect an adequate health component and can it develop a curriculum more appropriately geared to developmental needs of one and two-year-olds?

Sweden created an age-integrated and philosophically unified child care program in the 1970s. The only issues are internal to program development: What programmatic considerations justify segregation or integration? The assignment of this effort, covering children up to age seven, to the Social Board involves a decision (also taken in Finland) to create a new administrative entity that will be more oriented to child development than to traditional education, health, or traditional social welfare service "for the disadvantaged and troubled." Staff qualifications are based on task, not administration, so the dominant staff groups are early childhood education specialists and psychologists.

In the United States the administrative split is between social service agencies and education departments, day care versus nursery school and prekindergarten. Health departments have major roles in certifying center facilities and family day care mothers, but they are not assigned to funding or programmatic initiatives or responsibilities characteristic of the several countries, other than Sweden, that have been cited. Since public social service functions are central to the funding of most public day care, public welfare (public social service) departments are in the lead at federal, state, and local levels in the United States and there are no cut-offs at age three. However, private nurseries and public prekindergarten classes are in the educational stream (early childhood education), whether for regulation or for operation, and most day care centers, public or private, are directed and largely operated by personnel trained in early childhood education. Since children under three are not in public prekindergartens, it is the nursery school (defined as school-like, and education-oriented), and the day care center or family day care home (social-service based, if variously oriented) that constitute the overlapping systems. Head Start, a compensatory program for the deprived, is sometimes lodged in education, sometimes in social service.

The evidence is very strong that parent-consumers in the United States do not make these distinctions. They consider their children to be in a schoollike setting if it is a group setting, whether called "nursery school" or "day care." Family day care is seen differently, often as baby sitting.

Currently few people question the predominant role that health agencies play in inspecting family day care or centers. In most countries it is considered proper for centers to be regarded operationally responsible to social welfare or education and family day care to health. However, the situation could change if the initiatives toward integration of family day care and center programs were to develop further. Then, programmatic emphasis could affect administrative prescriptions and choices would need to be made.

Summary

The emerging picture is not without shape, but there are issues still to be settled:

- There is experimentation with full age integration in the preschool years, and it clearly is experimentation worth continuing.
- If there is to be a dividing line in center programing for the under-fives, experience argues that is probably around two or two-and-one-half and not age three, as at present.
- The issue of age-grouping or age-segregation in family day care deserves exploration and study.
- It is difficult to justify a split administrative pattern such as that in the United States (and in England) in which some under-fives (or fives-and-under) are in an education-related facility and some in a social welfare-related program. The preschool center requires programing elements of both, drawn upon by personnel oriented to child development and early childhood education, and not dominated either by excessive health routines or the culture of the elementary school classroom.
- If maternity-parental leaves continue to follow their present course, and if all countries (like the U.S.) which currently do very little were to join in offering them, child care programs might generally plan for an entry age at six or nine months, or a year, and careful, staged, gradual transitions into care—whether family day care or center care. This would assume a readiness in each country to ensure benefit-service coordination, whether or not there is an explicit recognition of their policy relationships.

The age debate implies some assumptions about program, of course. For purposes of the present presentation only we have relegated this to the next section.

IS THERE A CURRICULUM? SHOULD THERE BE?

The term "curriculum" is used here broadly to mean the conscious program focus that goes beyond physical care, health protection, and feeding. Are centers to be concerned only with providing good "care" or must they have developmental goals for children entrusted to them?

The countries vary as between those who consider center care as a group arrangement for offering safe care (literally) and those who have come to see in it a significant opportunity to enhance the development, socialization, and learning of children. Several of the latter are tending to a theory and practice which can be described as curriculum development. Some even employ the concept. No country conceptualizes a family day care curriculum, even though several are beginning to seek ways of affecting the care pattern and stimulation available in the family day care setting and, as already noted, are even experimenting with family day care-center cooperation and integration.

Among these countries, Sweden, the GDR, Hungary, France, and the United States have each taken steps toward a curriculum concept, using different terms to convey it, and not meaning a formal curriculum in the elementary school sense. The U.S. and French systems are so pluralistic and decentralized as to make characterization difficult. Sweden's ready acceptance of the need for programing strategy may derive from its administrative pattern which brings all children to one center from earliest infancy until elementary school at age seven. The staff inevitably faces the issue of curriculum, as do all kindergarten-nursery systems for three- to five-year-olds.

The guiding document in Sweden was the report on preschools published in 1972 by a national commission. Drawing upon the work of Piaget and Erikson, the commission held that children learn and grow best by exploring their surroundings with the help of experienced adults. The core process is a "pedagogical dialogue between children and adults" regarding experiences, feelings, and knowledge. This philosophy calls for attractive surroundings, indoors and out, for active play and for quiet activity. There must be opportunity both to participate in the group and to move toward a quiet corner. There should be stimulating toys and equipment. The caretakers bring not a formal curriculum but an attitude and a way of relating as they participate in play, feeding, reading—with the group and with individuals. The Swedish system does not mandate this program, yet national leadership and subsidies in a small country have led to general and enthusiastic endorsement. Excellent curriculum and programing guides have been issued and are available for international use.

While the Swedish program is oriented to adult-child interaction and is premised on high staffing ratios and small groups, the sibling groups (all children ages two-and-one-half to seven in one group) also assume mutual benefits from child-child interactions. As noted, there are, too, some experiments which add the infants to these sibling groups. Even more recently (perhaps, cynics might say, as costs of the high staffing ratio become overwhelming and programs do not expand rapidly enough), there have been some voices raised in Sweden to state that child-child interaction is most important and should not be discouraged by the high adult-child ratios. Political observers doubt that norms will be changed to permit less staffing against the strong combined pressure from staffs and the parents of currently enrolled children.

The GDR center program is the largest, relatively, and its curriculum the most formal. The program is characterized as "playing and learning." A recent statement in the GDR characterizes *Krippen* as "institutions of the health service designed to care for and educate (*erziehen*) healthy babies and infants." (*Erziehen* is translatable into English both as "educate" and "rear." Both meanings are apparently intended.) *Krippen*, in this interpretation, "constitute the bottom stage of the integrated socialist educational system and, together with the parents, bear a great responsibility for the harmonious ... development of their charges." Daily routines and staffing provisions are oriented "to stimulate the children to age-specific play, independent activity, and to help them develop their linguistic, physical, mental and musical faculties."

The careful empirical work of Dr. E. Schmitt-Kolmer and her successors in comparing home- and center-cared-for infants and toddlers led to adoption of norms for physical, social, emotional, and cognitive development. Child care personnel in the *Krippen* now monitor and report a child's development on standard forms that focus on all these dimensions. These guide individualized attention to children by personnel. To encourage even more extensive cognitive growth, the *Krippen* are actually guided in a daily "cognitive stimulation" program of brief duration, for children, during which specific programed activities are introduced for ten- and twenty-minute periods, the latter for the toddlers approaching preschool age. (See accompanying charts for daily program routines for children six to ten months old and for children two years old.) There is continuous research and curriculum innovation in these elements, as there is in physical care and activity. Yet visits do not yield any sense of greater uniformity of behavior by the children or of more control by staff than at most centers in the other countries studied. Only in the experimental programs and cooperatives with very strongly permissive philosophies does there seem to be any greater spontaneity.

In the United States, early childhood education, rather than nursing, is the professional identification of the leadership of centers that care for young children, including those that serve infants and toddlers. The professional ideology stresses a "developmental" experience, which is seen as different from custodial care. However, many different specific child development theories and program philosophies are found in the educational institutions that prepare personnel. It is, therefore, not surprising that at the level of operations there are many types of programing approach. Experts do not often use the term "curriculum" but they certainly accept the idea of a philosophy that includes concern for cognitive stimulation and rich socializing experiences, as well as health, mental health, and physical development. Also relevant is the fact that infant and toddler center care, not widespread in the United States, tends to concentrate in geographic areas where staff salaries and qualifications are low. Whatever the leadership aspirations, therefore, there can be only limited implementation, in most places, of curriculum in the Swedish or GDR sense.

In the period from 1948 to 1968 the center (*crèche*) was Hungary's only child care provision; thus, there is some continuity of program development and experimentation. Specially notable is the pioneering effort of Dr. E. Pikler, who has stressed the capacity of the very youngest infants to interact with peers and who opposes excessive adult interference with self-generated infant development generally. For reasons already explained, Hungary's policy orientation over the past dozen years has focused on downplaying center care and making at-home care financially possible; the popular culture apparently still defines at-home care as superior. The observer is nonetheless impressed with the careful work done to identify ways to successfully introduce infants and toddlers into the *crèche* experience; the linkage of each *crèche* to a "methodological *crèche*" for supervision and on-the-job training; the work of a national methodological *crèche* on methods and norms; the sense of program form and content. In short, a de facto "curriculum" has developed. Moreover, despite the Dr. E. Pikler tradition, the typical center offers an atmosphere and program routine not very different from what one encounters in many places in France or the United States: not a structured curriculum but staff attitudes, equipment, setting, and program to stimulate emotional, social, and physical development as well as cognitive

ILLUSTRATIVE KRIPPE SCHEDULE FOR CHILDREN
6–10 MONTHS OLD

6:00– 8:00 A.M.	Arrival of children Morsel feeding of older babies; bathing in connection with health-promoting measures (e.g., cold-water pouring); playing activities in the crib or on playing mattress; lap and finger games; singing songs to the babies; if necessary, changing diapers; getting babies ready for first sleep
8:00– 9:30 A.M.	First sleep with windows wide open or in open air (in winter with headgear, in sleeping bag or similar outfit)
9:30– 9:45 A.M.	Taking babies out of crib; changing diapers
9:45–10:00 A.M.	Individual activities
10:00–11:00 A.M.	First meal (vegetable pap)
in between until 11:30 A.M.	Playing activity with material and toys, didactic material, lap and finger games or individual activities; if necessary, changing diapers; getting babies ready for second sleep
To 1:30 P.M.	Second sleep with windows wide open; taking babies out of crib when awake; changing diapers
1:30– 2:30 P.M.	Second meal (porridge)
in between until 6:00 P.M.	Playing activity with material, toys, didactic material, lap and finger games, singing songs to the babies; individual activities; if necessary, putting to sleep; if necessary, changing diapers; parents fetching children

In good weather, playing activities can be organized in the garden or on the terrace, in open-air cribs or cots.

SOURCE: GDR Report

capacities. The main "program" is the personal contact and demonstration of affection of the adult for the child during bathing, diapering, and feeding of the very young. As the children reach age two, there are more caretaker-initiated experiences—but peer interaction is considered important.

The nursing orientation of most of the staff leaders and the supervisory role of the health ministry create an atmosphere in the French *crèches* that stresses care, and does not have a cognitive or developmental emphasis.

ILLUSTRATIVE KRIPPE SCHEDULE FOR CHILDREN
TWO YEARS OLD

6:00– 7:30 A.M.	Arrival of children; playing in group room, in cot, on large playing mattress (crawling lawn) with various toys and didactic material; lap and finger games; singing songs to the children, looking at picture books, etc.
7:30– 7:45 A.M.	Breakfast
7:45– 8:15 A.M.	Using the washroom, chamber pot, undress for first sleep, health-promoting measures (e.g., dry-brushing, shower, or cold rubbing) with some children
8:15– 9:45 A.M.	First sleep with windows wide open
9:45–10:00 A.M.	Using washroom, chamber pot, dressing
10:00–10:10 A.M.	Individual or group activity
10:10–10:15 A.M.	Dressing for open-air activity
10:15–12:15 P.M.	Playing in garden, on terrace, in open-air cots, in sandbox with various playing material, with balls, on playing installation (slide, crawling tunnel), bathing in pool on hot days, movement games; on rainy, cold days playing in group room
12:15–12:20 P.M.	Undress, using washroom
12:20–12:40 P.M.	Lunch
12:40– 1:00 P.M.	Using washroom, chamber pot, health-promoting measures with some children; undress for second sleep
1:00– 2:30 P.M.	Second sleep with windows wide open, in winter with adequate facilities like sleeping bags, hoods, etc.
2:30– 3:00 P.M.	Getting up, dressing, chamber pot, washing hands
in between 2:45– 3:05 P.M.	Individual or group activity
3:05– 3:20 P.M.	Afternoon meal
3:20– 3:25 P.M.	Using the washroom
3:25– 6:00 P.M.	Playing in the open air (s.a., 10:15 A.M.); plus individual educational promoting measures, singing, lap and finger games. Parents fetch children

Good weather provided, all measures and activities may be organized in the open air.

SOURCE: GDR Report

France has some distance yet to travel as it departs from the health tradition of its *crèches*. Until as recently as the 1960s, the long-unchallenged dominance of medical routines persisted. The purpose of the *crèche*, literally, was to care for children while their mothers worked. There was much concern with the danger of infection to children, so much so that parents and others were not even admitted to "deliver" a child; the child was taken in nude and dressed in *crèche* clothing, no plants or animals were tolerated, outside toys and games were excluded, the meal and toilet routines were very rigid—and so forth. The program was administered by public assistance authorities (from a health and welfare ministry), directed by hospital nurses and run by hospital personnel.

A change began in French programs in 1968. While still under a health ministry, they are administered at the prefecture and municipal levels. They began to employ *puericultrices* as directors (pediatric nurses who are required to have experience with well children and to learn about child development). Psychologists were brought in as counselors and to help with staff training and program development. Early childhood educators were added, too. Medical ideas and the concern with physical well-being are still of major influence and many of the personnel are said still to regard children under age two as needing physical care primarily. However, psychological concerns are becoming more visible. There is no one pervasive doctrine, but one notes attention to adult-child interaction and concern with the children as a group. Some *crèches* emphasize the importance of talking to children and of individualizing responses to them. Parents are free to visit and to join the group in the more advanced centers.

In recent years, as psychologists and early child educators have made their influence felt, all of the currents of research and theory known in Europe and North America have, of course, been experienced in France, too. Thus, as in the United States, one encounters some custodial and some developmental *crèches*, *crèches* that deliberately create group experiences and peer interaction, or adult-child exchanges, and others content to offer safe and wholesome care. There is no standardized *crèche* program content and the standard-setting bureaus stress physical setting, group size, staff qualifications—but not program content.

As noted earlier, the *école maternelle* actually serves more children under three than does the French *crèche collective*. Here there is no question about the appropriateness of having a specific program or curriculum, even though, like the *crèche*, it deals with two-year-olds (most of them two-and-one-half or older in the fall, when they enter). The *école maternelle* is essentially an educational setting, conducted in what is an international nursery school tradition of learning in and through play. Depending on school and teacher, these can be formal and rigid, or comparable to the most relaxed and permissive of experimental nursery settings. Because it is historically an "old" program this system must cope with old, inappropriate buildings in many places and the dominance of educators oriented to controlling very large groups (35–45 children to one teacher) in settings that follow kindergarten routines. At their best, the toddler classes resemble the best of child care centers in their physical setting, equipment, staffing, and learning-through-play routines. But the current reality is often quite different.

The FRG is not sufficiently accepting of center care for children under age three and is too decentralized in this regard for one to expect any explicit general program norms or even tendencies toward this in the *Krippen*. Health supervision is still dominant and most daily care is by personnel identified as "nurses." Whereas the FRG has legislated the right to an "educational" experience in *Kindergärten* from age three, and implemented this philosophy with a high percentage of coverage, the *Krippen* are seen as providing care for children while their mother works (and as second-best to family day care). Because the mothers who must use such care are considered to have or to be problems (and are often poor, foreign, and/or troubled) the stress is on health and hygiene. The dominant view does not justify the experience as valuable for children.

There are other currents on the FRG scene, however. A recent summary, from the country report, states:

There are more and more initiatives to change the mere substitute care functions of the *Krippen* into a function as a family-supporting but independent socialization agency. For the first time in the FRG, Berlin (with a third of the *Krippen* places) has formulated (but not yet implemented) explicit educational objectives in the fields of cognitive, emotional, and social behavior as guidelines for the work in the *Krippen*. This is the first step towards a socialization-development mission for the under-threes, something long guaranteed to the 3–6 group in *Kindergärten*. Recent research on enriched center care by Beller in Berlin is promising and may encourage other initiatives .... The "groups of 15" [Nordrhein-Westfalen] are programmed to offer the children "more opportunities for interaction and cognitive growth as well as for language and social-emotional development."

To this we add the fact that local cooperative programs and individual *Krippen* are often led by personnel who have mastered current child development research and program theory. Some of these programs, too, share their major characteristics with all the other countries that have been experimenting with enriched social-emotional developmental experiences.

Not by design, apparently, but because birth rate declines have made space available, the FRG now has more under-threes in *Kindergärten* than in *Krippen*. The differences in program orientation of these two institutions must (as in France) lead ultimately to a confrontation about programs.

To conclude: very little that is systematic can be said about the content of family day care. On the other hand, whatever the ideologies and rationales, those who provide group (center) care for infants certainly do see the need to go beyond health and safe custody. Caretaker behavior, planned activities, equipment, setting, support for peer interactions constitute—variously—curriculum and program for *crèches*, *Krippen*, day care centers, and integrated preschools. Only the GDR seems to be developing what may be considered a formal overall "educational" component for an entire country, but it does not seem to be creating great pressure to "learn," and individual differences are respected. Hungary is next in the continuum, followed by Sweden. Similar initiatives exist in some programs in the United States and France, and some, but fewer, in the FRG, depending on philosophy and leadership in these more decentralized and pluralistic systems. There is general convergence on the nature and meaning of development, whether among those who believe somewhat more in growth from within or those who stress outside stimulation. This is a far cry from the image of hospital corridors lined with cribs full of apathetic infants conjured up by the names Spitz and Bowlby and employed by opponents of group care of the very young.

None of this is to ignore those important differences everywhere, between centers with rich program content, and an emphasis on adults talking to children and responding to them as individuals, and those environments still offering *crèche-Krippen*-center children little stimulation or individual attention at all. We cannot statistically estimate the numbers of each type, but the dominant philosophies clearly favor the former, and advocates of center expansion favor such programs, not nurse-dominated mass nurseries without developmental programs.

Center programs clearly are undergoing change, and the direction is positive. The tension between programing in *crèche* and *école maternelle*, *Krippe* and *Kindergarten*, day care center and preschool, will continue the process as at least three countries consider the meaning of program differences for two-year-olds, depending on the program they enter. And if family day care should be connected to group programs in the long run, the integration process may raise questions of program for those facilities, too.

Several countries have been wrestling with the question of how child care programs do and should deal with handicapped children. A consensus is emerging here, as in other fields, in favor of maximum "mainstreaming," integrating all physically and emotionally handicapped children into the regular programs as much as possible. Here Sweden is in the lead, adding resources and specialists to many centers to make such integration possible. Impressive equipment and routines have been observed for the hard-of-hearing and the blind, for example. All countries are moving toward integration, however. In France the actual admission decisions in each *crèche* are under the control of the local directress, so there is great variation. However, since 1975, policy has provided for admission of the handicapped, given the *crèche* doctor's agreement. Recent U.S. legislation stating the right of the handicapped to preschool from age three (a right not recognized for the normal child below elementary school age!) may create leverage to expand resources for everybody.

We close this section by noting that there are those who oppose socially sponsored child care arrangements as a form of politically inspired takeover of parental child rearing prerogatives. What, in fact, is the picture? Do programs support such abuse?

The possibility of such use of child care programs is advanced in two quite different forms, with very different backers. Noting that it is the children of the most disadvantaged families who are more often physically, cognitively, and emotionally deprived (and who thus do not do well, no matter what social policy does to protect equality of opportunity), there are those who urge early exposure to child care programs with clear compensatory goals. Head Start began in the United States with such a goal. There are some such programs in several of the countries. Sweden offers priority to children in several deprived categories. There is no evidence that such programs are potent enough to be able to take over the parental prerogatives, however, or that they have such goals in the first place. Sweden stresses parent involvement. Those in the United States concluded quite early that active parent participation in all program aspects would contribute to program effectiveness. There are several Head Start spinoffs with even more emphasis on programing for an entire family: Parent-Child Centers and Home Start, in particular. Programs are voluntary and children are certainly not separated from their parents. Indeed the pace of work with children is controlled by parental preference in a significant number of places.

While one can find in the literature proposals that group experience from early childhood become a vehicle for more intensive intervention than this, indeed for complete resocialization and reeducation of problem-laden "underclasses," there is nowhere in any of these countries any advocacy of such views by articulate policy makers, programmers, or staff personnel. In a sense there is general recognition that "life chances" for children are framed by familial and neighborhood environments but there is no readiness to argue that equality or equity objectives can justify substantial usurping of family rights.

Along similar lines there are some who fear group programs for the very young as creating a vehicle for an all-powerful state bent on political indoctrination. While allegations about the practices elsewhere should certainly be pursued, since the possibility is obviously present where children are in care for long hours from early ages, there is no evidence of such goals or practices among the particular countries here reporting. Everywhere, it would appear, the goal is to supplement parental care and contribute to development, not to drive a wedge between parents and children. However, parental participation is a very important safety factor and, as noted below, it is difficult to implement and is poorly developed in some places.

None of this is to deny that the fact of family day care, center care, preschool represents a change from the child rearing of the past. As does the intimacy of the urban neighborhood and the salience of its street life and peer groups, out-of-home child care must inevitably affect families and create a new shared community culture. As much may be said for TV, radio, elementary and secondary schools, the mass press, or travel. What is relevant, however, is that the family shows no signs of losing its centrality in the countries studied, and pluralism is not threatened by child care programing in those countries where pluralism has been a value. The programs which we have studied and visited, and those reported on in available research, lack the uniformity, potency, and salience needed to supercede families. We have not found evidence that they are attempting deliberately to do so. Parents retain their influence with children and have options to exercise.

Family day care and center care always do pose the possibility that family day care mothers, teachers, nurses, and caretakers will regard themselves as superior to parents, creating confusion and conflict for children. Many such difficulties have been observed in the history of this field. Tension and conflict are reported in some places where child care workers may feel superior and in their zeal or lack of insight appear to contest parental rights with children. This, however, is an administrative and programing problem demanding careful staff selection, training, supervision. Clearly it is real but it is not in most places out of control. Certainly, it is not in these countries the result of policy. Nor is it a political danger.

In brief, then, there are problems in any program arrangement for the young, ranging from the risk of unintentional undermining of parental roles, to cognitive overstimulation and pressure, to the offering of dull and unstimulating physical care, to the creation of health hazards and physical dangers. Those who would develop such services cannot, therefore, ignore program specifics—or regular, ongoing inspection and evaluation. And parent participation is of highest priority.

IS PARENT PARTICIPATION REQUIRED?

There was a time when a parent who delivered a child to a *crèche* was not permitted in. The child was delivered through a window, slot, or doorway. The health personnel in charge had real worries about infection. They took many precautions, kept parents out, stripped the child of his home outfit, and provided *crèche* clothing. But the practice continued even as disease control and immunization grew, for there was also exclusion as a way to exercise control: if parents called upon communal care, they might as well leave it to the experts.

Today, in these and other countries, it is recognized that policy does not support superceding parents and that children have a better experience if centers promote parent participation. But there are still in many places infant care centers that allow all parents only into one waiting room, that require smocks (and occasionally special slippers) on staff and visitors, that require a change of clothing for the child, and that never admit parents to the activity rooms. Many other centers have given up policies that hold parents at arm's length only during recent years. On the other hand, there also is a search for effective modes of parent participation and a debate as to the most promising approaches.

In most centers, in most countries, participation means having a parent drop off and pick up the child and use the center's communication system (a chat with the care worker, reading or writing in a book provided for the purpose, observing for a few minutes at the start of the day or at the end, and asking, listening, and telling about the child). It also means periodic group meetings and election of a parent committee which can be more or less influential in an advisory role, in supporting the center, and in running special events and projects. Quite frequently one sees rooms where parents change their own children from street clothes to *crèche* clothes, corners where parents leave or pick up messages and materials. Less often, care workers visit all homes at the start of the year. In some places there now also is mandated parent attendance and joining in the program until the newly registered child has adjusted to the change. (see figure 4.2.)

There is, in fact, little discussion of center care as program or policy in any of these countries now without mention of parent participation. The significance of the topic for policy is perhaps illustrated by a discussion of *Krippen* with GDR personnel. Asked whether a comprehensive national system of *Krippen* with high rates of usage and a centrally initiated curriculum does not become a vehicle for the state to take over parental responsibility and to diminish the role of the family, GDR experts respond as follows:

- Available research suggests that family background, especially the education of the child's mother, is a far more influential factor in determining a child's future than is attendance at *Krippen* or other variables.
- In any case, the posture of the *Krippen* is that they are there to help the parents. The parents are expected to participate in the support of the program by working with their children evenings and weekends. To facilitate this they are kept informed as to the content of the daily program and the materials employed.

The GDR official position is that the parents, as vehicles for their children's development, protect their roles through such participation. The professionals formulate the program on the basis of ongoing research and expertise.

Figure 4.2

The Parent Participation Continuum

1. Hand the child in, through a slot or opening
   ↓
2. Deliver the child
   ↓
3. Bring the child, communicate, perhaps visit
   ↓
4. Bring the child, communicate, attend meetings and visit
   ↓
5. Plus an elaborate transition routine before the child attends alone
   ↓
6. More intensive participation involving 4, plus elements of the following:

   Parent remains or drops in from time to time as she/he wishes to participate in elements of the program

   Parent serves as a part-time staff volunteer

   Parent required to "volunteer" for part-time staff role or to perform some service-administration-building-management tasks

   Much of staff rule and administrative-management carried out part-time by parents (with one or two paid staff)

   Parents control all or some elements of staffing and program through a policy board

On the operational level, everywhere, the problem remains ever present: parents may defer to "expert" professionals or to staff members from more advantaged backgrounds; professionals may succumb, however consciously or unconsciously, to the occupational hazard of arrogance. While the six-country review uncovered no evidence of a staff "plot" to supercede parents, the very institutional roles and relationships are such that constant programmatic and supervisory vigilance is clearly needed. Parental participation should be encouraged as a valuable "antidote," and defined in terms appropriate to its core functions of ensuring center-parent cooperation around the child's development, and center programing attuned to parental and community values.

As will be noted in the "standards" discussion, one set of U.S. norms mandates a form of parent participation that goes well beyond this and gives parents a very active voice in center governance: this includes participation in the selection of staff, and/or budget review, and/or a role in fundraising.

Of all centers studied in a U.S. national survey in 1976-77, some 43 percent of the small centers (fewer than forty children) and 51 percent of the larger centers met one or more of these criteria. The compliance rates reached 49 and 57 percent, respectively, if parent volunteering was also expected as "participation." All U.S. centers also are expected to allow parents opportunity to observe and participate in the care of their child at the center.

Participation rates are low for the U.S. private, profit-making centers. They are higher in nonprofit centers, especially in those with federal financial subsidization.

But the tendency of many parents—especially those paying their own way and thus feeling more independent—in all countries not to participate is not to be ignored. Given the choice, many parents seem content to leave their children in the care of center experts for the day and not to insist on (or respond to the opportunity for) extensive personal involvement.

In family day care, especially the family day care which is not agency-operated (and is therefore most like the marketplace), parental preference most often is for two-way communication. Having chosen a family day care mother, the "consumer" expects opportunity to hear what the child has done and to be reassured by some aspects of the care routine. There is no assertion of a right to control or influence very much. If the parent is not satisfied, he or she goes elsewhere, and there is much entering and leaving of family day care arrangements.

Along similar lines, parents who choose center care may think of it as an essential support in permitting them to meet their heavy home, work, and child care responsibilities. If it demands considerable time from them, it would appear, the center becomes less helpful and another source of pressure. Participation and expectations about participation therefore tend to be geared to the realities of the clock. Nonetheless, there clearly is an authentic effort in all the countries to encourage parent participation to confirm that they are not taking over the major child-rearing responsibilities from parents. Many child care theoreticians and researchers hold that mutually supportive home and center approaches to socialization and development are essential if the experience is to be positive.

In most of the countries studied, center care thus reflects a series of tensions: 1) between the expert who "knows" and tends to take over and the parent who wants to assure her or his own primacy with the child; 2) between the center personnel and their leadership who want to work in the context of family goals and who believe it undesirable to supercede parents and who want only to supplement, and parents who are pressed or who, in any case, are content to leave children with qualified people; and 3) between those parents who see day care centers as vehicles for change in societies, families, children and want to call the tune by guiding the centers, and those who consider it enough to ensure that centers provide satisfactory care. The countries inevitably mirror their cultural, political, economic, and historical differences in these matters. This, in turn, has no small influence on the roles assigned to group care in their different policy outlooks.

The specifics are of some interest.

The *GDR*, as noted, expects parents to cooperate, not to control. On the other hand, *Krippen* facilities are so constructed that each group has a "drop off" room (as it has an activity room and a sleeping room) so that parents see their child's group and have easy interchange with personnel. This is a far cry from the old pass-through for children at *crèche* doors in many countries, yet in its provision of a room for changing clothing and turning the child over it shows some survival of the old modes. Similar survivals are visible in many countries. In the GDR, parents work full time, care staff is professionalized, and it is rare to find more evidence of parent participation than such informal communication and attendance at periodic meetings.

In the *United States*, although practice varies significantly from place to place, participation ideology is at the "maximum" end of the continuum and much more than this is called for in "requirements" for parental participation. In actual fact, practice ranges from parental "control" of policy and administration (most common in cooperative centers and in some centers for Head Start, a compensatory day care program serving largely children of low-income mothers, and in a limited number of public day care programs), to the more common communication and cooperation with the care personnel as well as attendance at occasional meetings, to rather substantial rates of volunteering, as already noted.

In *Sweden*, ideology about center care also supports considerable participation, but the results are considered unsatisfactory. As in all countries, parents give and receive communications about their own children, often daily, but do little more than attend the occasional social gathering or party organized by the center and attend the annual or semiannual meeting. Staff are concerned, but it is difficult to insist on very much more where parents work even part time. In the search for increased participation, some Swedish programs have insisted that parents work at the center at least one day each fortnight. A special benefit within the parental insurance now allows even the busiest parents compensated time for center visits.

In *France*, programs vary substantially, ranging from active involvement of parents in *crèche* affairs (but not quite the "community control" of some U.S. centers) to a continuance of the pattern of exclusion that prevailed long ago. In general, the local *crèche* directress is all-powerful and sets the pattern. She calls parent meetings. Most French *crèches* have not yet fully undone a tradition of staff dominance, inherited from the era of health control and parent exclusion. However, this tradition is tempered with the participatory democracy and the new child development theories which are more current. Change is under way.

FRG programs do not yet reflect new modes of participation except in nonpublic parent cooperatives and experimental initiatives in some jurisdictions. The preschool law actually mandates provisions for parental participation. However, according to reports, most programs have not implemented such policy and parents "do not show interest" in participation.

Hungary, influenced by a health tradition, does not generally make it easy for mothers to drop in and wander about the center, but does work hard at slow introduction to the center for children by insisting on parental attendance for the transition period (and the care allowance facilitates this).

No countries are entirely without procedures for slow introduction. This, then, and two-way communication about the child's experiences, is rock-bottom participation. The policy question for countries is how much more to require to assure program values consistent with parental values and to assure that care supplements the family rather than superceding it.

Advocates of increased parent participation are attracted to the idea of *cooperative child care centers*, especially in the United States, the FRG, France, They are joined in their position by people generally concerned about increased "interference" by government in family matters and convinced that child care professionals will always wrest control over child rearing away from parents, unless either replaced by volunteers or tightly supervised by parent boards. Thus the question arises: if parent participation is important, why not organize parent cooperatives instead of center care under public or voluntary agencies?

Comprehensive, reliable statistical data do not exist as to the numbers of cooperative child care centers in the countries which have seen most of such development among these six (U.S., FRG, France). It does appear obvious, however, that parent cooperatives offer little available coverage and hold little promise of major expansion. The self-confidence as to the ability to carry out a program and the requisite acquaintance with child care theories are largely confined to the middle class. And only members of the middle class do not have a problem with the daily out-of-pocket costs of volunteering. In any case, it requires a family economy based on only one out-of-home wage earner to make available a parent with sufficient leisure to volunteer for a significant number of hours weekly—and to fulfill this duty reliably.

The major potential exception to middle-class dominance could be the parent with adequate income from means-tested social assistance to devote full time to child rearing. Such single mothers, a large group in the United States (AFDC) and a small one in the FRG (social assistance) are not representative of the community and are not at work—so their children are less likely to attend child care. When the children from such families do attend there is an inclination to assign program control to experts in compensatory programing and not to rely on cooperatives.

Thus, while parent cooperatives are often attractive and innovative—and of course represent a solution to the participation goal—they are hardly the answer for most child care in most places.[9] Working parents cannot participate adequately. The cooperative mode cannot count on continuity or ensure sufficient coverage. The alternative forms will need to be developed on the assumption of more or less bureaucratized administration, more or less professionalized staff, and more or less otherwise-preoccupied parents. Each country will need to establish its participation minimum and its own modes, however, if it would ensure a child care system that supports, cooperates with, and respects families and guards against apparent or real disregard of their prerogatives and inherent roles and responsibilities.

ARE THERE STANDARDS FOR CHILD CARE PROGRAMS?

Standards and regulations have enormous cost consequences and are often the battleground in child care policy debates. They also affect actual or imagined program quality and therefore influence public and professional attitudes toward specific programs. After health and safety provision has been made and building space provided, the two largest cost items debated are group size and staffing ratios.[10] Staff qualifications follow as matters of concern.

For the past several years, much of the U.S. discussion in the Congress and in the administrative units responsible for family day care and center care policy has focused on standards and regulations. The process began with increased social services funding and the recognition that a significant portion of it would be spent for child care. The Congress (1974) mandated implementation of federal standards, Federal Interagency Day Care Requirements (FIDCR), long on the books and not enforced. Questions of feasibility arose (Would there then be enough care?) as did a basic challenge to the validity of existing requirements (Were they adequate, reasonable, necessary, affordable?). A good deal of American research and discussion addressed these matters between 1975 and 1978. There have been delays in enforcing existing requirements and a flurry of publications, hearings, task forces. A report was sent to the Congress in the summer of 1978 and a redrafting of standards, to be enforced in connection with federal financial participation, was completed in 1979. After further delay and hearings, new regulations were issued, effective October 1980.[11]

In each of the other countries, those who work in and administer child care service programs are aware of the likely significance of staffing ratios, group size, staff training, and standards for health protection and safety, both in their effects on costs and in their possible impact on children. No country has been as preoccupied with the issue in recent years as is the United States, however. An overview of operational patterns and plans leads to the following general interim conclusions: While it is now possible to state firm criteria for the type of automobile tire required by a car of a given weight, to operate on standard roads at standard speeds, similar norms cannot now be objectively formulated in the child care field and validated for a country-to-country transfer. No one debates the importance of health, fire, and safety standards or of attractive surroundings and sufficient space for each child, although the specifics will and probably can vary with culture and wealth. Among these countries, France and the GDR actually have space and facility standards of great specificity already. The GDR, for example, offers specific and elaborated norms under such categories as hours open (6:00 A.M. to 7:00 P.M. maximum), health supervision and checkups, regime, temperature, nutrition, health education, physical space, open-air space, safety, time out of doors, ventilation, lighting, staff training and qualifications. The French also have regulations for many such areas, whether for *crèches, écoles maternelles, crèches familiales,* or licensed *nourrices.* Nor does anyone question the impact of group size or adult-child ratios on programs, but experience, theories, and methods of calculating vary enormously—enough so as to suggest that it is not universal child development wisdom but rather, again, social context, culture, history, and labor force realities that now are determining factors. In any case, there is now no basis in existing research or practice for specifying *particular* adult-child ratios and group sizes, applied to children in different age groups, and validated for international application.

One concludes, in short, that countries need not and probably cannot forego eventually developing and promulgating their own safety, fire, building, space, and health regulations for center and family day care. But the specifics cannot be stated now for many countries and certainly not internationally. Similarly, it is possible to state that groups "should not be too large," the numbers of children in the care of one adult should not be "too many," that the child-adult ratios should be "smaller for very young children," and that "staff providing direct care for children should have education/training in child development." However, one cannot justify at this time any specific numbers or detailed operational criteria of such validity that they should be carried from country to country.

The specifics of present practice are nonetheless of interest as indicators of emerging trends and as offering perspectives in the evaluation of experience within each country.

We have summarized the main staffing standards components (group size and adult-child ratios) in table 4.2 and have differentiated goals/regulations, on the one hand, from realities, on the other. Attention is given both to centers and to family day care. The types of categories required and the table's incompleteness reflect the state of the field. Since standards take several forms, not all countries are covered on all items and the U.S. situation requires a separate table (table 4.3).

The *GDR*, with the largest commitment to center care in this group of

TABLE 4.2

Group Size and Staffing Patterns: Recommendations, Regulations, and Practice

	GDR	FRG	Sweden	France	Hungary	USA
Group Size						
Children under age 1	12 (R)	6–10 (A)	10–12 (R)		10 (R)	7.1 (A)
Children age 1–2	15 (R)	7–12 (A)	10–12 (R)		10 (R)	
Children age 2–3	15 (R)	8–15 (A)	10–12 (R)		10 (R)	11.3 (A)
Recommended Center Staffing Ratios (Adults/Children)						
Children under age 1	3/12		2/5	1/5 nonwalkers	2/10 (R)	1/5.1 (under 1) (Y)
Children age 1–2	2/15		2/5	1/8 for walkers (crèche)		1/5.7 (to 18 mos.) (Y)
						1/5.8 (to 2) (Y)
Children age 2–3**	1/15		2/5	1/35 école maternelle		1/9 (to 3) (Y)
Current Actual National Center Staffing ratios	1/6 (A)	1/6.5 (A)	1/4.6 (A) (all ages)		1/11	1/3.9 (under 18 mos.) (A)
						1/5.9 (to 24 mos.) (A)
Unlicensed Family Day Care				1/6*		
Licensed Family Day Care			1/4 (R) (inc. own)	1/1.56–1/2 (A)		
Center or Preschool, age 3–6 (Ratios)			1/5 (R)	1/35*		
Center Size (under age 3)	90 (R) or 54 (R)	36.5 (A)		45 (A) 60* max	49 (A)	

NOTES: See text for cautions in regard to comparability of these numbers. See table 4.3 for U.S. standards effective October 1980. Here we report an incomplete sample survey.

R = recommended
A = actual
* = required
** Sweden = to 2½
Y = state *average* standards, 1979

TABLE 4.3

U.S. Federal Regulations for Group Size Limits and Child-Staff Ratios

Age of Child	Group Size Based on Enrollment[a]	Group Size Based on Attendance
Birth to 2 years	6	6
2 years	12	12
3 to 6 years	18	16
6 to 10 years	16	14
10 to 14 years	20	18

Age of Child	Staffing Requirement Enrollment[a]	Staffing Requirement Attendance
Birth to 2 years	1:3	1:3
2 years	1:4	1:4
3 to 6 years	1:9	1:8
6 to 10 years	1:16	1:14
10 to 14 years	1:20	1:18

SOURCE: Reprinted from *Federal Register*, March 19, 1980. Effective October 1980.

[a]In each case the enrollment numbers are based on a 12% absentee rate and have been rounded off to the nearest whole number.

countries (and no officially recognized family day care), takes as its current norm a center (*Krippe*) with ninety-six registered children under age three at the maximum:

under age 1	3 groups of 12 children = 36
ages 1–2	2 groups of 15 children = 30
ages 2–3	2 groups of 15 children = 30
	Total 96

These numbers represent recommended registration; the space plans are for *Krippen* with either fifty-four or ninety places. Daily attendance would be lower. Staffing norms are as follows:

under age 1	12 children, 3 staff
ages 1–2	15 children, 2 staff
ages 2–3	15 children, 1 staff

The GDR reports that at present the national average overall is twelve children and two staff per group in daily attendance.

These numbers call for some explanation and digression. Upon examination, ratios for all countries prove to be tricky. In most places staff work "normal" shifts, certainly no more than eight hours, often less. Some work part time. Centers, *crèches*, and *Krippen* are variously open for nine to twelve hours a day. Nursery schools are open half-days or for short days in many countries. The usual practice is to begin and end the day with low staff coverage, since only a few children come very early and a few are picked up very late. The potential ratio of coverage obtained by computing the child totals and the staff totals reflects the true situation only briefly and at the height of the program day, if ever.

Nor is it clear that countries all count the same things. Does one report the ratio of staff to the *crèche* total child capacity, registration, or actual average attendance? Practice varies. Some countries overregister, taking account of average daily absence, so as to assure full space utilization; *crèches* inevitably have high absence rates given the frequency of childhood illness and other contingencies. Thus registration or capacity is a useful number in some countries and not in others. Average attendance, if stable, is probably a more valid way of computing group size and ratios in most places, but is not always known.

There are other issues to be determined in precise measurements—most countries do not have the same interpretation of these variables in all jurisdictions: Should one observe ratios group by group or compute for the center? What norms apply in mixed-age groups? Does one compute staff coverage and child attendance on a daily or on hourly basis? Does one count staff members as present even if they are not in the room with children at certain times?[12]

Where the entire staff have known training or qualifications, as in the GDR, the ratio has specific meaning. GDR *crèche* attendants complete the tenth grade of the general polytechnical secondary school, at about age sixteen, and then attend a three-year course at a medical-technical school. There are similar requirements for French *crèche* personnel and higher requirements for Swedish care personnel and French *école maternelle* teachers. (In most places experience is credited and alternative routes exist or have in the past.)

But what of the United States, where 26 percent of the staff are volunteers and where there are levels of training: professional, paraprofessional, and aide? And whom does one count: the seamstress in the French *crèche* who interacts with and is loved by all children and staff and helps feed the infants? Cooks and cleaning personnel? The locally employed service personnel in the French *école maternelle*, who vary in numbers and quality but do change the teacher-child ratios? Most countries in this grouping, in most places, count only child-caring staff in their ratios. However, because it is a program principle in Sweden that all staff (cooks, maintenance personnel, etc.) interact with children in the course of the program day in accord with the child care program philosophy and curriculum, no distinctions are made there and all adults are counted. The U.S. tabulations include volunteers.

These cautions and caveats make it possible to summarize the rest rapidly. *Hungary*, with a significant space shortage and backlog, tends to overregister. Average *crèche* registration is forty-nine and average attendance is thirty-six. The target for a staff-child ratio is two adults for each ten children, but this has not yet been achieved. In 1975 the average ratio was one staff member to eleven children, but there were places it was as high as one to seventeen or eighteen. Child-caring personnel, called "nurses" quite often, as they are in the GDR and other countries, attend a standard vocational secondary school course with a specialization in health care. This is supplemented by a ten-month on-the-job training experience. The work is regarded as hard and as offering low pay. Many of the young staff members are out at a given moment on their own child care leaves. The result is high turnover, staffing instability, use of temporary personnel—all of which must be considered in examining group size and staff-child ratios.

Of all the countries in the group, *France* has the most elaborate system of regulations, norms, goals—and they cover both family day care and *crèches*, since the French have the most diverse and comprehensive of the systems here described. (The United States is as diverse but coverage is far lower.) Moreover, the French have the most complete enforcement machinery, considered as appropriate given the public role in financing. Even private family day care, with a large unregulated component everywhere, is now increasingly to be brought under public surveillance as the French begin to implement their law requiring licensing more vigorously. *Nourrices* (the official term is *assistante maternelle*) are licensed by the official ministry unit and are under the supervision of social workers. Standards are not very demanding: a medical examination indicating freedom from TB or venereal disease and a social worker's judgment that the home is adequate. In most of France there is a follow-up visit once a year, but in Paris the visits average three annually. There is legislation calling for some training for these women who care for children in their own homes, but it has not been implemented to any significant extent as yet. However, in the instance of the *crèche familiale*, in effect what others might call agency-operated family day care, the *nourrices* are on the agency payroll and some thirty to forty women are supervised by a directress who is trained, and who admits children and collects the fees. If more than forty *nourrices* are supervised, the directress has an assistant. This presumably raises standards; however, because *nourrices* earn more on their own, they have a tendency to leave the *crèche familiale* and do private family day care work after they are experienced and have made contacts.

In contrast with relatively high U.S. and Swedish family day care numbers, the average licensed French *nourrice* on her own cares for two children and the *nourrice* in the *crèche familiale* cares for 1.56. (A *nourrice* may care for one to three children in addition to her own, officially.)

As noted there are significant numbers of two-year-olds in the public nursery school, *école maternelle*, in France. Group size may reach thirty-five, forty, and even more (forty-two is a recent average)—with one qualified nursery teacher and untrained aides for feeding, clothing, and cleaning —often the equivalent of one per group. Currently each *école maternelle* class must enroll thirty-five children and should be closed out if it enrolls fewer. However, there are plans to convert the thirty-five from a minimum to a maximum. Staff qualifications for the before- and after-school and holiday coverage vary enormously and are not standardized.

The French *crèche* maximum is not to exceed sixty children and, as indicated, the national average is forty-two. The range is twenty to one hundred. The regulations, which are enforced, specify one qualified child care person per five children who cannot walk and one per eight who can walk. The staff-child ratio remains the same in the *mini-crèche*, which tends to have twelve to fifteen children and two to three staff. Staff in the *crèche* and related facilities (*haltes-garderie* and *mini-crèche*) originally had training much like the child nurses of the GDR and Hungary, but upgrading of recent years has created positions of *puericultrices* and assistants, essentially pediatric nurses who must gain experience with "average," well children on the job. *Educatrices des jeunes enfants*, more oriented to early childhood education and development, also have entered the system.

Sweden's only formal requirement, in its child care system, is for twelve square meters of space per child, high by international standards. However, given great emphasis on program quality and especially on the quality of adult-child interactions, Swedish programs tend to translate recommended staffing patterns into realities. For the infant groups under age two-and-one-half, the recommendation is for a group of ten to twelve children, with two staff members for every five children. (For children ages three to seven, in the "sibling" group, fifteen children per group, with one staff member for each five children is proposed.) The present operational reality is 4.6 children per staff member, nationally, all ages included; but as we have seen, there are relatively few very young children in group care. For family day care which is publicly funded and supervised (in a pattern not unlike the French *crèche familiale*), it is recommended that one family day care mother not care for more than four children, including her own, and that only one should be under one year old.

There are few comparable data for the *FRG* given the considerable decentralization of responsibility to the states, the tendency to ignore officially the large unlicensed private family day care program, the limitation of new *Krippen* initiatives to a few states, and the recent government preoccupation with a very small family day care experiment called *Tagesmütter*, which does not offer a standard pattern and was changed in the implementation. Under one interpretation, in their failure to require registration, state authorities are responsive to a parental preference for *informal* family day care, as expressed in a 1975 survey.

We can report only that *Krippen* groups tend to range as follows in size: six to ten infants; seven to twelve children aged one to two; and eight to fifteen aged two to three.

By contrast, the *United States* provides substantial volumes of data, state by state and nationally, about standards, actual ratios, the gaps between previously promulgated federal standards and the reality, the costs of achieving compliance—and the empirical validity of available norms. Indeed, the series of relevant reports is being completed only as we write.[13] Here a preoccupation with standards for several years preempted any comprehensive attention to quantity of care.

Between 1968 and 1980 U.S. day care in which there was federal financial participation was governed by FIDCR which were not feasible for some jurisdictions and thus not rigidly enforced—even though influential. In addition to standards as to group size and staff-child ratios, the FIDCR provided for:

- adequate meals and snacks;
- a health examination when the child enrolled;
- counseling and guidance to parents on the appropriateness of day care for their child and a periodic assessment of the child's development and adjustment;
- social services, especially aid in receiving public assistance and community services as needed;
- parent participation, which could mean *either* an active voice in the governance of the center, *or* some participation in the center's decision process and opportunity to volunteer. Centers were required to offer opportunity to observe at the center and participate in care while present.

The quality of compliance with federal requirements varied in the United States by the type of standard (health examination and meals, as contrasted with parent participation) and the type of center (profit or nonprofit, with or without federal financial participation).

Day Care Centers in the U.S. illustrates with much specificity the importance of decisions on topics cited earlier: how to count staff, children, coverage—as well as how to monitor and how often. The conclusion has general relevance: "The stringency of the monitoring guidelines used to interpret and enforce a set of day care regulations can have as large an impact on the characteristics of day care services as the stringency of the regulations themselves."[14]

States and localities also have regulations and standards, some enforced uniformly, and some not. With exceptions, federal standards are more demanding on the indicated items, but localities have assumed fuller responsibility for standards of safety and fire protection. Especially in staffing requirements, FIDCR exceeded the states. As a result there was overall compliance with state child-staff ratio requirements by 93.9 percent of centers but compliance with FIDCR child-staff ratios was only 50.9 percent.

Especially relevant to policy is the question of compliance costs. There are no calculations possible in relation to elements other than staffing ratios.

However, with reference to such ratios the U.S. studies showed that with "relatively lenient" compliance definitions, it would have cost an average of $19 per child per month, or $227 a year, to bring care of children in centers which did not obtain federal funds (nonfederal financial participation centers, non-FFP) up to the FIDCR standards for children in their care. Also for 1976-77 it would have required 5,500 more full time caregivers to bring into compliance all FFP centers; the cost estimates range between $33 and $44 million, not large in the scale of current expenditures. Thus the larger standards issue relates to the non-FFP centers, where there is no subsidy source. In general FIDCR standards created a disincentive to the mixing of children for whom public social service funds pay part or all fees, with other children.

There is no comparable higher cost for FIDCR family day care (day care for which there is federal financial participation) as compared with private-pay family day care. In the family day care field cost differentials are affected not by staffing ratios but by training, support services, licensing, and monitoring.

During 1979, U.S. authorities released a report of the most ambitious effort anywhere to interrelate quality and cost of day care and to generate staffing norms in the context of a cost-benefit analysis.[15] While great precision is not possible, and while policy proposals obviously reflect judgments about quality-quantity cost trade-offs, this effort was used to propose *for U.S. use only* the following guidelines:

- One achieves the most positive impact on services for the three to five age group by enrolling groups no larger than sixteen and staffing them at a ratio of one to eight (the attendance on average would be fourteen and the ratio thus one to seven).
- Costs could be reduced and quality of care for four- and five-year-olds improved moderately at an enrollment ceiling of eighteen per group and a ratio of one to nine (attendance average then is sixteen per group and ratio one to eight).
- There would be greater savings yet good quality service for those three to five at a group enrollment of twenty and an enrolled ratio of one to ten (attendance eighteen per group and a ratio of one to nine).

Between 75 and 90 percent of all U.S. publicly funded centers were found in compliance with all three of these possible standards for the three to five group and 30–60 percent of private centers were in compliance—depending on the option. All three options were less costly than full enforcement of existing regulations would be.

All the options were premised on suitable "child-related education/training" for staff (little detail is specified).

For children under age three the findings were that a ratio of one to five should be maintained in setting *enrollment* standards (one to four *attendance* average) and that the group limits should be eight for infants and twelve for toddlers. While caretaker backgrounds clearly matter, it is not possible to be specific about education or training levels.

Although the research on which these conclusions are based cannot predict long-term effects, these standards are derived by measuring such things as: the teachers' amount of social interaction with (or passive watching of) children; children's cooperation, verbal initiative, and reflective/innovative behavior; children's cooperation, hostility, conflict and aimless wandering, versus involvement; scores on standarized test. Most of these measures are focused on preschool children, not the under-three group, but they meet current child development criteria and have face validity as relevant to long-range positive child development, socialization, and intellectual growth.

The research, public debate, and hearings which led to the group size and staffing choices outlined in table 4.3 also resulted in somewhat more flexible requirements for staff training (personnel without child care credentials must take part in in-service training), parent involvement (a variety of opportunities), information about and help in obtaining social services and health care. When operational, these standards in fact will govern only 8,000 of some 18,000 U.S. centers which provide only a small portion of all U.S. child care.

All countries set their unique group size and child-adult ratios through a mix of *their* knowledge base, resources, and cultural elements. For policy makers everywhere, then, the standards and licensing issue is tied on one side to the extent to which programs ensure that they offer safe, sound, and stimulating supplementary care environments. At the other end there is the pressure of a trade-off between quantity and quality at a given resource level. Among the countries here reviewed, France has elaborate guides and standards in all areas, but its staffing ratios in *écoles maternelles* seem quite inadequate to many child development experts. Sweden has maintained tight quality control (even though only by recommending standards) and has expanded slowly in relation to a large unmet pool of demand. The FRG has focused its *Tagesmütter* project on all aspects of quality control—but this remains a small controlled experiment. In general, all the countries appear to be pragmatic: expansion is consistent with policy; standards rise slowly, and new quality targets are kept in view.

WHAT DOES IT COST? WHO PAYS?

Three cost questions emerge in considering out-of-home care as a public policy: Who pays? Is the level of costs assigned to consumers reasonable and acceptable? Is the public cost reasonable and acceptable? One might also explore and assess distribution of costs among levels of government, on the one hand, and between government and enterprise, on the other—a subject beyond our immediate scope.

It is assumed that budget authorities and planners carry out analyses of all these matters in most countries, despite the relatively limited amount of published research reported by the six countries. There has also been an effort to develop relevant cost-benefit studies. Despite major differences in the completeness of country analyses and reporting, enough of the essential picture does emerge to advance the discussion.

GDR

Center care is the standard way to care for children of working mothers in the GDR, as we have seen. All new housing developments include space for a center, as they do for *Kindergärten* and schools. It is flexibly constructed space so as to allow for conversion from one use to another if demographic developments change the need. *Krippe* attendance is free to all children admitted but parents pay .35 DME daily for meals, a fraction of actual costs, and even that may be waived or reduced for large families or those at the public assistance income level. Before 1976, when a general preschool policy was enacted, *Krippe* meals were more expensive than *Kindergarten* meals, but now there is one program.

In short, in the GDR a universal concept of program creates a free service (the meal policy actually adds to family income), makes *Krippen* as "normal" as *Kindergärten*, and places the full costs of provision on the public and enterprise treasuries. The "real" costs of *Krippen* are not reported (outlays plus opportunity costs) any more than they are for *Kindergarten* or elementary education. Nor do we have reports of the financial contributions that come directly from enterprises and those from local communes and national budgets. The policy and provision is an organic requirement of the larger economic, labor market, and family policy in which it is embedded, and there is no serious question about the expenditure or "investment" involved.

Sweden

Parent-users of Swedish child care facilities pay income-scaled fees. Since space is limited, it is rationed in accord with public priorities and not by the fee structure. While a significant part of the bill for care is picked up by the central government in Sweden, municipalities have an important role, too, just as they collect a significant income tax total. Payment of part of capital costs at an attractive rate (and in accord with countercyclical public construction strategies) was the main way in which central government rapidly implemented its child care center expansion targets at several points in the 1960s and 1970s. The distinction between operating and capital subsidies ended by 1976.

For those admitted, the child care fees are low. Average parent payments for center care were 3,000 S.Kr. in 1975 and 3,400 S.Kr. in 1978; payments for municipal family day care were 1,500 S.Kr. in 1975 and 3,200 S.Kr. in 1978. In 1975 the average gross female salary for full-time employment was 38,000 S.Kr. Thus, the 1975 fee was 4 percent of the female wage for family day care and 8 percent for center care. Except for single mothers or where the children had special handicaps or problems, the families using such care were two-earner families.

The "ultimate" 1975 and 1978 costs for *center day care*, per place, were paid for as follows:

	1975	1978
Central government subsidy	7,500 S.Kr. (37%)	16,500 S.Kr. (51%)
Parent charges	3,000 S.Kr. (15%)	3,400 S.Kr. (10%)
Municipality	10,000 S.Kr. (49%)	12,600 S.Kr. (39%)
Total	20,000 S.Kr.	32,500 S.Kr.

(In 1975 the central government subsidy included an additional 12,000 S.Kr. for building costs, intended to speed up expansion and play a countercyclical economic role. The total was thus 19,500 S.Kr. There was no 1978 supplement for building.)

At the expenditure level, per place, this meant:

	1975	1978
Salaries	15,400 S.Kr. (75%)	21,300 S.Kr. (66%)
Building	2,100 S.Kr. (10%)	7,300 S.Kr. (22%)
Equipment, furniture	650 S.Kr. (3%)	750 S.Kr. (2%)
Other (food included)	2,350 S.Kr. (12%)	3,150 S.Kr. (10%)
Total	20,500 S.Kr.	32,500 S.Kr.

At the time of the above 1975 operating and general costs, a new "place" cost 19,916 S.Kr. to construct, plus 4,787 S.Kr. for site purchase and 3,000 S.Kr. for initial equipment. These investments were among the highest in the countries here represented, and purchased high-quality plants and service. As we have seen, coverage rates were and are modest.

Because capital costs are not covered, costs of family day care are somewhat lower for central government. It provided an annual per-child subsidy to the municipality of 1,000 S.Kr. 1977, 1,500 S.Kr. 1978, and 2,500 S.Kr. 1979 and subsequently. To this is added reimbursement of 35 percent of municipal expenditure for salaries, social benefits, and cost reimbursement to the childminders.

Operating *family day care costs* were:

	1975	1978
Childminders' salaries	9,000 S.Kr. (60%)	13,700 S.Kr. (59%)
Childminders' social benefits	3,600 S.Kr. (24%)	6,100 S.Kr. (26%)
Cost reimbursement	2,320 S.Kr. (16%)	3,700 S.Kr. (16%)
Total	14,920 S.Kr.	23,500 S.Kr.

Municipalities met such costs from the following sources:

	1975	1978
Central government subsidy	2,600 S.Kr. (17%)	10,000 S.Kr. (43%)
Parental fees (actual)	1,500 S.Kr. (10%)	3,200 S.Kr. (14%)
Municipality costs	10,820 S.Kr. (73%)	10,300 S.Kr. (44%)
Total	14,920 S.Kr.	23,500 S.Kr.

While the following considerations are not directly relevant to the Swedish policy process as conducted, we may note that total center costs per place for 1978 (including capital costs) were 86 percent of an average female wage—and family day care costs per place were 62 percent of such average. French data are subsequently provided in similar form, but do not include the same treatment of capital costs. Even given the recognition that the families using subsidized care are two-earner families (unless defined as problem families needing special help), and noting too the more favorable Swedish ratio (wages for women are higher), it is clearly necessary to revert for justification of the expenditures to a broader calculus: the offsetting value of the labor market contribution of women and of the investment in supervised care of children.

Of special interest is the fact that parents pay the municipality directly, whether for center care or family day care, and the fees have gradually been made practically identical. No other country is program-neutral in the same sense. Nor do municipalities appear to "tilt" toward center care and central government toward family day care—despite some apparent financial incentives in that central government meets a larger portion of the center care budget than of the family day care budget—and center care is overall more expensive at present both for municipality and for central government (because of both capital costs and salary rates).

France

For the French family using child care facilities, there are real cost differentials, too. The ranking is as follows, from most costly to least costly: private family day care (*nourrice*), center care (*crèche*), agency-operated family day care (*crèche familiale*), public nursery school (*école maternelle*). In Paris the "market price" of the private *nourrice* was 50 FF per day in 1978, more expensive to the user than any care mode except scaled *crèche* fees for high-earner families. Centers and family day care in the public system adjust fees to income. For those at the bottom end of the income scale the family allowance supplement (see chapter 2) in effect pays the child care fee. Fee scales are set in consultation with the regional units of the National Family Allowance Fund, which keeps them in line. Its leverage for influencing fees comes from its substantial contribution to costs of all programs except the private *nourrice* (see below).

Capital costs apart, recent operating costs per day, per child, have been 77 FF for centers in Paris (1977), 87 FF for centers for the country as a whole, 60 FF for *crèche familiale*. If these costs are related respectively to the gross annual earnings of the median female worker (24,000 FF per year) the operating costs are, respectively, 85, 94, and 65 percent of earnings. Fees, which are income-scaled, are of course much lower (roughly a third of this), and care users in these programs are members of two-earner families. If one adds a median male salary for 1978 of 33,600 FF to the median female salary of 24,000 FF, the operating costs have the following relationships to family earnings: 35 percent for the Paris *crèche*, 40 percent for the average national *crèche*, and 27 percent for the average *crèche familiale*. Again, we note that actual fees are income-related and the parents' actual payments, except to private *nourrices*, are at a small fraction of the actual costs. The society is apparently willing thus to invest in the labor force participation of its women and/or the socialization and development of its infants and toddlers.

The investment is considerable in the *écoles maternelles*. While groups are very large, the teachers are better paid than are the child care workers in centers or family day care, and the weekly hours of coverage are fewer. Nonetheless, there are here no parent fees at all (except for the supplementary lunchtime, Wednesday, and holiday coverage). There is no requirement that the mother be at work. Clearly society is investing in child development—as it is in elementary school as well. While many parents are agitating for more centers and municipal family day care, since the groups are smaller, there is no major debate about extending *école maternelle* to more two-year-olds and about lowering group size a bit so that thirty-five becomes the maximum.

As indicated, an average daily per diem *crèche collective* cost is 87 FF, but the range is 70 to 110 FF, given regional variations. Personnel costs account for 80 to 85 percent of the total. The parental fees range from 12 to 37 FF. The construction of a sixty-place *crèche* in Paris involved 2,200,000 FF in 1976, for all except land and exterior space. By 1977 the price was 3 to 4 million. Of this the national government (Ministry of Health) paid 40 percent; the Family Allowance Fund (CNAF) 40 percent; the municipalities amounts which varied by locality; and the local operating organization the rest (public departments, local children's allowance funds, nonprofit voluntary organizations, hospitals, or enterprises).

The rate of national subsidy to the *crèches* through the CNAF is set annually by the Finance Ministry (16.20 FF out of an average daily price in 1976 of 54 FF, subsequently increased by 30 percent in 1978). Funds not provided through CNAF, local government subsidies, and parent fees must be raised by the managing board (local government, firm, or private associations). Some local government subsidies are larger than others. Since the CNAF scale is a standard one, the difference is seen in local parent fees around the country.

Because of the larger group size, the per-child space costs for the *école maternelle* may be only one-third or one-half those cited above for the sixty-child *crèche collective*. Early in 1976 the building costs amounted to 6,490 FF per child-space (land, provided by the municipality, not included and varying from place to place). Annual operating costs were 52,853 FF per class, on the average, and 1,419 FF per student (ages 2-6) in a class of a little over thirty-seven children, including building maintenance. Of this sum, 83 percent was assigned to the salaries of teachers and maintenance staff. The state paid 55 percent of all staff salaries, the municipalities 45 percent. The state also paid 48 percent of capital costs. Parents, through their organization, supplement public contributions to supply and equipment costs. They pay indivdually for the complementary care outside of the official hours, as indicated. The locality pays for the service personnel who assist the teacher in the daily care routines with the children. Although the function is mandatory, the quality and scale of this coverage vary by the wealth of school and community.

The *crèche familiale*, the centrally directed family day care program in which a directress recruits and supervises forty childminders and places children with them (national average 1.5 per childminder), has a different cost structure because of low capital costs. Space costs are met, there is medical supervision and administrative overhead, including directress costs. The same scales and approach to fee setting are employed as for the *crèches*; therefore, for the parent this is far less expensive than the private family day care. These family day care mothers are permitted to work up to sixty hours a week, offering the same weekly coverage as the *crèche*.

The program is relatively small (343 units at the end of 1975, 21,856 children at latest report). The costs range in the various units between 40 and 88 FF per day, with an average of 60 FF in 1976. CNAF, local government, parents, and management share costs in a complex formula.

Capital costs for this form of agency-operated family day care are lower than for the center—the local office costs are met by *départements* ("counties") and the local operating body and not at all by the state or by CNAF.

While the lower cost of family day care does figure in the French debate, those who favor it stress particularly the view that it is more familylike and less "collective." Proponents of group care respond that family day care is cheaper only if capital costs are ignored, childminders underpaid, and central services not offered. They challenge the notion that family day care is really familylike and argue that centers offer safer and healthier environments.

Hungary

In Hungary, center and preschool fees are identical, and are the same throughout the country. The rates are reviewed annually. The income-related scales take account of husband-wife earning and the number of dependent children. In general, parents of an average income level will pay, for twenty-five work days per month, a sum equal to 10 percent of the mother's earnings or 6 percent of the father's—or some 4 percent of the common earnings. These are not unlike costs to Swedish parents for center care and much lower than French fees on the average. While not actively encouraging center attendance, Hungary makes it more manageable, relatively, from a family budget perspective than does France (a tentative generalization since salary has different roles in Eastern and Western Europe). On the other hand, the Hungarian child care allowance is even more significant, economically, to low earners.

Overall center costs are met out of: state funds (via the locality), 68 percent; parent fees, 15 percent; and enterprise contributions, 17 percent. Specific data are not published on capital costs but it is of interest that enterprises have not constructed *crèches* in recent years; they do provide 6 to 10 percent of the funds used by local communities for capital investment.

United States

The U.S. cost and funding patterns (insofar as there are data) reflect the market-public sector mix, the public payments for the welfare poor and income eligible, and the great diversity of points for initiative, control, and information.

It has recently been estimated that annual child care costs in 1975–76 for social service day care (but not including locally subsidized preschool) were $8.8 billion, of which government paid $2.5 billion and parents $6.3 billion. There is no way to identify expenditures for children under three specifically in these totals.

TABLE 4.4

Federal Child Care Expenditure, FY 1977

Program		Amount
Social services day care (Title XX)		$809 million
Social services day care (Title IV-A)		84 million
Social services day care (WIN)		57 million
Social services day care (Title IV-B)		5 million
Head Start		448 million
Elementary and Secondary Education Act		172 million
Total, Dept. of Health, Education, and Welfare		$1,575 million
Total, Dept. of Housing and Urban Development		43 million
Total, Dept. of Agriculture		150 million
Food	120 million	
Food stamps	30 million	
Tax credits for child care		517 million
Grand total		$2,299 million[a]

SOURCE: Congressional Budget Office, *Child Care and Preschool: Options for Federal Support*, September 1978, table 1, p. x.

[a]State matching funds for social service would bring the public expenditure over the $2.5 billion reported in the text.

An alternative tabulation given in table 4.4 shows the federal expenditure for fiscal year 1977.

Most of the federal reimbursement to states is for work-related programs for the welfare poor or to meet some of the costs of the working poor, not for universal programs. The federal government reimburses up to 75 percent of state costs for social service day care, up to a state social services ceiling, and the state (or state-locality) shares the remaining 25 percent. While user fees are income-tested, states may adopt scales somewhat over the poverty level and in fact have—but most thus serve the working poor or near-poor principally, permitting "partial" or "full fee" eligibility. Those on welfare rolls for support or in assistance-related career training have free service, whether center or family day care. Others are reimbursed at a low rate for in-home care by neighbors or relatives, an informal unlicensed type of day care.

The expenditure totals cited include fees for in-home care by nonrelatives, and relatives, care in licensed and unlicensed facilities, brief and all-day care, centers and family day care.

Federal financial participation in programs eligible for income-related reimbursement under social service and work-training provisions of the Social Security Act (Titles XX, IV-A, IV-B) purchased service for some 500,000 children in fiscal year 1977, some three-quarters of it full time, at a cost of almost $700 million. Children of all ages are included, mostly those three to five. Federal financial aid in these categories was distributed as follows (late 1976):

center care	55 %
family day care	23 %
in-home care	21 %
other	2 %

As noted, the private ("market") care bill is substantially larger than the public because of the significant quantity of private, especially proprietary, family day care and center care.

When surveyed from the centers' perspective (again including children of any age, and in the United States *most* are three to five), fees cover 70 percent of costs, government 29 percent, and contributions the rest. Average annual operating expenditure for a full-time enrollee in all types of centers in 1976–77 was $1,630 for a full year, when the average annual expenditure per public elementary or secondary school student, attending thirty-six weeks per year, was $1,480. Profitmaking centers were less expensive than nonprofit centers with federal financial participation. The latter spent $2,190 per child per year. For all centers collecting fees from parents, the average charge was $26 weekly; where welfare programs reimbursed, the average was $31 weekly. If one inputed cash value to donated resources, the average costs per full-time enrollee rose to $1,940. At the time, the median U.S. gross income for a woman was $145 weekly and for a man $234 (annually $7,540 and $12,168). The $26 fee constituted 18 percent of the women's wages and 7 percent of the combined wage where both worked. The center cost average for a year, $1,630, was 22 percent of the female wage and 8 percent of the combined average wages of men and women. (If the calculation is made on the basis of $2,190 per child per year, the cost in centers with full federal support, the center's average cost was 29 percent of an average female wage and 11 percent of the combined average wages of men and women.)

In comparing these to the French and Swedish data it should be noted that in all likelihood capital costs are computed differently in each case.

Full-time center care is clearly the implicity preferred federal aid arrangement, as reflected in Title XX payments. On the other hand, in-home care and family day care are apparently more heavily subsidized through tax credits and grants to public assistance recipients (chapter 2). In general, nonprofit center care (not limited to children under age three) with federal financial participation involves lower child to staff ratios, higher wages, extra services (meals, transportation, social services) and tends to raise the costs of such care above the costs of "for-profit" providers receiving federal funds. The 1976–77 monthly costs were: public care, involving federal financial participation, $190; for-profit care, involving only private fee-payment parents, $120. In general, the largest cost factor is the child to staff ratio, and a tendency to enforce federal standards creates an incentive for some centers to serve only children eligible on a means-tested basis for federal aid, and thus to segregate by income group.

Tax credits for child care (as seen in our benefit discussion) create an incentive to use in-home care, albeit a small one, and are available only to the middle class. The tax credit constitutes a considerable portion of resources expended (about $700 million in 1978).

The importance of day care as a social service in the country as a whole is seen in the fact that it commanded 20 percent of the funds from the only general social services funding stream (Title XX) in the 1977 fiscal year. There are, however, major state variations.

Available U.S. data show how public policy affects the distribution of forms of care and the care specifics—but full interpretation is limited by the quality of the data and the fact that children under three are not separately identified.

State variations are such as to suggest that the differences in table 4.5 are in part the reflection of consumer preferences, in part the result of choices by state agencies administering social service funds, in part a reflection of the well-organized day care provider lobbies.

Cost studies are in many ways unsatisfactory in the United States too, and there are major geographic differences. States tend to have maximum and minimum reimbursement rates for centers, family, and in-home care, and they award payments in accord with quality and number of service elements. In 1976, states averaged $25 to $30 per week for center care and $15 to $20 per week for family day care and in-home care. Consumers in the marketplace on their own were reported in a 1975 survey as paying less for center care (mother working full time):

Weekly Care Costs

In-home

| by relatives | $16.75 |
| by nonrelatives | $16.24 |

Other home

by relatives	$17.00
by nonrelatives	$20.71
Nursery school	$24.31
Day care center	$22.49

One might sum up the U.S. picture in another way by stating that costs to parents for proprietary care, as reported in a national consumer study, were about 12 percent of a 1975 average wage ($10,892) for the most expensive private care and 8 percent for the least expensive (average annual costs, $1,264 and $844; most families using care, of course, had two wages). Not too different from the other countries listed—offering subsidized care. It is, however, the U.S. subsidized care and its higher standards that raise costs somewhat, especially center care with higher staffing ratios. But even there, discounting initial capital investment or paying it over a long time frame, costs are reasonable if work by a parent is thereby made possible and no other strong case against care is made.

In the United States, a case against care has been made in recent years by comparing high-cost urban day care with low depressed area salaries for un-

TABLE 4.5

Title XX versus Private Child Care Expenditures

Care Mode	Title XX[a]		Private[b]	
	Dollars	*Percent*	*Dollars*	*Percent*
In-home Day Care	$87	14%	$2,144	34%
Family Day Care	$104	17	$2,464	39
Center Care	$418	69	$1,711	27

SOURCE: *FIDCR Report*, p. 10.

[a]Title XX data as of late 1976, federal and state. Totals in millions of dollars.
[b]This is from 1975 consumer study. *Some* of the family and in-home care is by relatives. *Most* is not. But very brief care and baby sitting is included. Again, in millions of dollars.

skilled women. While that may have been the real choice in the U.S. welfare reform debate, it is not the basis for policy decisions for all working families. Despite the likely large error factor in our calculations and inconsistent treatment of capital costs, U.S. reluctance to use more out-of-home care can hardly be explained in cost terms, when compared with several of these countries doing more.

FRG

How does the final country affect the picture? Basically, it offers no further enlightenment. If family day care or center care on a small scale becomes services for the deprived or the neglected, they are financed as social services, with many local and regional variations, reflecting parental means or lack thereof.

The cost distribution for FRG operations is as follows:

State	26%
Locality	26%
Provider agencies	33%
Parents	15%

Krippen fees are income-tested, with a top monthly fee of 300 DM (3,600 DM annually) in big cities like Munich or Hamburg, but less in town or rural areas. Some 75 percent of working women in the FRG earn 1,000 DM monthly or less. Here the unique factor is the voluntary provider agencies, but much of their contributions is ultimately governmental, from central government. Land and capital costs are provided as follows:

Sponsors	25%
Locality	25%
State	59%

The FRG relies heavily on state and locality and allows less leverage for central government initiatives. As we have seen, there is also a constitutional inhibition on federal service delivery initiatives, except for experimental demonstrations. Apart from a few states or large cities the care system is not heavily supported by government.

General Comments

The data do not permit any rigorous statements about individual country costs and do not justify any confidence about intercountry comparisons.

Table 4.6 provides an imprecise and general point of departure if the following caveats are recalled:

The construction costs for centers are variously included, not included, or partially included in annual operating costs.

The data refer largely to center care, whereas everywhere, except in the GDR, family day care predominates as the care mode, for the under-threes at present.

U.S. cost data, in the form reported above, do not differentiate children under age three, since day care services mostly those aged three to five.

FRG calculations are for high-cost centers, and wage data calculations used here are uncertain.

We have everywhere artificially added average female and average male salaries, hardly ever a real situation in a real family.

Crèche fees for France are actually reported as being in the range 12–37 FF, and we have artificially used 25 FF per day for lack of a validated average.

Several alternative U.S. cost figures are available (but will not change results very much).

From the parents' point of view it would appear that fees are everywhere reasonable where there are two incomes—a very tentative statement since these are averages, gross wages, and theoretical calculations. On the other hand, in many places wages are supplemented by social benefits. Since the care resources are concentrated on two-earner families, the point is relevant, however. Moreover, the countries encouraging care as a policy (GDR, Hungary, Sweden) have made it free or reasonable even in relation to one wage. France, the United States, and the FRG reflect their ambivalence; the fees are high in relation to one wage, especially a female wage. However, French fees are adjusted significantly to meet the special situation in a one-parent family.

The cost picture also is interesting. Care costs are not low. But what is "high" or "low" if one considers total labor market, population, equality, or child development objectives? These countries variously value women's work (the product of which offsets a large part of costs), opportunities for women, what children learn or gain in care, and the family policy components of what they are doing. Preschools and elementary schools are also costly, per capita, as compared to wages, although less so than child care at

TABLE 4.6
Child Care Fees and Costs as Related to Wages: An Overall Summary (In Country Currency)

Country and Program	Fee per Year	Cost per Year	Female Avg. (Full-time) Wage	Male Plus Female Avg. Wages	Fee as Percentage of		Costs as Percentage of	
					Female Wage	Female + Male Wages	Female Wage	Female + Male Wages
GDR Krippen	—	—	—	—	—	—	—	—
Hungary centers	—	—	—	—	10	4	—	—
Sweden								
centers	3,400	32,500	38,000	93,000	8	4	86	35
f. day care	1,500	23,500	38,000	93,000	4	2	62	25
France								
crèche (Paris)	6,500[a]	20,020	24,000	57,600	27	11	83	35
crèche (avg.)	6,500[a]	22,620	24,000	57,600	27	11	94	40
crèche familiale	6,500[a]	15,600	24,000	57,600	27	11	65	27
private *nourrice* (Paris)	13,000	?	24,000	57,600	54	23	—	—
USA								
all centers	1,352	1,630	7,540	19,708	18	7	22	8
centers with federal financial particip.	1,612	2,190	7,540	19,708	21	8	29	11
FRG[b]	3,600	—	12,000	—	30	—	—	—

NOTE: We have used data for various years, 1975–78, wherever maximum consistency among categories existed for a country.
[a] Approximate. See text re fee range.
[b] This is a questionable calculation: high cost centers and better-than-average female wages.

a one to six staffing ratio in a good physical setting, well serviced by complementary programs.

Given the planned growth, consolidation, or improvement of publicly sponsored or operated care in most of these places, it seems reasonable to state that *either public policy or the private market has created care at a cost acceptable to low-salaried parents, whether for licensed or unlicensed family day care or for center care. And societies themselves have taken on center care or family day care costs,* usually in a central government-local partnership with parents in which (although we lack data for full accounting) the available level of provision is managed *at a price acceptable to parents and to taxpayers in the light of the country's particular policy thrust.*

In short, costs are not a deterrent to the development of out-of-home care at the current levels for children under three—and there is no reason to believe that as labor market and/or political pressures create added need, they will not also ensure comparable resources for expansion.

MORE COST-BENEFIT RIGOR?

The question may be raised: why not a more rigorous cost-benefit analysis? In general, a careful review of what has been attempted leads to the conclusion that despite the availability of several impressive individual studies, especially in the United States and Sweden, it is in the nature of cost-benefit work in this field that conclusions do not hold across country lines, and comparisons are even less reliable than those in table 4.6. As noted earlier, the United States has been able to show that modest investments in group size and staff qualification improvements (and for infants and toddlers, also the adult-child ratio) do produce better programs and, perhaps, better child results. This is useful to know. On the more basic question of whether child care is a worth-while social policy from a cost-benefit perspective, a Swedish contribution is helpful. (See figure 4.3.)

Gustafsson reviews the Swedish cost-benefit literature and develops an interesting analysis.[16] To the question, "What is the social profitability of educating and giving good care to small children? The answer must be: it depends." Obviously, there are the issues of the alternative chosen (home care versus type of out-of-home arrangements), the quality of personnel, the type of physical plant, the estimation of other-than-labor-force outputs

Figure 4.3

Cost-Benefit Analysis of Extra-Family Day Care

(Alternative of comparison: mothers take care of their children at home)

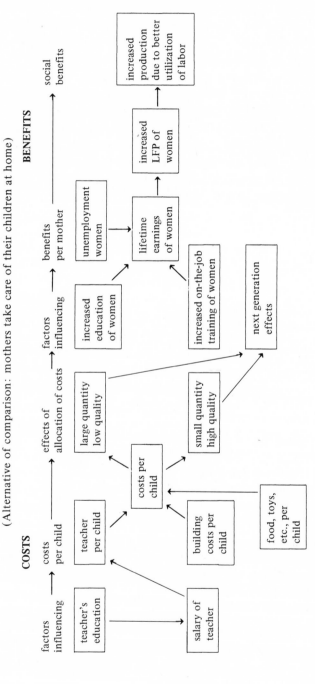

SOURCE: Gustafsson, "Cost Benefit Analysis."

of mothers thus free to work, the value of the increased lifetime earnings of these mothers, the estimates of values for the children—and the costs for all components, especially the costs of the home care which is foregone and the opportunity costs generally.

Available studies, with different assumptions, and different time horizons, yield contradictory results. But Gustafsson's chart is helpful. (Opportunity costs are perhaps not adequately considered, while nonquantifiable costs and benefits clearly are left out.) Often the result from the perspective of the parent-consumer is different from that of the municipality which pays a good part of the costs. Staff qualifications and numbers can be critical. Day care *can* be cost-effective—but *need* not be—depending on program decisions, women's own labor market behavior, and decisions made in setting up the analysis.

The critical question ultimately relates to values—the country's objectives and how it ranks various costs and allocates them. What is considered relevant?

The analysis should balance the costs of care with the costs of *noncare* and its effects, positive and negative, on children and on families. What we have summarized certainly is incomplete and not definitive on the cost-and-effects side. Clearly, however, societies that want to offer care are able to do it at a monetary cost not prohibitive to the economy, to government, or to consumers. Among these countries, if one observes practice, all but the FRG have decided that the price is acceptable. Several of the societies obviously feel the care investment to be economically attractive. And there is no evidence of harm to children, and some developmental advantages may be present—in an admittedly inconclusive research picture.

But we also must mention, if only briefly, the possible high costs to societies if many women are forced to remain at home for lack of child care resources. Although with widespread unemployment the labor market case may at a given moment be weak (it is only a short time ago that Sweden, for example, undertook a major care expansion as it sought to facilitate widespread female labor force entry—and a mix of "equality" and labor force factors led to the expansion), the GDR has long seen this as an urgent consideration and it is operative in the United States today. Labor market projections in the FRG and the United States suggest this as a serious consideration in the 1980s, and it may hold true in other countries as well, unless they import large numbers of workers from the poorer countries of the world.

There is yet another aspect, the psychological and role "costs" for women of the nonavailability of care. Here research is sparse and not definite, but it is suggestive. Studies reported from Sweden, the United States, and England indicate high rates of depression in isolated mothers of young children.[17] A research review by Rhona and Robert Rapoport and Ziona Strelitz concludes that the conventional picture of the "happy and fulfilled mother" of young children, caring for them at home, is hardly complete. Significant subgroups of educated parents report "mixed feelings." For such subgroups the

picture of the housewife/mother . . . is so pervasively indicated to be unsatisfactory that it can no longer be attributed to sensationalist journalism, neurotic feminism, biased sampling. . . . Literature from medical practice has documented the "tired housewife syndrome" as relating neither to organic illness nor psychoneurosis but to overloads and strains in the role—producing feelings of loneliness, self-deprecation, depressive and psychosomatic symptoms. . . .

Epidemiological literature documents the increasing prevalence of depressive symptoms, suicidal attempts and other associated complaints among women in all advanced industrial settings. . . .

. . . Reanalysis of data from the National Stress Study conducted by the Tavistock Institute indicated that in Britain the most vulnerable population for psychosomatic stress symptoms. . . is married women, 35+, at home with no hobbies.

Much of what is found in the research literature is generalizable as a hypothesis:

Conceptualizing the predicament of modern women as entrapped people, suffering the consequences of having chosen a valued option in a situation that entailed excessive constraints, particularly but not exclusively for the more highly educated.

Available research, much of it small-scale, suggests that the strains seen in the housewife role reflect the nature of the marital role more than they do social class or gender:

While working-class wives had more economic stress to cope with, middle-class wives had greater frustrations at being strait-jacketed by the housewife role after having been educated for a broader range of interests and activities. The nature of the "couple" relationship often is a critical intervening variable.[18]

There is, of course, plenty of evidence of depression and strain in many variants of the male and female roles in the modern world, and we would hardly argue that the case has been made for depression as the price of no child care. On the other hand, the social changes affecting women and men, and their families, create need for child care resources as a prerequisite to satisfactory lives for many parents. To fail to offer child care—and thus an important lifestyle *option*—is to assign significant costs to some parents, especially mothers—costs not precisely quantified. These costs are in addition to the price of keeping precious skilled and unskilled labor from the marketplace when it may be needed.

TRENDS: SUMMING UP OUT-OF-HOME CARE AS A POLICY

Care programs for children under age three exist and are growing. From a policy perspective center care and family day care are the major *service* responses, explicit or implicit, both to the two-worker family and to the one-parent family in which the parent works, or to the desire to expose children to a group experience even if the mother does not work. While Hungary gives priority to a cash grant which permits mothers who have a labor force attachment to remain at home for three years, center care is a respectable and growing option there. The FRG stresses at-home care until the child is age three and offers few care facilities. The United States has no national policy but both formal and informal care arrangements are expanding rapidly. Sweden is committed to offering sufficient care but has not yet reached its goals. France gives care and cash equal formal policy status but in fact for most families the care option is the attractive one and the French care coverage for under-threes leads Western Europe. The GDR exemplifies the policy of care, particularly center care, as the major response.

Does this mean that there is enough out-of-home care? Clearly not. While the GDR projects only modest growth to assure balanced regional coverage, the others are further behind. Since France and Sweden report waiting lists and expansion plans at their present levels of coverage, the current deficit for Western countries would appear to be somewhere between where France and Sweden are and the GDR, with its significantly higher female labor force participation rates. Hungary has a specific, modest expansion target because the center is second in line as a policy priority, but neither the United States nor the FRG has adopted any specific expansion goals, and expansion is quite controversial in the FRG.[19] However, if the criterion is "where the children are" and consumer demand, some expansion is needed everywhere to a coverage level which each country will define dynamically. In short, there is more debate about the types of care (family day care or centers), about who will pay, and, in some places, about sponsorship (public or marketplace) than there is as to the need for more facilities.

Will needs be met through center programs or through family day care? Surprisingly, given the importance of the psychiatric tradition in this field, family day care is not everywhere dominant, and centers lead in most expansion. Family day care is quantitatively well ahead of *crèche* coverage in France despite much demand for center expansion. Municipal family day care is not less important than center care in Sweden, and private family day care matches municipal provision. A continuing (if eventually more specialized and individualized) role is projected for family day care in Sweden. It is dominant in the FRG and probably at least equal with or exceeding center care for infants and toddlers in the United States. Both policy and labor market realities make family day care insignificant in the GDR and Hungary. Increasing concern with child development, standards, safety, and peer experience, as well as labor market factors, suggest an ever-growing center role elsewhere and a more specialized use of much-upgraded agency-operated family day care for the future.

Particularly in center care, there is a tendency to a later entry age than was (or was assumed to be) the case in the past. Infant-toddler programs have few children under six months of age.

At the other end of the under-three age continuum, experience in four of the countries raises questions about the age boundary. As a policy matter, France admits two-year-olds (mostly $2\frac{1}{2}$) to *écoles maternelles* as well as to *crèches*. Hungary and the FRG have done as much in their preschools, as space has become available. The United States has two competing systems, social welfare and education-based, and two-year-olds may be in either. Moreover, U.S. day care centers serving children under age three tend to recognize an age break at thirty months. The most comprehensive recent study states: "Two-year-old children (24 to 35 months) are in transition from infant/toddler care to preschool care."[20] Sweden has one system, with special infant groups, but two-and-one-half is a more frequent dividing line, and there is experimentation with full age integration. Such experimentation is also found in the FRG.

Should this "push" from the bottom and the top continue, the special group programs for children under three will gradually concentrate on ages six months to two years (or $2\frac{1}{2}$). Such a tendency raises operational as well as policy questions.

Opponents have cited negative consequences for children and families. While the research base for policy is not yet adequate, whatever is known does not justify the view that child care programs will harm either. There is some evidence that specific benefits are derived. Similarly, costs, while high, are assumed consciously and are apparently offset by female productivity and child gains. Here the analysis is at best suggestive. Deliberately or not, country fee levels make the care affordable by two average working parents. Where care is considered desirable (three countries), the fee is even reasonable in relation to a female wage alone. The French situation, as the French policy, is here not completely clear. The GDR expresses its policy by offering a free system. The others all scale fees to income. However, where facilities are in short supply and market arrangements are essential, costs can impose a heavy burden—but only in some places.

Family day care is largely "care" and not "child development" and much of it is as yet invisible. A tendency to agency operation and central services for family day care make it increasingly a planned and enriched experience and potentially a specialized resource. Integration with center care may occur. *Centers* formulate their program goals increasingly in child development and socialization terms. They refer to a diversity of theories and employ many different techniques; they are more or less willing to talk about program and curriculum guides. Yet staff qualifications are improving, and all clearly share objectives for enhancing the experiences of children in environments encouraging speech, self-expression, growth, play, stimulation, and emotional support by adults who are knowledgeable and sympathetic. To avoid takeover of parental rights and responsibilities, they all acknowledge the importance of protecting the parent-child relationship and ensuring parental cooperation with, as well as participation in, center programs. Here there are different levels of expectation and limited successes: parental participation faces serious obstacles given the time problems of working families and the practical daily pressures of living.

Child care programs thus are a growing, valuable, accepted—if imperfect and still debated—resource for the care of children under age three. They need improvement, and certain administrative and programmatic questions should be answered as their policy role is shaped further.

NOTES

1. Research reports and guides are found in Eva Schmidt-Kolmer: *Pädagogische Aufgaben und Arbeitsweisen in der Krippe* (Berlin, DDR: VEB Volk und Gesundheit, 1972); *Zum Einfluss von Familie und Krippe auf die Entwicklung von Kindern in der frühen Kindheit* (Berlin, DDR: VEB, 1972); *Der Einfluss des Lebensbedingungen auf die Entwicklung des Kindes im Vorschulalter* (Berlin, DDR: Akademie Verlag, 1963); (with others) *Leitfaden für die Erziehung in Krippen und Heimen* (Berlin, 1957).

The full experimentation currently involves room humidity, temperature, and other aspects of the physical environment, as well as the "thermal treatment": using cool water pools for wading and cool showers, keeping classroom temperature relatively low, regular fresh air exposure, etc. Several countries in Eastern Europe are pursuing such research, which was initiated by a Bulgarian physician.

2. Jay Belsky and Laurence D. Steinberg, "The Effects of Day Care: A Critical Review," *Child Development* (1975), 49:929–47. The review contains many citations from the literature, which will be of interest to child development scholars.

3. *The Appropriateness of the Federal Interagency Day Care Requirements (FIDCR)* (Washington, D.C.: U.S. Department of Health, Education, and Welfare, 1978), pp. xxi–xxiii. The empirical base, to the extent that one exists, is the Abt Associates *Report of the National Day Care Study* in six volumes (Cambridge, Mass., 1979), published and distributed by the Department of Health, Education, and Welfare, Washington, D.C. A summary is given in vol. 1, *Children at the Center.*

Since completion of our work, a comprehensive review and interpretation of the literature has appeared—see Urie Bronfenbrenner, *The Ecology of Human Development* (Cambridge, Mass.: Harvard University Press, 1979), ch. 8, "Day Care and Preschool as Contexts of Human Development." This review does not contradict our work, but underscores the need for future work in this field by child development researchers.

4. Dr. Irving Lazar and the Consortium on Developmental Continuity, Cornell University, *The Persistence of Preschool Effects* (Denver, Colo.: Education Commission for the States, 1977), and Comptroller General of the United States, *Early Childhood and Family Development Programs Improve the Quality of Life for Low-Income Families* (Washington, D.C.: General Accounting Office, 1979), ch. 4.

5. Suzanne H. Woolsey, "Pied Piper Politics and the Child Care Debate," *Daedalus* (Spring 1977), 106: 127–45.

6. Thomas W. Rhodes and John C. Moore, *American Consumer Attitudes and Opinions on Child Care* (Washington, D.C.: Office of Child Development, HEW, 1977), pp. 1–3.

7. See "Policies for Children: Analytical Report" (Paris: Centre for Educational Research and Innovation, OECD, February 1980).

8. Richard Ruopp, et al., *Children at the Center* (vol. 1 of Abt Associates' *Report of the National Day Care Study*), appendix B. See also Abt Associates, *National Infant Day Care Study*, draft (Cambridge, Mass., 1977), ch. 5.

9. British playschools are often cited as evidence of the success of the voluntary alternative. These programs have had a spectacular growth since their development in the early 1960s. By 1975 some 13,600 groups of many types and sizes served 328,000 children aged three and four for varying numbers of hours. (Two-year-olds are not served; five-year-olds are in elementary school.) In Britain the state has not yet supported a large expansion of public nursery schools, despite a policy thrust favoring it. The playschools are locally organized, but many are in a national association. Parents and children come together for play, usually for a half-day, but in many places only on specified days. Groups vary greatly in size. Over half are run by parent committees. Some are fully cooperative, while others are run for profit. All charge fees. Some are subsidized. The development is relatively smallest where there are sufficient good day care centers or nursery schools. The playschools are viewed as a stopgap.

See *The Under-Fives: Report of a TUC Working Party* (London: Trades Union Congress, 1977).

10. Sheila B. Kamerman, "Licensing, Standards, and Regulations in Child Care Programs in Europe, Canada and Israel," report prepared for the Office of the Assistant Secretary for Planning and Evaluation, HEW, November 1976.

11. *The Appropriateness of the Federal Interagency Day Care Requirements* (Washington, D.C.: HEW, 1978). The United States receives disproportionate attention in this section because of the extensive recent preoccupation with standards, the availability of relevant research, and the large number of publications on the subject. See reprints from the *Federal Register* for March 19, 1980 as circulated by Office of Human Development Services, Department of Health and Human Services, Washington, D.C.

12. For a relevant research report, see Abt Associates, *Day Care Centers in the U.S.* constituting volume 3 of National Day Care Study (1979).

13. Abt, *National Day Care Study.* Our comments here are based on vol. 1, *Children at the Center;* vol. 3, *Day Care Centers in the U.S.: A National Profile, 1976–77;* and also *Appropriateness of Federal Interagency Day Care Requirements.*

14. Abt, *Day Care Centers in the U.S.,* p. 95.

15. Abt, *National Day Care Study.* The summary here is from *Executive Summary,* published in March 1979.

16. Siv Gustafsson, "Cost Benefit Analysis of Early Childhood Care and Education," unpublished draft (Stockholm: Industrial Institute for Economic and Social Research, 1978). Chart (figure 4.3) reproduced with permission.

17. For example, see George Brown and Tirrel Harris, *Social Origins of Depression* (New York: Free Press, 1978); Ann Oakley, *Housewife* (London: Allen Lane, 1974); and Nickie Fonda and Peter Moss, eds., *Mothers in Employment* (Uxbridge, U.K.: Brunel University, 1976).

18. Rhona and Robert N. Rapaport and Ziona Strelitz, *Fathers, Mothers, and Society* (New York: Vintage Books edition, 1980). We have summarized and paraphrased from pp. 221–27. The volume contains full research citations. Quoted with permission.

19. For the U.S. debate see Sheila B. Kamerman and Alfred J. Kahn, "The Day Care Debate: A Wider View," *The Public Interest* (Winter 1979), no. 54, pp. 76–93.

20. Abt, *Children at the Center,* p. 252.

Five

THE BENEFIT-SERVICE PACKAGE

Five of the countries provide income supplements to families with children, some more significant than others. Five also offer important statutory supports for the expenses of childbearing. Only one country in the group offers sufficient income substitution to make an at-home role for an average working woman possible for a significant length of time beyond the maternity-paternity leave period.

Each of the countries also has some child care provision for infants and toddlers, but the programs vary in type, quality, and coverage. One country offers enough child care for under-threes to meet much of the current need, two have significant coverage but also have visible deficits in facility capacity. Two are obviously far behind, and one country is somewhat behind in coverage.

As we have seen, however, these two elements, benefits and services, do not operate in isolation from one another. Each needs to be weighed and evaluated with reference to the other. In developing an approach to an overview and assessing societal learning it is in fact useful to employ the *concept of a country benefit-service package*.

The provision of a cash or of an in-kind benefit may be viewed as a choice between two alternative strategies for achieving the same goal of income support. The conventional distinction between the functions of the two has usually focused on the question of which values are to be maximized in relation to an objective. Where freedom of choice is most important, the policy has been to provide cash; where the goal is to guarantee access to a particular good (food, housing) or to a service (health care) or to constrain a recipient's use of a grant, an in-kind benefit has been preferred. We do not ignore other motives, such as ensuring farm product sale, constraining choices of people believed not to be reliable, and so forth.

In recent years, an equally useful further distinction has been made about one aspect of in-kind benefits: between 1) an entitlement to use a service and 2) the offer of financial supports, fee payments, or a voucher with which to purchase the service. The enormous expansion over the last ten years of Medicare, Medicaid and food stamps in the United States, as well as the expansion of health insurance generally in several European countries, has highlighted the latter approach. However, a debate has emerged regarding the costs and benefits of what may be characterized as demand or consumption subsidies for in-kind benefits: Do they really increase or protect user choice? Do they really stimulate needed expansion of supply? Do they strengthen demand in a situation where supply is relatively inelastic, thus generating cost inflation? Do they protect standards adequately? What criteria should be employed for deciding whether such a policy works well, or if it is preferable to subsidizing service providers and thus ensuring the supply?

Considerations such as these are relevant to policy development in the field here under discussion. However, there is an even more fundamental point: providing cash benefits and categorical vouchers for child care is not necessarily the same thing as supplying and guaranteeing services and access to them. Put differently and more explicitly: cash benefits and services are not necessarily alternative pathways to the same result. In fact they may be used to achieve different goals. Thus, for example, a cash benefit may be provided to offset loss of income when a mother withdraws from the labor force to care for a child at home, while an entitlement to a free or partially subsidized child care service in a day care center may facilitate a mother's entering the labor force by assuring the right to out-of-home (or in-home, but other-than-mother) child care. Or, another illustration: a tax credit for child care costs may help solve the financial burdens of care arrangements, whereas public operations of or subsidy of care programs may help shape their modes (center or family day care), their policies, their standards.

The boundaries between benefits and services are not so sharp as initially believed. Government can operate a child care program, subsidize a provider, give parent-users a tax break for child care expenditures, or include money to help pay for services in a general cash grant, as in the French family allowance supplement. Yet the distinction remains useful, and the understanding that each strategy is somewhat different, even though all involve child care, is essential.

We began with the hypothesis that countries would see services and benefits as alternatives, would choose a larger emphasis on one as opposed to the other, and would substantially trade them off against one another. The material assembled changes the reading somewhat, but not completely: countries that actively concern themselves with the issue discover that the reality is far too complex for a simplistic approach. Each country eventually employs a cluster of benefits *and* some services, or a range of services *and* some benefits.

The particular balancing of benefit and service components to meet a country's objectives is what we have described as a benefit-service package. A country's benefit-service package is responsive to its own realities, as perceived by its policy makers and/or manifested through consumer behavior. While some countries may tilt more toward benefits and others more toward services, the combined benefit-service package (even though not everywhere perceived or conceptualized as such) is the vehicle for each country's explicit or implicit policy for families with children under three. For a package to implement goals successfully, the blending of the two components must be subtle, for they interact and are not the clearly separable categories initially expected or often debated. The picture which emerges thus also supports a hypothesis of convergence: a policy "solution" to the societal ferment described in our first chapter requires a certain minimum of each, of benefits *and* services, and makes the countries more alike as time passes—without fully eradicating the policy differences reflecting divergent objectives.

WHY ARE THERE DIFFERENCES?

The major task of this chapter is to summarize each country's unique benefit-service package and to place that package in its broader societal context. However, we first attempt to locate these responses generally in the broader framework of developments in industrial and urban societies. To what extent are the "packages" identifiable as the direct consequences of labor market trends, demographic trends and population-related policies, equality objectives, economic growth or decline, or other known variables?

To take literally each country's own formulations is to forgo the full advantages of the six-country comparisons. Thus we begin here with an effort to see whether in fact, whatever the formal rationales, some of the major single-factor explanations usually cited do account for country provision. Such presentation requires some caveats:

In some instances, causation could run in either or both directions.

Our benefit-service characterizations, justified in the previous two chapters (here largely treated as dependent variables), could be debatable to some analysts.

The indices employed as independent variables are far from perfect.

Data are not always complete.

The number of countries is relatively small for some of the usual and relevant more sophisticated statistical manipulations (multiple regression generally, path analysis), so that we are limited to rank-order correlations.

It is not fruitful in this type of cross-national study to attend to some of the usual variables favored by American political scientists for U.S. research (voting patterns, unionization rates, type of leadership). It is more appropriate to look at variables which are surrogate for needs and resources.[1]

Nevertheless, we do feel called upon to offer interested observers the opportunity to consider modest statistical analysis of the societal dynamics at play. After looking at some of the variables which generally occur in discussions of the subject, we shall turn toward an integrated characterization of the countries, one by one—which, in fact, proves to be more fruitful.

Five tables (2.6, 5.1, 5.2, 5.3, 5.4) summarize the essential data for this phase of the discussion. We explore, sequentially, the ability of a large group of independent variables to account for first, a few of the country policies supporting (with cash) an at-home role for mothers of young children, and then, the country policies facilitating a work role for these women by providing a sufficient out-of-home provision for children under three. (The reader will note that none of the rank-order correlations in the tables in this chapter are statistically significant. However, the data in the tables are useful for observing trends.)

Family Benefit Systems (Tables 2.6, 5.1, 5.2, 5.3)

The descriptive material in chapter 2 takes account of such important elements as male and female participation in benefits, the relative values of benefits as short-term or long-term replacements or substitutions for market-place income, the real value of income supplements supplied to families through government programs. As we have seen, Hungary and the GDR, with their high female labor force participation, including high rates of working by mothers of very young children, support and facilitate such employment with important family benefits. However, France also has a major benefit system despite its less impressive labor force trends; and Sweden, which outranks France in labor force developments, does less in its income supplementation system but has an unmatched parental insurance. The FRG and the United States do not address the under-three question explicitly through family benefits, but the FRG does more than the United States for families with children in general, even though the United States has higher female labor force participation than the FRG and France and is not far behind Sweden. And more of the Swedish female employment is part time. (All these comments about female labor force participation should be read with awareness of the different percentages of part-time work in the different countries [table 1.1], as well as the different definitions of full time.)

Birth rate is cause (it encourages pronatalist policies as in the GDR, Hungary, and France) and perhaps also is effect. Results of policies and programs in Hungary and the GDR are shown in table 5.1. But the United States and France, while their birth rates per 1,000 population have gone down, have not yet fully experienced the major decline which reached most of Eastern and Western Europe in the 1960s. (At this writing U.S. and French rates appear to have ended their decline. France still leads in fertility and the United States is relatively high.) The FRG's low rates are actively discussed but have not yet overcome the historical hesitancy to deal with the issue. Here, clearly, there is no single pattern.[2]

If we turn from the global, descriptive overviews of chapter 2 to the specifics of a few objectively comparable (because they are simply quantifiable) benefits of tables 5.1, 5.2, and 5.3 we note that no one program or benefit is an index. The countries are clearly different in their emphases among package elements. Thus, Sweden's parental insurance is outstanding and reflective of a strong overall equality posture and labor market goal, but the FRG far surpasses France in the length (and value) of its maternity leave—yet in other elements of the package the FRG has not gone as far. One cannot explain this through efforts at correlating such responses with a host of independent single variables (table 5.1); a country's mode of

TABLE 5.1
Extent of Coverage—Maternity or Parental Leaves Paid

Independent Variables	Sweden	GDR	FRG	Hungary	France	USA	Spearman Rank Order Corr.
No. of Days	270	182	224	140	112	None	—
Replacement Rate[1]	100	100	77 (plus employer supplement)	100	100	—	—
Index (days × replacement)[2]	27000	18200	17248+	14000	11200	—	—
FLFPR[a]	69%	85%	52%	75%	48%	56%	.4875 ns
Females as % of Labor Force[b]	43%	49%	38%	49%	38%	41%	.3825 ns
Mothers Work, Child Under 3[c]	58%	80%	32%	82%	43%	35%	.3143 ns
Mothers Work, Child 3–6[d]	64%	85%	34%	75%	44%	48%	.3714 ns
Birth Rate, Per 1,000 Population[e]	12.6	10.8	9.7	18.4	14.1	14.8	-.6000 ns
Birth Rate, Per 1,000 Females 10–49[f]	53.3	54.8	41.3	67.3	72.0	58.5	-.6571 ns
Child Care Coverage 0–3[g]	23%	50%	3%	12%	31%	10–11%	.3143 ns

Child Care Coverage 3–6[h]	28%	85%	75%	78%	95%	64%	−.2571 ns
GNP Per Capita[i]	$8150	$3910	$6670	$2150	$5950	$7120	.1429 ns
GNP Growth[j]	2.3%	3.7%	1.9%	3.2%	3.4%	1.6%	.3143 ns
Population Size (millions)[k]	8.2	17.	62.	10.5	52.6	213.6	−.7143 ns
Population Growth[l]	0.4%	−0.3%	0.2%	0.4%	0.8%	0.5%	−.6714 ns
Government Share[m]	49.4%	—	42.1%	—	40.3%	34%	—
Female Earnings[n]	69	65	60	62	65	60	.6179 ns
Natural Increase[o]	+1	−3.5	−2	+5	+3	+6.5	−.7714 ns

[1] For this purpose all replacement which covers *net* income up to the maximum wage under social security (salary minus social security deductions) is treated as roughly 100 percent.

[2] The employer supplement places the FRG replacement rate somewhat above that in Hungary even though exact specification is not possible with the data available to us.

[a] Female labor force participation rate: percent in labor force during what country defines as productive years (see table 1.1)

[b] Women as proportion of labor force (see table 1.2)

[c] Mothers of children ages 0–3 in labor force (see table 1.4)

[d] Mothers of children ages 3–6 in labor force (see table 1.4)

[e] Fertility: crude birth rate per 1,000 population, 1975 (U.N. Demographic Yearbook, 1977)

[f] Fertility: birth rate per 1,000 women ages 10–49, 1977, except the FRG and Sweden 1976. (U.N. Demographic Yearbook, 1977)

[g] Child care coverage, 0–3, 1975 (table 3.1)

[h] Child care coverage, 3–6, 1975 (table 3.1)

[i] GNP per capita–U.S. dollars (World Bank, 1975)

[j] Real growth–1970–75–U.S. dollars (World Bank)

[k] Population size 1975 or closest year reported.

[l] Population growth rate 1970–75 (World Bank)

[m] Government share of economy, percent of GNP (*NYT*, 2/4/78 from OECD and *Economist* 1975)

[n] Female earnings as percentage of male

[o] Natural increase (Westoff–*Scientific American*, Dec. 1978; birth rate minus death 1976, except U.S. 1978).

TABLE 5.2
Generosity of Child Allowance in Relation to Wages

Country	Allowance if 2 Young Children, One Under Age Two (monthly)	Child Care Allowance	Average Female Wage (monthly)	Total Child Allowance as Percent of Avg. Female Wage	Child Care Allowance Plus Child Allowance as Percent of Female Wage
Hungary	720	1,920	2,525	29%	105%
Sweden	417	—	3,167	13	—
France	550[a]	—	2,000	28	—
GDR	40	—	390[b]	10	—
FRG	130[c]	—	1,000	13	—
USA	—	—	—	—	—

NOTE: All numbers and relationships relate to the local currency for each country.

[a]Family allowance plus *complément familial*.
[b]*General* average wage is 600 DME; female wage is 65 percent of this.
[c]As of July 1979, this is 150.

responding and its pacing of the specific elements are and must be idiosyncratic.

Similarly, Hungary and Sweden are by far the most generous in leaves for care of a sick child, but in fact the more important Hungarian benefit is the child care allowance. Given the large percentage of mothers at home until the child is age three, the Hungary benefit allowing care for a sick child is probably less important, per se, than the Swedish or GDR provisions. France, quite generous about and concerned with family benefits, does not offer the right to working parents to remain at home with a sick child, yet the FRG does. Both France and the FRG are more concerned with income supplementation for families than with substitution or replacement, but the FRG clearly has selected a significant benefit in beginning to respond to the needs of working parents. As can be seen in table 5.2, the child allowance is a major supplement in two countries (Hungary and France) and of secondary but coequal value in three other (FRG, Sweden, GDR). In these domains the United States has no statutory provision at all. And given such divergent concerns and different vehicles of response, one is not surprised at the lack of significant correlation between provision for care of sick children and the usually postulated indicators.

Family allowances or child allowances redistribute income in favor of families with children. The responses of these several countries reflect implicit or explicit family policy, perhaps natalist concerns or hopes, but are not specific to the issue of parents at work. Thus there is no relationship between the generosity of family allowances and the generosity of the maternity-paternity leave arrangements or of the provisions for care of a sick child (except that the United States does least in all these fields). The countries do in their fertility rates rank as they do in their family allowance generosity, except for the low FRG rate; here we note that FRG family allowance rates were very low until July 1979, and that the gap between France and the GDR was substantial in 1975 and remains so with the increase in 1979. The U.S. birth rate is third among these countries despite the lack of a family allowance (see table 5.3).

What is here important is that while the Hungarian and French family allowances are by no means small where there are two children, their significance is as supplements and not as adequate substitution for income from work. (We compute table 5.2 on the basis of two children because labor force participation rates for women are significantly lower where

TABLE 5.3
Examining Children's (Family) Allowances in Relation to a Diversity of Variables

Independent Variables	Hungary	France	FRG	Sweden	GDR	USA	Spearman Rank Order Correlation
Child Allowance Index (table 5.2)	29	28	13	13	10	—	
FLFPR[a]	75%	48%	52%	69%	85%	56%	-.1286 ns
Females as % of Labor Force[b]	49%	38%	38%	43%	49%	41%	.0149 ns
Mothers Work, Child under 3[c]	82%	43%	32%	58%	80%	35%	.4143 ns
Mothers Work, Child 3–6[d]	75%	44%	34%	64%	85%	48%	-.0429 ns
Birth Rate, Per 1,000 Population[e]	18.4	14.1	9.7	12.6	10.8	14.8	.3286 ns

Birth Rate, Per 1,000 Females 10–49[f]	67.3	72.0	41.3	53.3	54.8	58.5	.4143 ns
Child Care Coverage 0–3[g]	12%	31%	3%	23%	50%	10–11%	.0714 ns
Child Care Coverage 3–6[h]	78%	95%	75%	28%	85%	64%	.3857 ns
GNP Per Capita[i]	$2,150	$5,950	$6,670	$8,150	$3,910	$7,120	-.4714 ns
GNP Growth[j]	3.2%	3.4%	1.9%	2.3%	3.7%	1.6%	.3571 ns
Population Size (millions)[k]	10.5	52.6	62.	8.2	17.	213.6	-.4714 ns
Population Growth[l]	0.4%	0.8%	0.2%	0.4%	-0.3%	0.5%	.2206 ns
Government Share[m]	—	40.3%	42.1%	49.4%	—	34%	—
Female Earnings[n]	62	65	60	69	65	60	.2239 ns
Natural Increase[o]	+5	+3	-2	+1	-3.5	+6.5	.1286 ns

NOTE: See table 5.1 for definitions and data sources for the independent variables.

TABLE 5.4
Coverage Rates for Out-of-Home Care for Children under Age Three, by Country (1975)

	GDR	France	Sweden	Hungary	USA	FRG	Spearman Rank Order Correlation
Coverage Rate 1975	50	31	23	12	10–11	3+	
Independent Variables							
FLFPR[a]	85%	48%	69%	75%	56%	52%	.3714 ns
Females as % of Labor Force[b]	49%	38%	43%	49%	41%	38%	.4119 ns
Mothers Work, Children 1–3[c]	80%	43%	58%	82%	35%	32%	.6000 ns
Mothers Work, Children 3–6[d]	85%	44%	64%	75%	48%	34%	.6000 ns
Birth Rate, Per 1,000[e]	10.8	14.1	12.6	18.4	14.8	9.7	–.0286 ns

Birth Rate, Per 1,000 Females 10–49[f]	54.8	72.0	53.3	67.3	58.5	41.3	.3714 ns
Child Care Coverage, 3–6[h]	85%	95%	28%	78%	64%	75%	.5296 ns
Per Capita GNP[i]	$3,910	$5,950	$8,150	$2,150	$7,120	$6,670	-.3143 ns
GNP Growth[j]	3.7%	3.4%	2.3%	3.2%	1.6%	1.9%	.8857 $p < .05$
Population Size (millions)[k]	17	52.6	8.2	10.5	213.6	62.	-.4857 ns
Population Growth[l]	-0.3%	0.8%	0.4%	0.4%	0.5%	0.2%	-.0429 ns
Government Share[m]	—	40.3%	49.4%	—	34%	42.1%	—
Female Earnings[n]	65	65	69	62	60	60	.7945 ns
Natural Increase[o]	-3.5	+3	+1	+5	+6.5	-2	-.3174 ns

NOTE: See table 5.1 for definitions and data sources for the independent variables.

there are three young children.) If they provide a work disincentive it could be for some very low-skilled, poorly paid women whose husbands' earnings are good. The FRG rates, even with recent increases, are not high enough to implement the mother-at-home goal, and the Swedish and GDR rates are quite consistent with their labor market policies. Given these diverse concerns, the lack of correlation with the indicators listed in table 5.1 is predictable.

The child care coverage data, when examined in relation to the totality of family benefit, as in chapter 2, and not merely with reference to any one specific benefit, reinforce the point about a blending of the two modes. With exceptions, countries responsive on one level are somewhat more likely to be responsive on the other. Except for Hungary with its exceptional child care allowance which was intended as an alternative to centers, three of the countries with relatively generous family benefit packages (France, GDR, Sweden) are clearly developing under-three care provisions, too. The FRG has not yet made the leap and apparently has been surpassed by U.S. market responses.

France and the GDR, with different histories, now offer virtually universal preschool care for the three to five group. Hungary and the FRG also have rather high preschool coverage rates in a similar pattern of provision, which is concerned with child development, education, and socialization, not merely with assurance of good care while mothers work. If they are a bit lower it is because of rural lags (Hungary) and late starts (FRG). Under the FRG pattern children attend for a "short" school day, whereas the Hungary preschool is scheduled for a full day, but the FRG is rapidly expanding the longer day and supplementary programs.

Those countries which have already achieved very extensive provision for children aged three and older tend to have *relatively* (not yet absolutely) high coverage for children under three, except for the case of the FRG, which is high for over-threes, and Sweden, which compares favorably for under-threes but lags for the older group, despite expansion plans.

Looked at from the country perspective, the GDR with its high center care coverage rates for both under-threes and over-threes also remain relatively generous in its family benefits—viewed as a system. Hungary, stressing benefits, is now adding to care provision, and France clearly is committed to both, even though the benefits are not a wage substitute for most families. The United States does less than Hungary, the GDR, Sweden, and

France both in out-of-home care for the under-threes and in family benefit systems. The FRG is high in *Kindergarten* care, low in *Krippe* and family day care rates, but has recently begun to add to its as yet modest family benefits specific to working families with young children.

Any effort to interrelate holistic overviews of family benefits or the provisions in tables 5.1, 5.2, and 5.3 with a group of other possibly relevant independent variables serves to caution against simplistic explanations. The higher *per capita GNP's* are associated with low or modest family benefit provisions, but the highest *GNP growth rates* parallel the most extensive provision in these categories. Population size, natural increase, and population growth also distribute in complex ways. Among Western countries, Sweden and the FRG, where government per se expends a higher proportion of GNP than it does in France, do not do more than France in family benefit provisions, overall, but do offer maternity-parental leaves, unlike France. (This type of statistic has no meaning in the GDR and Hungary.) There are not enough differences among the countries in relation to the female salary as a proportion of the male to justify any generalization or prediction from it.

Out-of-home Care (Table 5.4)

An examination of the rates of out-of-home care coverage for under-threes in these countries, in relation to similar independent variables, shows the causal dynamics to be complex or obscure. Hungary, the GDR, Sweden display the case for the argument that female (and mother) labor force participation lies behind the societal response through care provision or (if the causality runs the other way, too) is responsive to provision. But France, clearly, is responding to other considerations: a concern with child socialization and education. The United States and the FRG are in the expected rankings, when France is discounted.

Birth rate and fertility data shed no light on the pattern of provision of out-of-home care, perhaps because countries in this group are at several different stages in response to demographic trends, or perhaps because their policy responses have limited impact. The birth and fertility rates in the United States and France clearly reflect long-term demographic tendencies and show no evidence that family benefits and child care are major responses or causes.

Again, the other independent variables show the complexity of the larger

Figure 5.1 *Child Care Coverage—A Display of Some of the Relationships*

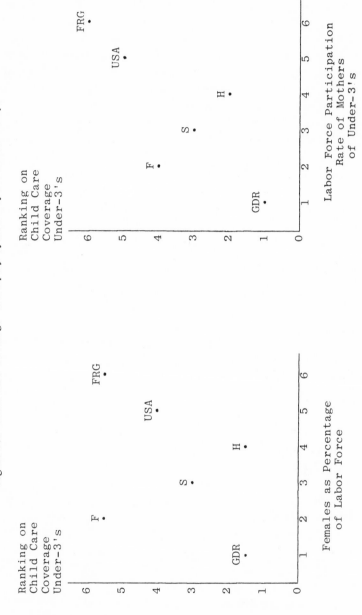

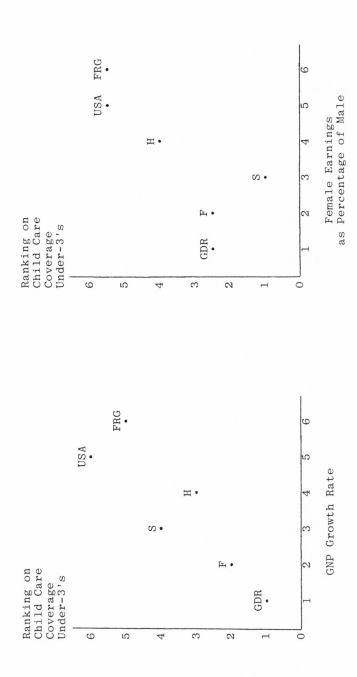

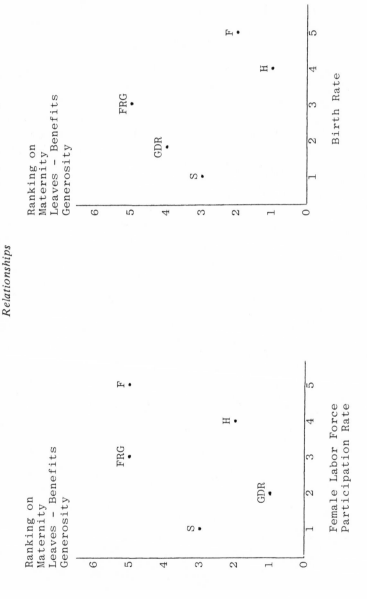

Figure 5.2 *Maternity Leave–Benefits Generosity—A Display of Some of the Relationships*

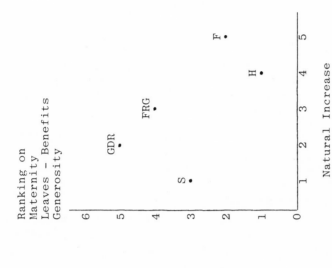

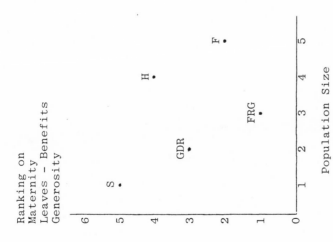

dynamics. Here, too, the higher-GNP countries are below the lower ones in overall provision, but among themselves, Sweden, the United States, and the FRG do have coverage rates similar to their GNP rank. But for the entire group of countries, GNP growth rates show some correlation with under-three out-of-home care provision. These are all suggestive, not definitive relations, and other variables defy clear patterning, yet there also is some imperfect relationship between under-three care provision, on the one hand, and the higher female salary ratios as compared to male salaries, on the other. Hungary's commitment to benefits, but not to center care, appears to contradict the pattern seen among the others—but its child care investment and coverage clearly are growing.

Certainly, it would be of considerable value in such an analysis to compare the individual countries as to their scales of investment in a combined benefit and service response to the needs of working families with young children. Unfortunately, we are here dealing with two different types of economic systems and, within each, very different degrees of government involvement in individual standards of living through commodity and other consumption subsidies and the provision of public goods. Valid comparisons have not been possible.

The need for a package, it would appear, derives from the requirement that a country attend to its birth rate and the quality of its parenting while supporting or at least responding to female labor force participation. The latter calls for child care provision and the former for measures which enable (or encourage) women who are working to have and to rear children. Both the objectives remain, and the package seeks to join, reconcile, or balance them.

If one were to construct a hypothesis based on these incomplete, suggestive, yet hardly random materials, it would be this: *the family benefit differences—on the one hand—and the child care service provisions—on the other—represent the various ways the individual country solves the contradictory pressures of labor market and demographic objectives.* There is interest in childbearing and in encouraging or facilitating female labor force participation; in parental nurturing and in labor force equality; in child development and in individualized life roles for women. *In the context of its own traditions, history, politics, and its economic and demographic circumstances, a country shapes its unique benefit-service package.* And given a dynamic world in which these causal elements change in their interrelationships with one another, the package, too, develops and changes.

This can best be seen by summarizing what we have found to characterize the countries individually; first, the benefit-service package and, then, what we understand of the societal dynamics.

THE COUNTRIES—THEIR PACKAGES AND DYNAMICS

In examining the countries and their individual packages as a whole, we begin with Hungary—which has been identified with a unique family benefit—and then turn to the GDR, which has achieved high center coverage. The contrast is informative. We then look at two countries in the middle of the distribution, France and Sweden; here the order has no significance. The final two countries have as yet no explicit "under-three" policy at all, but the FRG has provided somewhat more family benefits and the United States has developed—largely in the marketplace—more child care resources.

HUNGARY

Hungary, as we have noted, offers a universal, significant income transfer policy for women whose children are under age three and who have prior labor force attachment. While not equal to a full wage, the grant level is attractive, especially for low-qualification or completely unskilled female workers. This Hungarian invention, a child care allowance, is on top of a substantial cash benefit at childbirth and a five-month paid maternity leave— as well as relatively generous family allowances and a diversity of other cash and in-kind entitlements which ensure maternal and child health and lighten the financial burden of child rearing.

More than any other country here covered or any country we have identified, Hungary thus supports a policy which enables a mother to care for her own child until entry into preschool at age three, an almost universal occurrence. The requirement of labor force attachment for eligibility and the abrupt termination of the child care allowance almost ensures labor force return at that time, or after completion of a child care leave for a second child.

Even though this policy is further supported by the availability of paid leave to stay home with a sick child and vacation guarantees, it still does not meet all needs, preferences, and circumstances. There are women whose qualifications and personal career goals are such that they do not choose to

TABLE 5.5
Child Care Benefit-Service Package (Major Components) by Country

Benefits	Hungary	France	GDR	Sweden	FRG	USA
CASH						
Income Replacement	Maternity	Maternity	Maternity Supplementary maternity	Parental	Maternity	—
	To care for an ill child at home	—	To care for an ill child at home	To care for an ill child at home	To care for an ill child at home	—
Income Substitution	Child care allowance	—	—	—	—	AFDC
Income Supplementation	Family allowance Housing allowance Child health services	Family allowance Housing allowance Child health services Family allowance supplement Single parent allowance Family-based tax system	Family allowance Housing allowance Child health services	Child allowance Housing allowance Child health services	Child allowance Housing allowance Child health services	—
				Tax allowances for for dependents	Child care tax credit	Tax allowances for dependents Earned income tax credit Child care tax credit

EMPLOYMENT					
Right to Leave Work and Job Security	Maternity (20 weeks) Child care up to child's 3rd birthday	Maternity (16 weeks) Parental Education 2 years	Maternity (26 weeks) Supplementary (26 weeks)	Parental (9 months) Unpaid 18 months; 6 hour day up to child's 8th birthday	Maternity (7½ months)	—
Services (1975)						
Percentage of Cohort 0–3 in Out-of-Home Care	12% Mainly 1½–3 years old	31%	50% 80% of 1–2 year olds;	23%	3%	10–11%
Major Care Mode	Center care (almost completely)	Coequal in policy but family day care predominates	Center care (completely)	Policy favors center care but present reality is family day care primarily	Family day care primary in policy but coequal in provision	Family day care predominates

remain out of the labor force for three years. Others find it financially difficult or unattractive. Still others experience it as an obstacle to full gender equality. While such women have increased their claims on the child care entitlement since the beginning, they remain at home considerably less than three years. A significant portion of women seek out-of-home care arrangements for children at age one-and-one-half years and another large group for children at age two. Government responds, apparently to acknowledge diverse preferences, to meet the real career needs of the highly educated, but also to meet labor force needs in a labor market which has changed since the policy was enacted.

Since there is no significant labor supply for family day care (but this may change under a new policy permitting mothers at home on child care leave to care for the children of others), the response to the need for care arrangements for children under three is the child care center. Over 12 percent of the cohort is covered, but the real rate is much higher for children between eighteen and thirty-six months, the major users. Plans are in place for expansion to 15 percent coverage. While those who staff the centers speak of the superiority of at-home child rearing, they have systematically developed and implemented a quality center program.

Thus, in fact, the Hungarian benefit-service package involves significant cash and in-kind supports for those who remain at home until the child is age three; significant buttressing of child rearing generally by goods, services, cash, and other entitlements; and an increasingly available out-of-home child care option. Despite the society's positive stance toward sexual equality, these programs are largely mother-child oriented.

Hungary's response clearly is significant. It is a small, economically poor country in this group of six, but is sustaining good economic growth and perhaps making progress in what it defines as its fertility problem. Hungary began by offering an earned income substitute if a woman withdrew from the labor force while her child was under age three. The policy was a response to labor market needs (an excess of unskilled female workers) and to the urging of psychiatrists that young children not be reared in poor, large nurseries. Good facilities would be expensive and required staff which would remain in short supply.

By now the policy is functionally semiautonomous despite other labor market realities. There are, for example, labor shortages. More unskilled workers are needed. The child care grant remains a central element in a total benefit-service package that reflects the country's other social and political goals as well: to ensure the well-being of all children, reduce inequalities based on family education/employment, and increasingly, stimulate female work. The work-related nature of the benefit and its significant size, combined with its abrupt cut-off when the child is three years old, assures return to the labor force either then or at a similar point in time after the birth of a second child. (Relatively few people have three children.) And the availability of a growing number of child care centers, plus the planned center expansion (despite the unwillingness of officials to define the center care option as anything but the second-best alternative) contributes to uninterrupted career development for the more educated and successful woman, both a labor market and an equality goal. There also are proposals to open more of the entitlements to men as well, proposals which if enacted would enhance the equality drive.

Children in general are protected in their living standard by an overall social policy in which, while two-thirds of the costs of per capita, child-raising expenses are covered by parental earnings (1970), some 36 percent of such costs are met by statutory benefits. Two-thirds of the latter are via in-kind benefits and one-third are in cash. The Hungary policy stresses universalism and in-kind benefits to provide access to critical child-raising needs free from wage-level determination and vagaries of parental priorities.

In short, labor market and population goals create parameters, but ideology, political objectives, traditional attitudes to children create a unique policy mix in a particular cultural context.

GERMAN DEMOCRATIC REPUBLIC

The GDR has developed an extensive family benefit package designed to help women cope with maternity and childbirth costs and burdens while they are employed. Labor force participation is the point of departure. Just as Hungary has pioneered in a cash child care benefit as an alternative to work until the child is three years old, the GDR is in a leading role in its provision of extensive center care arrangements for children under age three in order to facilitate paid employment for their mothers after the briefer maternity leave. Thus, the services offer an essential complement to the benefits.

While the family benefit package is not offered as an alternative to out-of-home care, it is rich and varied, especially in short-term income replacement. Relatively generous cash maternity benefits and maternity leaves are given, and there is a right to a subsequent cash allowance for single mothers and extended job-protected leave for the others, where there is no opening in a child care facility. Other forms of family income supplementation are modest, since there is no intent to offer supplementation or substitution that would create a work disincentive. On the other hand, increasing concern with population matters has led to a series of pronatalist measures meant to encourage childbearing and to facilitate child rearing. In this category there are (for those with several children) housing allowances and loan write-offs. Also, there is a supplementary maternity leave which increases the time allowed from twenty-six to fifty-two weeks for second and subsequent children. A single mother with one child may also elect the second six-month period without pay and be assured of job protection. After mothers return to work, a parental right to remain home to care for a child too ill to go to a center, preschool, or school, and to be paid under social insurance, also supports the work role.

As evidence of the tendency in the GDR to plan for centers and cash benefits in relation to one another, we note the practice in all official reporting to compute center coverage rates for under-threes *only after subtracting children who are not yet twenty weeks old* from the cohort data, the rationale being that they are not eligible for center care. Because this is not generally understood, many international reports and our own early drafts reported that 60 percent of the under-three's in the GDR were in centers, in 1978, when the true rate was 48 percent. (Because center expansion did not keep up with the birth rate, there was a decline from 50 percent in 1975.)

The integrated family benefit-service package thus has the effect of protecting the childbirth and maternity period (six months for a one-child family and twelve months for those with two or more children), while ensuring care arrangements in infant and toddler centers (*Krippen*) for children from about six months to about three years of age. As we have noted, over 80 percent of the one- and two-year-olds are thus in care, but most children under age one are at home. This latter group constitutes 16 percent of those in *Krippen*. And because *Krippe* care is the centerpiece of the GDR package, there is considerable and systematic research attention to all innovations in program, physical environment, and staff training.

The package, to summarize, supports at-home care for six to twelve months through a stable, elaborate, and relatively generous family benefit package, labor-market-related, with pronatalist incentives. It ensures an easy transition to guaranteed center care arrangements. There are few support alternatives for women who do not wish to return subsequently to out-of-home work. An insurance benefit allows parents to remain at home when children are ill. There are no special measures to encourage paternal participation in childrearing.

These policies may be best examined in their historical context. The enormous loss of men during World War II, and the large migration to the West before the construction of the Berlin Wall in 1961, as well as a political context requiring a solution of the labor force supply problem from within, created a situation in which very high female labor force participation was critical. But because population decline was and is a source of concern, there was also a need for income replacement so that women could withdraw from work to have children, and also be assured that their children would have a good start—sufficient income and in-kind supplementation, plus care resources, to allow parents to continue to work both before and after a six-month to one-year withdrawal, while knowing that their children have adequate care. Consistent with such objectives are the operational policies of *Krippen*, meant to encourage parents to retain their primary responsibilities with their children and to regard the care arrangements as a supplement, not as a takeover.

The benefits and participation arrangements have not yet involved both parents on a more equitable basis despite widespread interest in the status of women.[3]

These components clearly are a coherent response in a country of modest means. Economic growth, recent progress on population problems, and positive research results on the role of the *Krippen* could encourage continued reliance on this group of interrelated measures.

FRANCE

As we have seen, the French benefit-service offerings reflect an explicit policy of supporting parental choice: that both parents work and have access to adequate child care resources, or that one parent works and the other remains home, with sufficient income supplementation for the plan to be economically viable. Compared to the other countries, the French provision is substantial: only the GDR offers more extensive child care coverage; only Hungary clearly offers a family benefit package more adequate for the under-threes. Yet neither of the two package elements, benefits or services, is as yet fully developed, so the options cannot be said to exist for most families.

More specifically, the extensive family benefit system in France differentiates the family with a child under three, but offers similar entitlements to benefits where there are three children of any age. Except for a paid maternity leave, the benefits are not contingent on labor force attachment or leaving work, but they are income-related. Thus, they represent significant income to low-income families, whether one- or two-parent. They are reinforced by a tax system which is similarly family-oriented, but somewhat biased to favor higher-income families.

These specially focused benefits and allowances are in addition to a large package of social benefits and services in support of maternal and child welfare and family life generally, ranging from significant family allowances to health services, pre- and postnatal allowances and maternity leaves, to social security retirement credits for the at-home mother.

The effect of all of this is to offer substantial income supplementation to *all* families with children, as well as special support for families around and shortly after childbirth (and until children reach age three)—almost all regardless of labor force attachment (except for the sixteen-week maternity leave period). All this is gauged for low-income families, and is not enough to discourage work by most mothers who want to seek out-of-home employment. The new family allowance supplement would not seem to support an economically attractive at-home role for any women except the unskilled whose husbands earn at least average wages. Yet a sufficiently high supplementary allowance would be consistent with the goal of making the at-home role a real option for both married and unmarried women with young children. However, women with workplace qualifications or low-skilled women with low-earner husbands would seem to be better off economically at work. Tax deductions do support use of child care by low-income families.

Given a family benefit picture which does not discourage an "at work" role for most mothers of young children, the French benefit-service package also includes extensive governmental and market provision for out-of-home care of young children. Public programs offer both center and family day care to the under-threes, apparently responsive to different population preferences and to supply factors. Increasingly, too, space has been created for children of this age in the public nursery school system. But none of these facilities meet the demand, and there are waiting lists. There is also heavy use of private market family day care, often more expensive for families, except perhaps for those of high income who pay graduated fees for the *crèches*. The poorest familes have their *crèche* or family day care fees subsidized, in effect, through the family allowance supplement, and the others meet the costs. *École maternelle*, essentially free (except for meals and supplementary care), is most popular with all groups. While public center care and family day care space is reserved for the children of working mothers, this is not the case in the *école maternelle*, which is growing rapidly in use and popularity. The mothers of 60 percent of the children under three now in *écoles maternelles* work outside the home, but 40 percent do not. Work affects priority rating in the latter but is not an absolute criterion, this again being the result of diverse objectives.

The child care picture for under-threes is pluralistic, much more so for the under-threes than for the older group. And there are some options between benefits and services, but neither arm of the system is yet fully developed. Finally, the French program is family-oriented but assumes traditional parent gender roles and makes no special efforts to engage fathers in child care.

France, we have noted, is higher in care provision and in family benefits than might be predicted by labor force dynamics, mother employment, or per capita GNP alone. But, of interest, if hard to interpret, is the fact that of this group of six countries, France ranked behind the GDR but above Hungary in GNP growth between 1970 and 1975. How does one account for the overall approach? Here one perhaps must turn to culture, history, and family ideology. In a comprehensive (if admittedly preliminary) analysis in which he sought to locate the "structural and ideological roots of public expenditures," Harold Wilensky has repeated an earlier finding by Henry Aaron to the effect that "the best predictor of the share of nations' income spent on social security was the number of decades since the first program was initiated." While Wilensky argues that program direction, per se, is "directly or indirectly a product of economic growth,"[4] our own materials suggest that, in the instance of child care, it may be an autonomous variable of some importance. The French middle class began to send their newborn infants to wet nurses in the countryside in the seventeenth century despite very poor results—infant mortality was very high. The process accelerated in the eighteenth century.[5] One traces a readiness to use out-of-home care in all social classes since then, including the later group day care stream for the working poor, nursery education, *école maternelle* (which began for workers but soon served all social classes), the unregulated family day care (childminder) for the poor and working classes, and the at-home nurse for the affluent. To this day France leads in the quantity of provision. Its universal preschool, *école maternelle*, began in the 1880s. It became a "given" in the 1950s for all social groups. There clearly is a readiness to offer child caring arrangements which are independent of a mother's labor force attachment and are responsive to public demand for both education/socialization and care. In short, the belief that care is acceptable and good is rooted in the culture and view of childhood. The psychological theorists and ideological contenders debate largely about program form, not about the need for provision. Public officials are also motivated by costs and by who bears those costs.

The other major element shaping the French response is the readiness to provide income redistribution in favor of families with young children. Here, too, France has had the longest history. Family allowances were initiated in the 1930s in an effort to be responsive to the serious economic problems of workers with children. Salaries, after all, are not calibrated to family needs. The allowances permitted a response which was less costly than general salary adjustments and therefore feasible at the time. They were endorsed, elaborated, continued for pronatalist reasons (however questionable their effectiveness in this regard). The French social security system continues to be guided by family concerns, focused on aiding families with child rearing costs and—especially in recent legislation—targeting on low-income families with very young children or several children. In general, family policy is a strong theme in France, and it is expressed mainly through income maintenance programs. In some sense, too, government is acceptable as a "moral guardian," as it is not in the United States.

Because of the long interest in childhood education and socialization (and much current conviction about the importance of the first three years of life), and a commitment to income supplementation in the form of redistribution to favor families with children, France thus emerges with a benefit-service package which is extensive yet not immediately and directly reflective of or completely tied to female labor force participation. (Both tax and transfer systems, as noted, create work disincentives for some women.) And because the dynamics are complex and the conditions of families diverse, the system (in tune with French culture generally) remains extremely pluralistic—but does not satisfy proponents of truly balanced choice, of an emphasis on adequate at-home care support, or of sufficient out-of-home arrangements.

SWEDEN

Unique among these countries is Sweden's *parenting* emphasis. The nine-month parental insurance is designed to involve *both* parents in child rearing, especially during the first year. There is a substantial effort to ensure optimal conditions around childbirth and for the child's first year of life. Apart from a universal health system, the parental allowance facilitates replacement of almost the full wage of an at-home parent, but a modest "houseparent" equivalent also includes those without a labor force attachment. There are similar generous benefits for subsequent use to remain at home from work to care for a sick child. Also, a new provision in the parental insurance allows the option of a shorter work day, without compensation, for some parents for part of the time when children are young, to shorten the day care day and allow more time for parenting. Family allowances are quite modest; they supplement income, but do not substitute for a wage. But an income-tested housing grant is a major instrument of redistribution in favor of families with dependent children. (It is alleged that this allowance may create a work disincentive for low-skilled married women with several children; in short, in this instance it may be a wage-income substitute. It clearly is very important for all one-wage families, whether with one or two parents.)

If one theme of explicit Swedish policy is the support of parenting by both fathers and mothers, another is the promotion of *equality* of the sexes. The former component is supported through the family benefits, the latter through a commitment to child care facilities, so that both women and men may find it possible to work and develop their own interests. Government has committed itself to providing adequate child care facilities, centers, and family day care homes. Thus far, however, coverage is limited by the GDR or even the French standard, if good as compared to countries which have not chosen a coverage care policy for under-threes. There is clear concern for high-quality programs; there has been some trade-off of quality for quantity as programs have been developed.

To summarize: the Swedish package emphasizes overall redistribution to favor families with dependent children, a general social minimum standard, specific measures to permit and encourage intensive involvement with children, by both parents, during the first year especially but longer if parents wish. In addition, on the assumption that during a child's second year (or after his or her ninth month) both parents should and will work, there is a commitment to extensive high-quality family day care and center care, each of which also is to feature parental participation. Growth targets have been established and considerable progress made.

While it has developed a somewhat more diverse policy scenario since the Social Democrats left office, Sweden does not seek the formal French neutrality about female labor force participation. The equality and parenting goals are still discussed in a labor market framework, even though Sweden ranks behind the GDR and Hungary in female labor force participation rates and in the rate of working by mothers of young children.

Crucial in shaping policy in this overall context are several elements unique to Sweden: first, there is generous response to and treatment of foreign workers and their families. Second, it is a homogeneous society with a strong political-party and trade-union system which ensures a relatively high degree of uniformity between central government and municipality policies. Third, a decision was consciously made some years ago that female labor force participation is more desirable and less costly than large-scale importation of labor. Other elements in Sweden's ability to develop and implement policy are: technical assistance and financial incentives provided by the central government; an equality debate focused on men and women (not on racial minorities as in the United States) and of sufficiently long duration so as to influence the attitudes of the current generation of young parents; a trade union movement concerned with creating a welfare society and willing to deal intensively with social policy; and a government that collects taxes on the highest GNP per capita and expends the largest share of GNP among these six.

However, the explicit policy themes of equality and parenting, and the benefits and services enacted to give reality to such goals, do not capture the full Swedish reality.

Swedish labor market conditions permit many women to work outside the home part time (1977 employment rates for mothers of children under age seven: full time, 28 percent; part time, 37 percent). Perhaps, as a consequence, the gaps in child care facilities remain tolerable. In addition, a tax reform was enacted during the past decade to create a neutral family policy by introducing individual (not family) income taxation. But, given the high Swedish marginal tax rates, this reinforces the tendency to part-time work by mothers of young children (the income losses suffered, as compared with full-time salaries, are modest).

There are those who are sure that more women will work full time as soon as there is more child care—and when current economic problems are solved. Certainly Sweden has expanded child care resources at a rapid pace, given its very late start, and has even surpassed coverage rates elsewhere. Nonetheless, an outside observer also notes that there is still an active debate about such matters in Sweden and that trends are not unidirectional. Proponents of Hungarian-type child care allowances have been increasingly heard from in recent years, and part-time work for women is often cited as a desirable thing, not as a transitional phase. After all, the parent insurance was recently reformed to allow either parent a shorter work day while children are very young.

The same developments may be seen in other lights, as consistent with the long-term explicit policy already reviewed. If there are lags in center development, it is because children pay too large a price for poor care arrangements. If more women work part time, it is because fewer women worked initially and part-time work protects children until good child care is available. The equality goal is constrained by other goals and by history. Equality and parenting do reinforce one another as themes, overall, on the premise that unless the fathers share parenting the mothers' opportunities are circumscribed and the growing child's models are inappropriate. Parenting in this sense is reflected in the provisions of the parent insurance, the work leave for either parent to care for sick children, a reassuringly high standard for all child care programs, and as yet unrealized goals of enough child care places in centers and family day care, and intensive parental participation.

Advocating more rapid progress are those young parents who have been reared during the equality debate and have simultaneously become committed to effective parenting. Amendments to the parent insurance even permit some workers the option of a shorter work day when children are very young—another contribution to parenting. All of this, as indicated, is consistent with the ethic of a relatively rich society concerned generally with the quality of life, pollution, and with narrowing the resource and income gap between high and low earners. It may also be an early element in an evolving response toward population issues.

FEDERAL REPUBLIC OF GERMANY

While the dominant ideological mood of the FRG is decidedly pro-family, a stance implemented in several ways, the sum total of the benefit-service package neither facilitates a labor market role for mothers of very young children to the degree accomplished in the countries reported earlier, nor does it make an at-home role economically viable (except, perhaps, for a limited number of single mothers).

More specifically, the child allowance is a significant supplement, especially for low-income families, and is not labor-force-related. For the poor there is further supplementation through income-tested assistance and for housing. None of these latter benefits are pointed specifically at the child under three. Maternity leave provisions have recently been improved to provide coverage for seven and one-half months (six months after childbirth), a significant period, which compares favorably with European trends. The income replacement index (benefit level times duration) is somewhat lower than that of several of the countries, but not by much—and it exceeds several others. This benefit and the provision to stay home with a sick child for five days are new and significant support for parenting by women who work. No steps have been taken as yet to involve men more actively in parenting, but discussion of such policy has increased. It remains to be seen just what the take-up will be of the new benefits and how adequate the benefits will be found as parenting aids. But they do appear to offer significant short-run income replacement for working parents. When they seek child care upon their return to work, the service picture is very modest: a preference for family day care, very limited center care or family day care coverage, little program enrichment in many *Krippen*, and a concentration on the poor and on foreign workers. The latter fact, in turn, stigmatizes the service. Of some interest is the fact that demographic trends have left space in *Kindergärten* which traditionally serve children ages three to five. Significant numbers of under-threes have been admitted recently, with unknown consequence. Here there is clarity as to an educational and socialization goal.

The recent public debate has been giving the subject of young children of working mothers active attention and has concentrated on the possibility of a child-rearing allowance during the child's first year (probably means-tested and for at-home mothers) and/or better family day care (also probably for poor children, as in a current experiment). There is also some innovation and experimentation in modes of center care.

In summary, the FRG has a benefit-service package which does not go very far either toward public support of an at-home parenting policy for parents of very young children by substituting statutory benefits for earned income for a significant time period, or toward support of the work role for the many mothers of young children who actually do work by providing sufficient child care facilities and a program of short-term income replacement in support of child rearing. Since many women work, nonetheless, many families continue to meet their needs within the primary group, or in the marketplace and by private arrangements in a fashion not yet fully described or reported.

The FRG and the United States have lower rates of female labor force participation than the GDR, Hungary, and Sweden, but not lower than France. Nor are the rates so far behind that child care is not a major issue. If we focus on labor force participation rates of mothers of children under age three, the United States and the FRG rank behind France, in that order, with U.S. rates rapidly approaching those in France. Moreover, when children reach the three to six group, higher rates of women participate in the United States, followed by France and the FRG. Perhaps the FRG and the United States still have an adequate labor force margin to offer the unlicensed, informal, and grandmother care which must pick up some of the deficit in formal and licensed care provision, just as licensed and unlicensed family day care—and care by relatives—seem to cover interim needs in France.

The discrepancy between the recent rapid *Kindergarten* coverage growth in the FRG, and the clarity as to the value of *Kindergarten's* educational and socialization roles, on the one hand, and the slow development of facilities for under-threes (which are mostly perceived as "care arrangements") on the other, creates a built-in tension and defines issues to be addressed. There also are scholars and advocates, thus far in the minority, offering new views of *Krippen*, family day care, and paternal roles in child rearing. They, too, may affect future policy. The core issues were deferred, denied, or defined otherwise (there are different interpretations) longer in the FRG than in several other places because the high rates of foreign labor may have deferred labor market questions. (It is not that foreign workers do the same jobs as women do, but their large-scale entry created an impact that affected the entire structure of the labor force and, thus, eventually, attenuated the demand for female labor. Sweden deliberately made the alternative choice.)[6] As current unemployment problems and economic difficulties pass, the choices will reappear. It is not clear which direction will be chosen, but either should lead to a fuller response to the situation of working parents and young children.

If the FRG's traditional family ideology is to remain dominant, one might expect serious efforts to develop provisions for income substitution for work, whether along the Hungarian pattern or at least through more generous and longer support for child rearing in low-income families. Or, if increased labor force entry for women is taken for granted and deemed inevitable, considerable investment in child care arrangements of high quality for children of all social classes becomes essential. A position offering choice would demand considerable activity along both lines. Thus far, family ideology joins with traditional poor law tradition: most of the cash aid is means-tested; the *Krippen* largely address themselves to the very poor and the foreign workers; and the two debated options, a *Tagesmütter* (family day care) program or an *Erziehungsgeld* (child rearing grant), are both being explored only on a means-tested basis and not for typical families. Nonetheless, its per capita GNP lead and "government share" statistics indicate that the FRG can and will be in a position to choose policies when labor market realities dictate them. Unlike the United States, it does not seem to fear government action. Increasing concern with fertility and a cultural transformation in which incentives to have children may once again be discussed publicly for the first time since World War II may generate further initiatives.

UNITED STATES

The United States, also, lacks a benefit-service package specifically addressed to children under three. As is the case in the FRG, the ethic favors an at-home role for mothers caring for children and has not adjusted to the reality of labor force participation rates for mothers of young children. However, unlike the FRG, the United States also lacks maternity benefits or maternity leaves as a statutory right, or a universal child allowance to redistribute funds and supplement family income in support of child rearing. The United States also lacks extensive publicly subsidized preschool programs for children aged three to six. However, an earned income credit in the U.S. tax system does buttress somewhat the economic situation of poor families with dependent children, and a tax credit helps middle- and upper-income families to a limited extent with the costs of market child care.

Most notable in the U.S. benefit scheme is Aid to Families with Dependent Children (AFDC), a large program which—despite contrary objectives—has the effect of offering income and various in-kind benefits (especially food stamps and medical services) for low-income women sufficient to substitute for employment income, and thus supportive of an at-home role until a child completes school. Stigma, disapproval, and (largely ineffectual) pressure to accept training and find work do not discourage most recipients, but may affect the experiences and self-images of these families. There are variations in grant levels and administrative practice by states.

A combination of 1) governmental initiatives to facilitate training and work for mothers in poverty, to assist in ensuring child care for children of working mothers, and to offer compensatory experiences for deprived children; and 2) marketplace demand by parents able to afford the fees (a small portion of which are recoverable as tax credits, as noted) has proven sufficient to sustain the growth of infant and toddler care programs. Family day care, licensed and unlicensed, is dominant for the under-threes, but center care is apparently growing, and federal policy in fact seems inadvertently to favor the group alternative.

To summarize, the United States has no formal policy and no deliberately created benefit-service package, but pragmatic public response and the marketplace have created elements of one package for the poor (AFDC and compensatory Head Start or day care to permit work and training), and a different package for others (industry-related maternity benefits and market-based family day care and private nursery school programs). Neither component is sufficient. Anything more is currently defined by some elements in the society as unwarranted governmental interference with families—despite an actual situation in which almost as many children under three are in out-of-home care as in Hungary, and half as many as in France. Some of this care is of the highest quality, imaginative and creative. Much of it is not visible or evaluated. The price of a nonpolicy is the lack of a framework of assured quality provision. Much U.S. energy has been invested in recent years in defining adequate child care standards, but the regulations to implement them will have applicability only where federal funding is involved.

As in Sweden, some U.S. programs make impressive efforts to engage fathers fully. The leading programs are not surpassed anywhere. Again, however, the overall impact remains limited.

Provision of infant and toddler day care has apparently been increasing of late; if this conclusion is correct, this is a response to demand by both the social and the economic markets, not explicit government policy at all. Thus while it now ranks fifth among these six countries in the amount of coverage of child care services for both the under-three and the three to six age cohorts, the United States seems to be improving in its responsiveness. This is not surprising, given the extraordinary growth in female labor force participation, particularly the participation of mothers with young children, in the past decade. Nor is the dominant family ideology opposed to this in most sectors of the society, to the extent seen in the FRG. The need to assure care while parents work is the main motive. Some parents appear to seek enriched group experiences for their children. Little of the equality debate overlap, as seen in Sweden, seems to be present.

The United States has tended to leave family policies relating to marriage, divorce, guardianship, foster care, adoption to the states, as a way to preserve harmony in a religiously, ethnically, racially, and politically diverse society. Increasingly, however, because of elements relating to the national interest (racial justice, antipoverty commitments) or because its monetary and fiscal policies and its taxing prerogatives give it great power and resources, the central government, too, has engaged itself in family-related issues. Federal courts have made equality rulings, which also have had impact. The results, in the form of educational aid to the most deprived school districts, family planning, abortion, and school integration programs, have often been difficult to assess, or controversial, or diverse, or restrictive. The experience sometimes feeds fear of government intervention as interfering with family privacy and options, or as creating insensitive and unresponsive bureaucracies. Action by government is sometimes defined as aiding racial minorities and (by the most bigoted) as encouraging them to have large numbers of children. Thus there are forces opposing more action, as there are others favoring it.

Also, as in the case of the FRG, the objectives to intervention of government in family-related matters are tempered in the case of the poor, the deviant, the dependent. Income-tested public assistance and related social services were inspired by social control objectives. Before government can successfully evolve a family benefit and service response to societal change, it must here, too, renounce an old poor law tradition.

At the right and the left, there are those who see the solution in the form of resources from the federal government and control and policy from the locality. But the ethic also favors accountability and equity.

All of this inhibits action and explains a thin and skewed family benefit package in the United States, which does not employ most of the instruments for family support used by the other countries. It also explains "pluralistic ignorance" as to the child care realities, a confused debate, and a policy vacuum—while the market meets urgent need.

On the positive side, a body of rigorous research has not found evidence that out-of-home care harms children, and has produced some evidence that it may have benefits. The society's per capita GNP level and its low ranking in governmental share of GNP suggest that if the current economic problems were to be overcome, there would be a resource base for implementing a benefit-service response to a clearly growing need. And both the equality movement and greater consciousness of labor market realities have brought new voices to the debate.

These unique benefit programs in the six countries are not fully accounted for, but they certainly do not occur at random. Moreover, there is a group of policy instruments and programs that recur across country lines and have known characteristics. We have identified and named policies, programs, and instruments and demonstrated how they are adapted or are adaptable to objectives. And we have pointed to obvious convergence in identifying the choices and the alternative pathways taken by countries as they shape their unique programs, and to some of the implications of choices that can be made. In short, we believe we have found that countries do have choices and that their answers are not fully shaped by uncontrolled forces. We also believe it possible to sum up what has been learned to this point and to pose the choices for countries that have not fully committed themselves to a direction. There are also alternatives of interest to countries further along which may consider mid-course corrections.

It is to the summation of such choices and alternatives, and our recommendations for a viable future policy, that the concluding chapter is addressed.

NOTES

1. See Martin O. Heister and B. Guy Peters, "Comparing Social Policy Across Levels of Government, Countries, and Time," in Douglas E. Ashford, ed. *Comparing Public Policies* (Beverly Hills: Sage Publications, 1978), pp. 149–76.

2. See Charles F. Westoff, "Marriage and Fertility in the Developed Countries," *Scientific American* (December 1978), p. 51: "Most of the world's developed countries now appear to be approaching zero population growth. Several European countries—Austria, *East and West Germany*, and Luxembourg—have already gone beyond zero growth: they have more deaths than births each year. The United Kingdom is right at the balance point. . . . If current trends in fertility continue, Belgium, Czechoslovakia, Denmark, *Hungary*, Norway and *Sweden* will reach or fall below zero growth in a few years. . . . If the trend should persist, . . . the *U.S.* population will stop growing in about 2015." [italic added]

3. See Herta Kuhrig and Wulfram Speigner, eds., *Zur Gesellschaftlichens Stellung der Frau in der DDR* (Leipzig: Verlag für die Frau, 1978).

4. Harold L. Wilensky, *The Welfare State and Equality* (Berkeley: University of California Press, 1975), pp. 10, 12.

5. Phillippe Ariès, *Centuries of Childhood: A Social History of Family Life,* Robert Baldick, trans. (New York: Vantage Books, 1962), pp. 373–74.

6. We do not wish to overstate this point or to deny some possible ambiguity. Data are not exactly comparable and do not refer to all countries in the study. The following are possibly relevant:

a) Components of net growth (percent) in economically active population, age 15–59, male, attributable to net migration: France, 1.9%; Sweden, 3%; Federal Republic of Germany, 4.9%.

b) Aliens as percent of total active population, 1970: France, 7.2%; Federal Republic of Germany, 6.5%; Sweden, 5.1%; Switzerland, 21.9%; United Kingdom, 7.3%.

c) Net migration as component of population growth, annual change per 1000 in mid-period population:

	France	FRG	Sweden	GDR
1960–70	4.5	3.4	2.9	−2.0
1970–75	1.6	4.5	0.1	−0.6

d) Increase in aliens as percent of population in labor force:

	First Date	Second Date	Change
France (1968–75)	6.3	7.2	+ 14
FRG (1961–70)	1.7	6.5	+282
Sweden (1960–70)	2.9	5.1	+ 76

Source:
United Nations Economic Commission for Europe, *Labour Supply and Migration in Europe: Demographic Dimensions 1950-1975 and Prospects*, constituting Part II of the *Economic Survey of Europe 1977*, Geneva, 1979. Table III 1, p. 133.

At the start of 1977 there were 2.1 million "guest workers" in the FRG, constituting 11–12 percent of the labor force. In 1976, 17 percent of all live births were to guest workers. However, in the early 1970s when 1 in 7 FRG manual workers was foreign, 1 in 5 in the French industrial labor force was foreign and French immigration was larger.

Six

SOCIETAL LEARNING

The question of how adults are going to manage work and family responsibilities emerged as an increasingly important issue in the 1970s, as more industrialized countries experienced a rapid growth in the number and proportion of women—especially young married women with children—entering the labor force. Those countries in which such behavior characterizes more than half the mothers of young children (and far more than half the women of childbearing age) have already selected some form of policy—or policies—in response to this development. Other countries which have yet to reach such a high level of female labor force participation may not have made a deliberate policy choice yet; however, it would appear that given the nature of current trends, pressure to make some explicit decisions will increase over the next few years.

This growth in labor force participation rates of married women with young children has served to highlight the tension between work and family life as a fundamental problem for industrialized countries. The conflict between work and family could be masked, and the tension between the two domains managed, as long as one parent was prepared to devote full time to unpaid work at home. But that situation has changed.

The rapid growth of sole-parent, female-headed families in several countries during the late 1960s and 1970s brought with it indications of work-family tensions as a problem for at least this kind of family. However, this could be interpreted as merely one more problem for single mothers, who clearly were a minority in the population in all countries and who were often viewed as a deviant group that should perhaps be expected to carry an extra burden. Moreover, the problem could be viewed as possibly containable (at least in those societies committed to a basic minimum living standard) by provision of a relatively low-level cash benefit to such families. Women, at best, could not be expected to earn as much as men in the marketplace and it would be cheaper to support them at home than to pay for a high-quality child care service. This view could be sustained especially for the many single mothers who were poorly educated and unskilled.

Once the work-family relationship became an issue for most two-parent families, however, a very different picture emerged. The two-paycheck family is already dominant in five of the six countries we have discussed. Today, women work for the same reasons that men work: for economic reasons primarily, but also for nonpecuniary reasons. Even though in most countries median female wages are still only 60 to 65 percent of median male wages (for full-time work, all year round) and the average working woman contributes only about 26 percent of family income (one-third of all working women work part time and thus earn a low wage), the percentage of women making this contribution to family income has expanded phenomenally during the past decade. Furthermore the percentage making a far higher contribution to family income has increased significantly also.[1] Nor is the pattern likely to be reversed. Indeed, the contrary is likely to be true. Temporary economic dislocation and rising unemployment may only serve to confirm families in their conviction of the necessity for two earners in a family.

Regardless of the reasons why specific, individual married women have entered and remain in the labor force, an immediate consequence is that the tension and potential conflict between work and family life has become more visible and more universal.

Thus far, we have described and analyzed the policies and programs through which each of our countries addresses or fails to address this new situation. We turn now, in our final chapter, to the question of *what can be learned* from the country experiences: Can we identify the components of an optimum policy? Is there a policy choice that, in the context of current realities, would appear to be good for children, women, men, families, and the society at large? What, if anything, can be recommended?

What follows seeks to be immediately relevant to all those countries that have yet to make a commitment but that, clearly, will soon have to deal with this issue, such as the FRG, the United Kingdom, and the United States. The review may also have meaning for still other countries, whether or not covered by this study, that may wish to make some mid-course corrections.

As noted, we launched our study with the assumption that the problem we were dealing with was a problem for women and children, primarily, and only individually a problem for men. Moreover, we assumed that the policy choices were relatively clear-cut. Thus, countries either wanted women in the labor force or wanted them home. Countries that wanted to facilitate female labor force participation would provide extensive out-of-home child care services, while countries that wanted women out of the labor force (and at home bearing and rearing children) would provide equally extensive cash benefits.

We discovered, as the study progressed, two things of significance: First, the fundamental problem goes well beyond the concerns of women or of women and children. It is more than a problem of changing sex roles, even when broadly defined. Instead, the most appropriate definition of the problem is that of the tension between work and family life for all adults who expect to—or want to—bear and rear children and for societies which, if they are to survive, need children.

The policy response cannot be simplistic, even if societies begin with concern only for working mothers. Whether or not women should be in the labor force is not a subject for a simple, clear-cut, unidimensional policy strategy. Actually, countries have multiple goals, and these goals may be inconsistent at the same time or over time. The ultimate policy choice a country makes represents a compromise—an amalgam of responses to complex and diverse factors within the context of distinctive historical and ideological elements. For example, a country may need women in the labor force but also want to be sure that they have children; a country may want to make it easier to rear children, but not be prepared to provide an alternative to earned income to more than a relatively small group; a country may have changing needs for an expanding labor force and therefore changing incentives for attracting women who have previously not been in the labor force; a country may recognize that highly educated, high wage-earning women will not remain out of the labor force for long, regardless of the policy system's preferences; a country may want to attract women into the labor force but not be able to expand child care services rapidly enough to meet the demand and, therefore, may be concerned about the consequences of inadequate provisions for children. And a country may value flexibility and diversity whatever its labor market or population trends.

Clearly, labor market and population concerns have been and continue to be paramount in the choice of responses. Influencing how these concerns become implemented in a specific explicit or implicit policy choice are the economic resources of the country; the need and degree of conscious desire to protect the quantity of future generations; the value placed on male and female equality; what child care already exists within the country; the relative emphasis on options and choices; the comfort with government action; and the time and authority it takes to initiate and implement major policy changes.

Thus, policy choice seems to balance labor market against population objectives, in a context of history, ideology, and existing resources. The issue for the future will be: What combination of which benefits and which services can best fulfill a country's objectives?

So far, the result, in each case, has been the visible emergence of what we have called a benefit-service policy package—a package that includes both cash and in-kind benefits to provide income, on the one hand, and out-of-home child care services, on the other. In other words, although the balance may vary, the policy choice is not cash *or* services but rather some combination of both. The issue is not whether to establish more services and provide less in the way of benefits, or vice versa, but rather, what should the particular mix be, and what is the best selection of benefits *and* services to assure the optimum mix. Such a combination or package may represent alternative options for *different groups within the same country* or, perhaps of equal importance, may represent a decision regarding the optimal policy choice for most women—or adults—*at different stages* in their own life cycles or at different points in historical time. The ultimate question then becomes: How much cash, for whom, for how long a period of time, under what circumstances, and how much child care services, of what types, for which children, under what circumstances, and how financed?

In reviewing current trends in all our countries, we would note in brief:

- The GDR is expanding benefits steadily, and expanding services—the former priority—somewhat slowly now, but steadily.
- Hungary is expanding services, albeit at a moderate pace.
- France is expanding benefits for low-income women and services for all.
- Sweden is expanding services as rapidly as it can, and discussing new benefits.

- The FRG is debating expansion of benefits still further, and experimenting with services.
- The United States is beginning to notice the issue.

Four of the countries studied have already made more or less major commitments and are now making some modifications or filling in gaps. The FRG has not shaped a definitive policy yet. Other countries, like the United States, have made no explicit policy choice either, and still assume the equitable functioning of the "invisible hand" of the economic and political marketplace. Under the latter circumstances, some women who want to have children and who have income which permits them to remain at home, do so. Others work and pay whatever the market price may be for care of varying—and often unknown—quality. Still others either work and do not have children, or they attempt both and "manage," often at serious cost to themselves—and their children, husbands, families. The choice is up to the individual. The consequences are borne by all the individuals involved as well as by the society at large. The consequences for society, thus far, are too rarely noted.

It is difficult to believe that the United States, which ranks low or last on much child care provision and in all family social benefits, can continue to ignore the consequences. The social and labor force trends we identified initially have continued. As of March, 1979, over 62 percent of the mothers of school-aged children, over 52 percent of the mothers of children aged three to five, and 41 percent of the mothers of children under the age of three, were in the labor force, and most worked full time. The labor force participation rate for U.S. women with children under the age of three increased more than 11 percent between 1977 and 1978, continuing the trend for these women to enter the labor force at a more rapid rate than any other group. Thus, these U.S. women, like women in may other countries, are increasingly trying to "manage" both having children and working. The policy-making system is challenged to respond in some way to the strain created for working mothers, their families, and their children.

RELEVANT TO CHOICES

What, then, have we learned from this study? Is there any clear societal learning as to an appropriate response to the work and family problem in a modern industrial society?

First, a summary of some of the specifics we have noted thus far, some of it assembled in this research, some reported by other researchers:

- Adult women—married or single, with or without children—are increasingly entering the labor force, with the greatest increase among married women with young children.
- Adult males—married, with young children—have for some time had the highest rate of labor force participation of all adults.
- There is some correlation between the extensiveness of out-of-home child care service and the rate of female labor force participation, but it is unclear which comes first.
- There is some correlation between low birth rates and high female labor force participation, but here, too, causality may run both ways.
- Although there may be some correlation between the growth in female labor force participation and the increase in divorce rates, the latter trend seems to be leveling off.[2]
- There is no evidence that children develop inadequately as a consequence of their mother's working or as a consequence of their experience in group care.
- There is some evidence that children develop *better* when their mothers work.[3]
- There is some evidence that women who are at home alone, with very young children, may become depressed.[4]
- There is clear evidence that women's wages and occupational progress—and male-female equality—are impeded by encouraging women to leave the labor force for an extended period of time.
- There is clear evidence that in-home child care will be less and less available over time—and indeed, this decrease in availability has been noticeable for some years.
- There is some evidence that family day care, long-term, is not a "cheap" child care option. As more women enter the labor force, while those who remain at home view care for others' children as a job, the latter come to expect equivalent wages and benefits.
- There is no evidence to suggest that women who try to manage both work and child rearing suffer negative consequences (or that their children or families do). But the history of this behavior is quite recent, and common sense suggests that as child care by relatives and informal child care becomes more difficult to obtain, the strain for those who cannot afford market care will increase—as will the strain for those who select care which they view as unsatisfactory but choose because they have no other option.

- There is some evidence to indicate that the husbands of working mothers contribute more in the way of time and labor to household, family, and child-related tasks than do men with full-time "at-home" wives.[5]
- There is general consensus (among more than just the countries included in this study) that it is better for the physical and emotional well-being of mother and child if women are able to remain at home for a brief time before childbirth and for a more extended period of time following childbirth, without the family suffering an income loss as a consequence.
- There is growing consensus that fathers can and should play a significant role in their children's development, even when children are very young.
- There is no evidence to suggest that most countries are prepared to provide a substitute for earned income to an adult who is healthy and employable for more than a relatively brief period of time—except when there are no jobs.
- There is growing consensus that any policy that provides income as a replacement for earnings while mothers remain at home to care for children should be designed in such a way as to avoid undue penalties for women in their work and family lives.
- There is general consensus that it is better for the overall development of children if there is available to them, after a certain age (the age is debated), a group experience with other children, for at least some portion of the day, if their parents wish it, regardless of whether their mothers work. (The consensus is that children are certainly deprived if such experiences are not available by the time a child is three. The debate focuses on which younger age is the most appropriate and beneficial for beginning a group experience for children). There is a growing trend in several countries to begin such care at age two or two-and-one-half.

SHAPING A FRAMEWORK

How does one put all this together? What are appropriate assumptions, basic values, which may be shaped into a policy framework?

Our first premise in choosing among the possible policy components is that the debate regarding whether or not women *should* work is over. Women are working, in growing numbers. The time when women remained at home, first for childbearing and rearing, and then in full-time leisure, has ended—or will end soon—for most women. This pattern, never complete, and concentrated among the more affluent, had a relatively brief history— about 100 to 125 years or so. Nineteenth- and early twentieth-century women had shorter life spans, longer periods of childbearing and rearing, and larger numbers of children. The present-day life cycle, in which women have a first child while in their mid-twenties and a second and last child by the age of thirty, means that the period of intensive child care demands is limited to a relatively few years. There is now a very long time between a woman's child rearing years and her death—even between the departure of all her children from the home and her own social insurance entitlement.

Women thus work for personal as well as financial reasons. Moreover, in several countries, women with one child are even more likely to work than women with no children. Only the presence of three or more children is likely to inhibit labor force participation of mothers, and this family size is increasingly rare in all industrialized countries.

In the predictable future, work is likely to continue to be a central part of the personal identity and life experiences of all adults. The prime labor force in all these countries is increasingly comprised of married adults with children. Although some adults will continue to choose traditional role models—one "at home" and one "at work" (and they should be able to do so)—it is likely that the number of people who choose this will become smaller and smaller. In any case, the society does not owe an equal standard of living to the families that prefer to trade the home contributions of one partner against income from work. Thus, any policy choice must be premised on the likelihood of labor force participation for most adults, regardless of sex.

For industrialized countries generally, the range of choice is certainly re-stricted. Women represent about 40 percent or more of the labor force among the Western European countries, and the only potential source of additional labor unless foreign workers are imported. In contrast to the 1960s, when young entrants—in addition to married women—flooded the labor market (and an astonishingly large number were absorbed despite the high rates of youth unemployment), the 1980s (because of demographic trends) will see a significant decline in the numbers of young people enter-ing the labor market. The likelihood is that many countries will experience a labor shortage by the mid-1980s, and female labor will be an increasingly important resource. Thus policy choice can be premised on the need for female labor by the society unless the unlikely choice is made of a slowdown in economic growth (beyond what may occur in the energy crisis).

A third and fundamental assumption is that whatever choice is made must ensure the well-being of children as well as their parents, men as well as women, the society as a whole as well as individual families. Indeed, much of the discussion of the need for a new policy perspective is predicated on the belief that what now exists in many countries is either "bad," or "not good enough," for children, parents, and society.

Clearly, any concern with adequate family income, and thus an adequate standard of living for children, highlights the significance of female earnings and points to the need for more equality of opportunity for women in the labor market. Inevitably, such an objective leads to more attention to provision of child care services. We are convinced, however, that providing child care merely to facilitate reentry of women into the labor force (for whatever reason) would be an error. In other words, neither labor market policy nor policy for women's interests should be the sole determinant of family policy.

We would argue rather that the well-being of children, parents, and society is not a "zero sum" game in which improving the situation of one always results in worsening the conditions of the other. What is "good" for women may not always be good for children, but certainly what is "bad" for children cannot be good for their mothers or fathers, and vice versa.

What assumptions, therefore, regarding what is good for children must underlie any ultimate policy choice?

With the decline in family size in recent years, children have much less opportunity for sibling relationships, peer group experiences, and the essential socializing activities with other children, such as existed earlier. The opportunity to be with other children in a group becomes an important developmental experience for children who are increasingly likely to be isolated at home, regardless of whether a parent works or not. Similarly, in homes in neighborhoods in which fewer and fewer adults are present during the day, preschool programs offer an important exposure to a variety of adults in a consistent and supportive manner, while providing relief from the intensity of a restrictive, all-encompassing relationship which previously did not characterize the family, but now often does.

The world as once known (let alone imagined) has changed, as have neighborhoods and families. Even for families with a parent at home the experience is very different for children growing up today. Increasingly, the young child kept at home may be a deprived child in relation to his fellows, just as the eight- or nine-year-old would be if he or she were kept at home instead of attending school.

Thus, we are convinced that it is appropriate for policy 1) to attempt to ensure good care for children when they are cared for outside the home (and not to undertake as a societal obligation the responsibility to maintain a parent at home for an extended period of time); and 2) to search for ways to maintain an appropriate balance between family and home, on the one hand, and child care services, for part of the day, on the other. It is also our belief that children can benefit far more from having the care and attention of both parents (when two parents are available) for some portion of the day than from living their days with one parent primarily.

Although the precise best age for benefiting from a group experience may still be debated, there is a high degree of consensus that such experiences are valuable even for the very young child.

The argument with regard to men seems clear-cut. We begin with the assumption that more gender equality is better than less and that many men believe this, too. Most married men are sufficiently rational to appreciate the economic contribution of their working wives—and the intrafamily "unemployment insurance" that results from having a second paycheck to fall back on in emergencies. We also are convinced that many men would enjoy the opportunity to be more active fathers, not just financial contributors, and would respond in particular to changes in the society that would make a more active family role possible, especially if the explicit values of the society supported such a role.

Thus, our ultimate policy choice must be one that 1) enhances opportunities for children to develop well; 2) expands opportunities for men to be more active at home, in the family, as fathers; and 3) increases opportunities for women to participate more fully in the labor force and the society at large, while attenuating the stress of having to carry full responsibility for home and family at the same time.

Underlying all this, of course, is an assumption regarding the need for children in all industrialized countries. Almost all of Europe is experiencing the consequences of a declining birth rate. Any further decline would serve only to generate a still greater demographic panic. Some countries already show evidence of such anxiety, and it is highly likely that others will too, whether for labor market, consumer market, tax base, or nationalist reasons. Thus policy choice must be premised, also, on the need for children to be born (and well cared for) even as adults are increasingly likely to be in the labor force.

We turn now to the question of how to select among the benefits and services, not only the appropriate mix, but the preferred components within the cluster of benefits and services that make up our package. We have already described and analyzed the existing array of benefits and services in each country, and indicated something of the advantages and disadvantages—the costs and benefits—of choosing among these. We do not intend to repeat here what has already been said earlier. Instead, to summarize, a desirable child care benefit-service package would:

- make it possible for all adults to participate in the labor market, not only in a search for a lifestyle pattern that could ensure an improved standard of living for families without concomitant negative consequences for children, but as part of a lifestyle in which children and adults would be provided with greater opportunities for individual and family development and satisfaction;
- expand the possibilities for men to participate in home and family life, for women to participate in the labor market, and for all family members—adults and children—to participate in the community and society in which they live;
- increase the value placed on children, childbearing, and child care in the society at large;
- ensure some equity in the treatment accorded different types of families.

We may now present our suggested model of a child care benefit-service package. Earlier chapters provide relevant detail.

THE CHILD CARE POLICY BENEFIT-SERVICE PACKAGE

THE BENEFIT COMPONENTS

If we have described the realities accurately and if the goals outlined are shared, they argue for a policy approach whose core component would involve: 1) entitlement to a leave from work at the time of childbirth or adoption: 2) a cash benefit providing short-term temporary replacement for earned income during that leave; and 3) eligibility for the benefit to cover either parent. More specifically, our recommended benefit component would be something akin to the Swedish Parent Insurance benefit. Such a benefit should:

- guarantee the right to a leave from work covering a period of not less than six months at the time of childbirth or adoption, including the right to take up to six weeks before expected parturition, and not more than one year at such time;
- assure job protection, seniority, and the continuity of pension and social insurance entitlements, as well as other employee benefits, throughout this period;
- provide a cash benefit for the period of entitlement at the level of full wage replacement, for the equivalent of any wage up to and including the wage covered under social insurance;
- be defined as the equivalent of earned income and, therefore, taxable at whatever the rate is in a country for personal earned income;
- include an option to prorate the childbirth-related portion over a longer period of time, to cover a shorter work day (half- or three-quarter time for those who would prefer this pattern);
- guarantee the right of employees to a specified number of days each year to permit a parent to remain at home if a child is ill, without loss of income;
- be financed in a manner consistent with the way in which health and unemployment insurance financing are carried out in the given countries.

Such a benefit would protect maternal and child health as well as family income; encourage fathers to play a more active role in parenting while assuring mothers of sufficient time to do so even when in the labor force; usually provide an incentive for women to enter the labor force early while providing a disincentive for extended labor force withdrawal by either parent; minimize the possibility of concomitant labor market stigma falling on women exclusively or especially; avoid contributing to increased income disparity among families while protecting against excessive horizontal inequities among different family types; and, finally, be within the realm of economic and political feasibility in all industrialized countries.

Virtually all major industrial countries have maternity benefit programs, some generous and some modest.[6] The United States has no statutory entitlement. An updated program along these lines becomes the cornerstone of any response to the question of child rearing and child care. It assures a good start for parenting and for child growth, with both parents able to participate, and in a financially viable way. It represents social endorsement of parenting, yet it is not so extensive as to create negative consequences for women who want to continue work, and it does not create financial incentives to stay away so long as to lose the continuity of the workplace attachment. It treats women and men equally and equitably.

THE CHILD CARE SERVICE COMPONENTS

The central component here would be the establishment of publicly subsidized child care services for all children under compulsory school age whose parents wish them to participate:

- provided as a separate program or under the aegis of the public education authorities, or perhaps (for children under two or two-and-one-half and for family day care) social service authorities;
- with priorities set (until there is sufficient provision) so as to favor the children of working parents (one-parent or two-parent families) and children with other special needs;
- free as in elementary school, or with subsidized but income-related fees, varying with country practice;
- covering the normal work day, but with some children staying shorter periods of time as needed and preferred;
- with some options among sibling and age-segregated groups and with whatever are the prevailing options for group size and staffing patterns and qualifications;
- including support of licensed, trained, and supervised family day care programs, in which the family day care mothers receive wages and fringe benefits comparable to similar staff in center or group programs, to serve some children from about the age of six months to two to two-and-one-half years, and older children with special needs. Here, parental preferences still vary. Moreover, time and resource constraints may require the use of family day care until sufficient space is available in group facilities. Thus, the principle would be to ensure good quality family day care for those who use it out of preference or be-

cause of temporary expediency. Or, if the costs can be met and it is preferred, it could remain within the programing repertoire, better integrated with group programs. Indeed, it is quite likely that some family day care will always be needed, whatever the cost, not so much for the parents who prefer the informality, flexibility, intimacy, and intensity of a one to one relationship (since if the quality is high it would be an extremely expensive form of care) but for children with special needs.

To the extent that there continues to be separation between preschool (from ages two-and-one-half or three to age five), on the one hand, and day care (ages six to nine months to two-and-one-half or three), the respective programs may be based in different systems, such as education (a *separate* department) and personal social services. Of course, there are models for one integrated free-standing system, as in Sweden, and other patterns may be invented to meet special country circumstances. What is needed is a child development orientation and a programing pattern attuned to the degree of age integration or age segregation which is preferred.

A CONCLUDING NOTE

SOME QUESTIONS

The kind of policy package we are recommending and the premises on which it is based inevitably raise questions. We have already commented on the most obvious of these insofar as our study sheds light on them:

- the trend for women to work and the value of their working;
- the consequences of women working;
- the effects—the costs and benefits—of out-of-home care for children;
- the impact of various cash benefits on family income;
- the consequences of any of these policies for fertility or for labor market behavior;
- the factors influencing differential policy choice.

Data are limited and knowledge is incomplete. Clearly, many questions remain unanswered, including exactly why countries did move in different directions initially (although it is easier to explain why policy choice seems to be converging in many ways today). Precise cost estimates of specific policy options cannot yet be made, although it seems clear that monetary costs alone have not been determining factors in the policy choice of individual countries.

Inevitably, however, in reviewing our conclusions and recommendations, other questions emerge. Some were raised by individuals who had an early opportunity to learn of our study and to review study findings.

1. *Why should society substitute paid work in a new "female" industry, child care, for unpaid work in another female "industry," at home?*

We would doubt that an expanded program of child care services would create a *new* female industry. However, it might be a substitute for a declining, but much lower status, lower skilled and lower paid female industry, namely, domestic service. Indeed, we would guess that jobs in an expanded child care service program would represent a higher status position for many women. Those who took on such work would be assured of some economic rewards and related status, but could also be provided opportunities for training and upgrading. Such a development might also serve to upgrade the existing nursery or day care center or child care service worker, too, who continues to be paid at a much lower level (with much less regard) than a preschool teacher (who in turn is of lower status than primary school teachers and so on up the ladder).

Despite this, we would urge continued attention to societal values about child care and child rearing, and encourage the entry of young men as well as women to this work. From the point of view of child development, increased participation of men in child care services would be almost as important as increased participation of fathers in the at-home care of their children. Certainly, any child care expansion plans must include attention to this matter. Some progress has been made in recruiting young men to work in elementary schools in some countries, and there are beginnings in child care.

2. *By making it easier for two-earner families to manage home and work responsibilities, are we not encouraging women with high earnings potential to work? Would not this add further to income inequities between educated/skilled and uneducated/unskilled women—and between one- and two-parent families?*

We recognize the potential problem here. Our concern is to protect the adequacy of family income where there is only one wage-earner, without offering an incentive for labor force withdrawal, on the one hand, and without creating undue stress for a sole parent who is coping with work and family on the other. Ultimately this issue must lead to further study of alternative policies for providing income to families with children. (Indeed such a study, codirected by us, funded by the Social Security Administration, DHHS, is a natural outgrowth of the work reported here. The study is expected to be completed in 1981.) It is our assumption here that all adults will probably be in the labor force. Where there is a sole parent, the need may be to supplement earnings as well as to attenuate the work-family conflict. Where two-parent families are concerned, some may choose a lower income and a lower standard of living for a period of time in order to permit one or the other to withdraw from the labor force. Such withdrawal might be for reasons of child care, but it might also be because of a desire to continue formal education, to return for retraining or a different kind of education, or for some other reason. Some assurance of adequate income for families with children is essential regardless, but the assumption is that except for relatively brief periods, most adults will work.

3. *Why develop a policy package premised on having more women in the labor force when, clearly, unemployment is on the increase—both because the economy is contracting and because technological advances will eliminate jobs?*

The technological "bogey man" has been announced before, yet despite the enormous advances in automation during the 1960s, more women entered the labor force, and the labor force grew everywhere. Although technology may eliminate some jobs, it may also create new jobs. Moreover, most of the jobs which have been eliminated are in the production of goods, not in the industries involved in the delivery of services, where most women work. Women were affected far less than men in the 1973-74 recession in the United States. Assuming that we may face a much more severe recession, we might hypothesize that even if women are affected, the existence of a wife's wages in the face of a husband's unemployment may make female contributions to family income even more important to some families. Regardless, the likelihood is that service jobs will continue to grow in availability for women. Long term, the question will be whether more women can move into the male-dominated occupations, not whether women will be in the labor force.

4. *Given the existing resource limitations, how can such a policy package be paid for?*

Here our assumption is that countries are constantly making choices with
regard to policies and programs. If the demand is large enough, a constit-
uency for such a policy package will emerge and press for a response. Given
the demographic pattern of the coming decade in the United States, with
the "baby boom" at the peak of its childbearing, child rearing, and employment responsibilities, such demand could reach significant proportions.
Even if economic constraints persist, the choice could be to move toward
a shorter work day and week rather than to press for higher wages or to
accept higher unemployment. This is a generation that for some time now
has shown a preference for an improved quality of life. U.S. taxes do not
yet approach those of most major industrial societies in Europe. But all
countries can and will decide what is important enough to afford and what
is not, and whether the obviously necessary constraints on spending should
affect one domain or another.

5. *If the ultimate objective of the proposed benefit-services package is
to facilitate the management of work and family life simultaneously, without undue stress for adults or children, while assuring adequate family income for families in which there is only one wage-earner—how will the
society support the decline in productivity of the work force?*

This is really a different aspect of the earlier question, just answered. If
there are advances in technology, there may be a concomitant offset in raised
productivity. If, on the other hand, this does not occur, the cost of a decline
in productivity may be viewed as being offset by an improved quality of
life. The productivity argument is not new. It has been posed every time
proposals have been made to shorten the work day or week. One could argue either the compensatory increased benefits, or the likelihood of technological advances, as offsetting this. Here, as in other areas, value choices
must be made. Our basic view is that the contributions here discussed to
child socialization, family life, and gender equality justify a claim on resources but will not necessarily decrease productivity overall: they will or
could be offset by more work by mothers, more productivity by working
mothers in the labor force more continuously, and even an end to the birth
rate decline!

THE LARGER VIEW

We end by noting that the evidence provided by the countries themselves
underscores the need for a larger perspective than we have proposed thus

far—a perspective that goes beyond the research here reported. We began by identifying a child care and working woman issue and suggested at the outset that what was really being discussed was a family policy issue in which the policy choice must be directed at the question of how all adults—men and women—can achieve fully equal status in society. In other words, how can all adults be productive both at work and at home? How can they be in the labor force and be able to marry and have children, too? Thus, our first finding of significance was that this problem we addressed went beyond the care of the very young child, under age three, to the larger question of how work and family life are to be related to one another and what the role of government should be in facilitating a closer relationship between the two domains, and in assuring broader support for family life as it is increasingly experienced in industrialized societies.

We noted subsequently that all countries other than the United States already provide income supplementation to families regardless of family type, labor force status, and, in some instances, regardless of income. For example, family or child allowances (cash benefits or tax credits) are available to parents regardless of income, as are health and medical services. Some income supplements may be targeted at low-income families only, but these are not restricted to certain family types (even if single parents may be entitled to higher benefits), and they are not reduced or withdrawn when parents work (unless wages are too high).

In contrast to such support for child rearing which already exists in many countries, attention to the interface of work and family life is only now emerging. Most countries provide a paid childbirth-related leave from employment, even if only three, thus far, have extended this entitlement to both parents. (Several countries provide an entitlement to an unpaid leave from work to either parent, with full job and pension protection for one or two years.) Some countries have statutory benefits that provide for a paid leave to care for an ill child at home; sometimes this benefit, too, is available to either parent. Clearly, this is an essential entitlement as women move increasingly into the labor force, and not just for parents with children under age three but for those with older children, too.

It is in this context that we would conclude by noting that we have concentrated here on the role of government in facilitating a closer yet less conflict-ridden relationship between work and family life. Our premise was that individuals—families and family members—had already made adjustments in managing the two domains, and that society had an obligation and responsibility to support these dual roles and to attenuate the stress. Clearly it was a matter of societal self-interest for government to respond in some way.

Now we conclude by underscoring that other kinds of adaptation are needed too, in particular within the domain of employment. Included here are such things as flexible working hours, part-time employment with proportionate entitlement to fringe benefits, seniority and so forth, longer vacations, and, the most fundamental adaptation of all, a shorter workday for all.

Moreover, until the standard workday becomes shorter, supplementary child care programs will also be needed for school-aged children, as well as preschool and day care attendees, when school hours and days do not coincide with parents' work schedules.

It is possible for adults to work and still build strong families. It is possible for mothers and fathers to share work and home responsibilities. It is possible for them to draw upon extensive child care services to help them in this, without sacrificing any of their rights and duties as parents. All this is possible, but only if the work world, along with government and communities, adapts and cooperates.

NOTES

1. For example, in the United States, in one-third of all marriages in which the wife has earnings, she earns as much or more than her husband. U.S. Bureau of the Census, *Current Population Reports: Special Studies Series* P23, no. 77, "Perspectives on American Husbands and Wives" (Washington, D.C.: U.S. Government Printing Office, 1978).

2. This may be occurring because 1) some marriages are not based on the woman's economic dependence on the male, her husband; and 2) some women may make a different marriage decision—or spouse selection—if they are in the labor force, and if they expect to stay in the labor force all their adult lives.

3. Lois Hoffman, "Maternal Employment," *The American Psychologist* (October 1979), 34: 859–65.

4. George Brown and Tirrell Harris, *Social Origins of Depression* (New York: Free Press, 1978); Ann Oakley, *Housewife* (London: Allen Lane, 1974); and Nickie Fonda and Peter Moss, eds., *Mothers in Employment* (Uxbridge, U.K.: Brunel University, 1976).

5. Joseph H. Pleck and Linda Lang, *Men's Family Role: Its Nature and Consequences* (Wellesley, Mass.: Wellesley College Center for Research on Women, 1978). See also Sheila B. Kamerman, *Parenting in an Unresponsive Society: Managing Work and Family Life* (New York: Free Press, 1980).

6. Sheila B. Kamerman, *Maternity and Parental Benefits and Leaves: A Comparative Review* (New York: Columbia University Center for the Social Sciences, 1980).

Appendix A

A CRITICAL REVIEW OF CURRENT RESEARCH ON INFANT DAY CARE

LOUISE SILVERSTEIN

(November 1977)

Group day care for children under the age of three is becoming an increasingly common child care alternative. As a result, the question of the developmental consequences of this type of group care experience has emerged as a subject of controversy in child development literature. Day care advocates include those who believe that center-based care is roughly equivalent to home rearing, and others who actually see day care as a healthier psychosocial setting for normal development than the nuclear family. At the other extreme are those who believe that normal development can take place only within the context of the mother-infant bond (e.g., Naguera 1973; Fraiberg 1977). These theorists express concern that day care, requiring the separation of mother and infant, by its very nature leads to pathological development. Research evidence on this issue is limited and difficult to interpret. Limitations in the conceptualization, design, and methodology of contemporary studies call many of the results into question.

This appendix reviews and assesses current research on the developmental effects of infant/toddler day care. The types of day programs evaluated and a summary of principal research findings will be presented. Methodological and conceptual limitations of the research will be discussed. Suggestions for improving future research efforts will also be presented. Two studies in process, the Stanford day care project (Ambron 1977) and the New York City day care study (Golden 1977) are described separately as examples of recent efforts to improve the quality of research on day care. The discussion closes with a summary of what is known about the effects of day care and what issues remain for research.

SUMMARY OF CURRENT DAY CARE RESEARCH

TYPES OF PROGRAMS EVALUATED

The research literature has concentrated almost exclusively on center care. Family day care, in which several children are brought to the home of a substitute caregiver, has not been the object of systematic examination. Thus the differential effect of family vs. center care is not known. (The New York City infant day care study and the Stanford day care project do examine both family as well as center care; see description of these projects below.)

The centers that have been studied are university-based, research-oriented model programs of higher quality than the majority of centers available to parents. In addition, university-based programs are often embedded within a larger system of family support services. Thus it is difficult to separate the effect of the day care experience per se from the more general experience of supportive services.

The objectives of the day care programs reviewed in the literature have included

1) care: custodial programs designed simply to be a substitute for home care;
2) remediation: compensatory programs intended to provide a corrective experience for high-risk populations;
3) supplemental experience: enrichment programs seeking to accelerate the cognitive development of normal children.

Thus the programs evaluated in the research literature have, in theory, included a wide range of objectives. In practice, however, only high-quality care has been studied.

PRINCIPAL FINDINGS

Historical Context

Day care in the United States has traditionally been negatively characterized as a form of "institutionalization." Frequently, day care advocates have attempted to demonstrate that day care does not lead to the adverse consequences of institutionalization documented by Bowlby (1951).

Bowlby developed the concept of maternal deprivation to explain both the emotional disorders and intellectual retardation characteristic of institutionalized infants. He proposed that 1) a close, intimate maternal relationship is the most important variable in normal development and that 2) any conditions that disrupt or dilute this relationship will lead to negative developmental consequences (1969, 1973). This position still occupies a central place in child development theory. It has most recently been reiterated by Fraiberg (1977).

The research evaluating the effects of day care has become preoccupied with this maternal attachment/deprivation controversy. Day care researchers have, for the most part, implicitly accepted Bowlby's assumptions that the mother-child relationship is unique, exclusive, and critical to normal emotional and cognitive development. These assumptions have primarily confined the research focus to testing hypotheses concerning potentially *adverse* effects of day care. The mother-child relationship and the child's intellectual development have been the major outcome variables examined, while other important aspects of child development such as individual differences, the development of social competence, and peer bonding have not been included in the research studies. In addition, few studies have formulated hypotheses concerning potentially *positive* effects of a day care experience.

Current research findings will be presented below in terms of the child's emotional, intellectual, and social development.

Emotional Development

The mother-child relationship has been the primary emotional relationship examined in research studies. Maternal attachment has generally been measured by the "strange situation" technique (Ainsworth and Wittig 1969). This is a laboratory situation in which the child is separated from its mother and/or a strange adult is introduced. The child's attachment to mother is rated, based on 1) protest reactions to mother's leaving, 2) exploratory behavior in the stranger's presence, and 3) positive reactions to mother such as proximity-seeking behavior. The results of individual studies are contradictory. For example, Blehar (1974) found that day care children manifested "anxious-ambivalent" attachments to their mothers; whereas Moskowitz and Schwarz (1976), attempting to replicate Blehar's results, found that home-reared children exhibited more distress reactions upon separation. Other studies failed to discern any differences between groups (Brookhart and Hock 1976; Doyle 1975). Taken as a whole, studies using the "strange situation" technique (Blehar 1974; Moskowitz 1975; Moskowitz and Schwarz 1976; Ricciuti 1974; Cochran 1976; Brookhart and Hock 1976; Doyle 1975; Kagan et al. 1976) have failed to show consistent, replicable differences between day care and home-reared groups.

Other techniques have also been used to assess the mother-child relationship. Caldwell (1970) developed a behavior rating scale to measure attachment to mother. She reports no differences between day care and home care groups. Unfortunately, her rating categories included subjective concepts such as "hostility" and "nurturance," rather than descriptive behaviors. Her findings are also subject to question because the ratings mixed data from both independent observations and parent-report interviews.

Some aspects of the effect on the mother-child bond of a relationship with an alternate caretaker have also been examined. Laboratory situations have been developed to assess whether an alternate attachment would weaken the mother-child bond (Ricciuti 1974; Ramey and Farran 1975, 1976; Ramey and Mills, 1975; Falender and Heber 1976). The findings indicate that 1) a familiar caregiver can attenuate the distress reaction to being left with a stranger and/or in a strange environment; 2) day care children continue to interact more with mother than with their alternate caretaker; and 3) when confronted with a problem-solving task, day care children prefer help from mother to help from their caretaker. Thus, these findings suggest that experience with a substitute caretaker can provide an additional attachment relationship from which the child can derive comfort when stressed, but which does not disrupt the primary attachment to mother.

Other dimensions of the child's attachment to substitute caregivers have not been explored, nor have the phenomena of peer bonding been the subject of systematic observation.

Given the research data currently available, day care does not appear to have adverse consequences on the mother-child relationship. While it seems clear that a day care experience will not disrupt the primary attachment to mother, such care may lead to subtle changes in the quality of that relationship which have not yet been identified. Positive consequences such as enhancing opportunities for mothers to pursue career goals or providing necessary support for single-parent mothers have similarly not been researched.

Intellectual Development

Intellectual development is generally measured in day care studies by traditional infant IQ tests such as the Bayley or Gesell. The empirical evidence generally suggests that day care has neither facilitative nor adverse effects on intellectual development (Doyle and Somers, n.d.; Doyle 1975a, b; Kagan, Kearsley, and Zelazo 1976; Fowler and Khan 1974, 1975; Keister 1970; Saunders 1972; Moore 1975a; Caldwell et al., 1970; J. Lewis 1975; Prentice and Bieri 1970).

The data concerning adverse effects of high-quality programs are clear. High-quality day care does not have a detrimental effect on intellectual development (Ricciuti 1976). The effect of poor-quality care is not known.

The evidence concerning facilitative effects is more difficult to evaluate. Many studies report initial modest IQ score gains for day care groups (e.g., Fowler and Khan 1974; Doyle 1975a, b; Keister 1970; J. Lewis 1975). However, these differences disappear either during the program or shortly after termination. Larger gains are more likely to emerge only after the child has reached eighteen months of age, even when day care is begun much earlier (Heber et al. 1972; Robinson and Robinson 1971; Ramey and Smith 1976). Significant differences between day care and home-reared groups emerge only in highly structured programs designed for children from deprived home environments (Heber et al. 1972; Fowler and Khan 1975). Some data do suggest that day care may reduce the decline in IQ score typically associated with children from high-risk environments (Lally 1973, 1974; Ramey and Smith 1976; Ramey and Mills 1975; Golden and Birns 1976; Garber et al. 1976).

A small number of studies assess intellectual abilities on measures other than infant IQ tests (Macrae and Herbert-Jackson, 1975; Schwarz, Strickland, and Krolick 1974; Kagen, Kearsley, and Zelazo 1976; Moore 1975). These indices, including tasks in problem solving, abstract thinking, and vocalization, have not been standardized. No consistent differences between day care and home care groups have been found in studies using these measures. Feine (n.d.) and Cochran (1976) (in a Swedish study) report more sophisticated vocalization in children from family day care than from center care. Both authors attribute the better performance of the family day care children to the larger number and variety of adult-child interactions and opportunities for exploring available in a home and family setting.

Taken as a whole, the research data suggest that the impact of day care on intellectual development varies, depending on the nature of the child's home environment. Day care is more likely to have a facilitative effect for children from deprived environments, where it provides compensatory stimulation. It appears to have a neutral effect on children from normally supportive homes. The Feine (n.d.) and Cochran (1976) data raise questions as to the ability of center care to provide the optimal conditions for promoting language development, a variable which has not been widely assessed.

Significantly, even programs specifically designed to provide intensive cognitive enrichment produce only modest, short-term gains in intellectual performance. This failure may be due to the fact, as Ricciuti (1976) suggests, that intellectual development in the early years is resistant to acceleration; or it may be that the program curricula are not appropriate to the structure of intelligence in infancy.

Social Development

The data on the effects of day care on social development are extremely limited. The studies have generally been designed to ascertain the potentially unfavorable effects of day care on peer relationships and responsiveness to adult socialization. Few studies compare day care and home care groups in terms of their ongoing social relationships with peers and adults.

Social behavior is typically measured either 1) by placing the child in a play situation with mother and observing the extent to which the child then leaves mother to interact with peers (Ricciuti 1974; Doyle 1975; Cornelius and Denney 1975); or 2) by behavior ratings of peer and adult interaction in a day care or school setting (Caldwell et al. 1970; Lay and Meyer 1973; Schwarz, Strickland, and Krolick 1974; Macrae and Herbert-Jackson 1975; Raph et al. 1964; Prescott 1973). There is general consensus that day care children interact more with peers and less with adults than home-reared children.

The interpretation of these data varies from seeing day care children as "aggressive, impulsive and egocentric" (Bronfenbrenner 1976) to Schwarz's

(1974) view that day care children are more assertive and independent. Thus interpretive conclusions may reflect rater biases more than objective reality. The findings may also be program-specific; that is, the behavior of the children may reflect the goals of the program developers. Datta (1969) reported that programs which stress social development produce children who are rated as better adjusted. Bronfenbrenner (1976) suggests that the "aggressiveness" of day care children may be culture-bound, i.e., typical of age-segregated peer groups in American society, rather than an outcome of day care per se.

Both the small number of studies and their narrow focus limit our knowledge of the impact of day care on social development. The focus on negative outcomes has ignored the possibility of positive social consequences from pleasurable group experiences or from practice in adapting to unfamiliar social situations.

SUMMARY

The focus of current research on day care, defined by the stigma of institutionalization, has been narrowly confined to examining the potentially negative effect of day care on maternal attachment and intellectual development. The findings to date suggest that day care has a neutral effect on these aspects of development. However, because of the narrow scope and limitations of the research, the existing data must be considered preliminary and inconclusive. It is still premature to conclude that raising children in day care vs. home care makes little difference. In the next section, a critique of the research literature is presented to emphasize the methodological and conceptual difficulties that limit the usefulness of this material as a basis for making policy decisions.

CRITIQUE OF CURRENT DAY CARE RESEARCH

METHODOLOGICAL LIMITATIONS

The basic methodological aspects of research design include 1) sampling procedures, 2) assessment techniques, 3) control of variance, and 4) statistical techniques used to interpret data (see Kerlinger 1973, for a detailed presentation of behavioral science research design). Each of these factors will be discussed separately.

Sampling Procedures

Adequate sampling procedure provides a basic cornerstone for the generalizability of findings from a research sample to a general population. Bronfenbrenner, Belsky, and Steinberg (1976) point out that virtually all the research data have been collected at day care centers offering high-quality care, rather than at centers which are more generally available to the majority of the population. There has been no research on the development of children enrolled in a broad range of day care settings. (The New York City day care study and the Stanford day care project are two studies that have attempted to correct many of the methodological defects discussed in this section. A detailed outline of the improvements implemented in these two programs will be presented below.) When a substantial segment of day care settings is omitted from evaluative research, the generalizability of findings must be considered tenuous. Thus the findings that infant day care does not lead to adverse consequences must be qualified, since there is a significant possibility that an unfavorable setting could lead to negative developmental outcomes.

Bronfenbrenner further notes that in studies comparing center vs. family-reared children, the children are not randomly assigned to either group. Some studies attempt to correct the effects of nonrandom samples by matching the samples on various characteristics such as sex and SES. However, the technique of matched sampling, while improving control of extraneous variance, is not a substitute for randomization. If the matched variable is not significantly correlated with the dependent variable, the matching is irrelevant. Ideally, subjects should be matched and then assigned to experimental groups at random, although this is difficult to implement in actual practice.

Since the equivalence of day care and home care groups is not assured, it is impossible to attribute reported differences to the impact of day care rather than to preexisting between-group differences. A similar problem exists in interpreting contradictory research findings, since the equivalence of groups in separate studies is also uncertain. Bronfenbrenner (1976) points out that the failure of Moskowitz and Schwarz (1976) to replicate Blehar's

(1974) results is probably due to the contrasting characteristics of the samples used in the two studies.

The meaningfulness of findings of individual studies is further weakened by the small sample sizes typically used. For example, in Ricciuti's (1976) review of nine studies on the effects of day care on maternal attachment, the size of most samples ranged between thirty and forty subjects, with some using as few as ten or twelve. This lack of representative and random samples, in conjunction with limited sample sizes, seriously limits the generalizability of results. With such small samples, the likelihood of achieving statistically significant differences in dependent variables is considerably reduced. Moreover, even when significant differences do emerge, the amount of the total variance of a dependent measure (e.g., IQ test score) which can be attributed to the day care experience per se is so small that the results do not actually provide any meaningful data.

Thus the lack of large, representative, and random samples in the day care literature considerably limits the meaningfulness and generalizability of existing findings.

Assessment Techniques

Assessment techniques are discussed in terms of the outcome variables they are used to measure: attachment behavior, cognitive functioning, and social development.

ATTACHMENT BEHAVIOR. Attachment behavior is usually measured by the experimental "strange situation" (Ainsworth and Wittig 1969). Bronfenbrenner, Belsky, and Steinberg (1976) discuss the limitations of this procedure in terms of its ecological validity, i.e., the tenuousness of generalizing from laboratory situations to real-life settings. The construct validity of the experimental "strange situation" is also questionable. Rutter (1974) observed a wide range of individual variation in reaction to separation which cannot be explained by the strength or quality of attachment to the mother. Kagan (1976b) concluded that separation reactions are related to cognitive maturity, rather than being a reflection of the strength of the emotional bond to the mother. Thus whether a child's reaction to separation in an experimental procedure can be considered predictive of his adaptation to more normal separation experiences or reflective of the quality of his attachment to mother is an open empirical question. The validity of the Ainsworth technique has not been documented.

Even if protest in response to separation were a valid measure of attachment, the question still remains whether this experimental procedure adequately measures the child's reaction to *separation from mother*. The design of the experimental situation seems to confound the experiences of 1) being separated from mother, 2) being left alone, 3) being left alone in strange surroundings, 4) being left alone with a stranger. Studies that have attempted to tease apart these questions have found that distress is less intense in the absence of the stranger and is considerably mediated by the presence of a familiar adult, even when the mother is absent (Ricciuti and Poresky 1973; Ricciuti 1974).

In addition to reaction protest, exploratory behavior during the "strange situation" is also used as a behavioral criterion for attachment. Escalona (1968) has found, however, that exploratory behavior is related to other organismic characteristics, such as activity level, reactivity to environmental conditions, and tendency to exhibit spontaneous behavior. Even if these other variables were controlled for, Escalona's data suggest that so much individual variation exists in this behavior characteristic that the differences among children in a day care group are apt to be as great as those between day care and home reared children. Consequently, interpretations as to the relations between attachment and exploratory behavior would be difficult to make.

Positive behavior toward mother, such as proximity-seeking, offering her toys, and so on, is the final criterion measure included in the "strange situation" technique. This category represents the most promising approach, since it can be limited to observable behavior and is appropriate for use in real-life settings. However, care must be taken to avoid Caldwell's (1970) subjective characterization of the behaviors.

Measuring "attachment" is a peculiarly difficult issue because of the degree of subjectivity involved in defining the concept, specifying its behavioral correlates, and rating the behaviors. Existing measurement techniques are so imprecise that it is difficult to make interpretive conclusions as to the positive, negative, or neutral impact of day care on the mother-child relationship. Standardized, observational assessment indices that describe the nature of adult-child and child-child relationships in a variety of real-life settings must be developed in order to obtain empirical information concerning the full range of emotional attachments available to infants and children.

COGNITIVE FUNCTIONING. Cognitive functioning in day care research is measured by traditional infant IQ tests, such as the Bayley or Gesell. Specific items typically consist of readily observable motor actions which are noted and summed into a single score. However, the construction of these tests is not based on a theoretical rationale which justifies examining motor development as an index of infant intelligence. Without a theoretical framework, the relevance of many of the item tasks is difficult to interpret. The utility of these tests is further limited because a single score is too gross an index to provide information about a child's cognitive functioning which could be useful in curriculum planning.

Although a premise of these tests is that intelligence is a permanent characteristic, they do not predict later IQ scores (Crano 1977). Thus, although these tests have been shown to be reliable psychometric instruments (Hunt and Bayley 1971), their validity for measuring the structure of infant intelligence is questionable. Bronfenbrenner, Belsky, and Steinberg (1976) further raise the issue of their appropriateness for minority and lower socioeconomic subjects since the population on which the test norms were based did not represent these groups.

The limitations of the infant IQ tests in turn constrict the meaningfulness of the research evidence which points to a neutral effect of day care on intellectual development. These tests may simply be unable to reflect the salient aspects of infant intelligence. Piagetian measures of cognitive functioning are presented below as more appropriate measures of intelligence in infancy. Standardized measures to trace the development of language in very young children do not yet exist.

SOCIAL DEVELOPMENT. No standardized approaches to assessing the infant's relationships with peers and with adults other than mother have been developed to date. The trend in this area has been to rate child-adult and child-child interaction in a real-life setting. However, standardized measurement tools to record objective behavior rather than ratings that are heavily loaded with rater bias do not yet exist.[1]

SUMMARY. The general approach to measurement in day care research has limited ecological validity. Dependent variables are not assessed in a longitudinal context. Experimental and laboratory situations rather than real-life settings are relied upon. Constructs are not assessed by multiple measures in several settings to verify impressions provided by one measurement instrument.

Control of Variance

Most day care studies define the day care experience as the only independent variable. Some studies, as mentioned above, try to control other attribute variables, such as sex and SES, by matched sampling techniques. However, other relevant variables such as birth order, father-present or father-absent family, age at entry into day care, total length of time spent in day care, and half-time vs. full-time day care experience, are not systematically controlled. Organismic variables such as developmental level (both cognitive and emotional) and activity level are similarly not part of the research design. Failure to control these variables leaves so much variance unaccounted for (and thus constitutes error variance) that the statistical power of any comparison is low (Kerlinger 1973). Consequently, the emergence of statistically significant differences in the data is highly unlikely, even when true differences do exist in the empirical situation.

Thus, the conclusion that an early day care experience seems to have a neutral effect on development may be an artifact of the design of the research studies. Since the design paradigms contain so much unaccounted-for error variance, empirical differences between day care and home care groups may be lost in the error term.

Statistical Techniques

Day care studies are generally univariate correlational studies. Multivariate statistical techniques such as multiple regression, nonparametric analysis of variance, or multivariate discriminant analysis generally have not been used. These techniques build more independent variables into the design to permit the investigation of interaction hypotheses, for example, the effects of day care on children of varying activity levels. Because these techniques control more variables, the total amount of variance accounted for is much greater than with univariate designs. Multivariate techniques are thus more powerful statistical measures, more likely to uncover existing empirical differences.

The discussion above suggests that many studies on day care fall short of methodological standards for good scientific investigation. The next section discusses conceptual limitations in the design of the research in this area.

CONCEPTUAL LIMITATIONS

In addition to suffering from methodological difficulties, current research on day care tends to oversimplify the issues involved in assessing developmental outcomes. Some important variables are overlooked, and others are treated too simplistically to yield meaningful results. This section discusses conceptual problems characteristic of contemporary research efforts. Relevant research from the broader field of child development literature is included to suggest future directions which day care research might take to remedy some of the conceptual limitations of existing studies.

Maternal Attachment Reassessed

Bowlby's maternal deprivation/attachment hypothesis has already been identified as the conceptual framework from which most of the research evaluating day care programs derives. Although Rutter's (1972, 1974) reassessment of the conceptual underpinnings of Bowlby's hypothesis is relevant to day care research, it has not been used for generating hypotheses. Rutter questions Bowlby's conclusion that the deprivation syndrome observed in institutionalized infants is attributable to separation from mother. He further critically reviews the empirical research supporting Fraiberg's (1977) and Bowlby's (1969) view of the mother-child bond as unique and exclusive. A summary of Rutter's work is presented below in an attempt to clarify the empirical evidence supporting the assumption that daily separations from mother necessarily lead to adverse consequences for an infant.

Bowlby observed the emotional and intellectual retardation of institutionalized infants and attributed these characteristics to the fact that the infants had been separated from their mothers. Rutter (1974), in a comprehensive review of the *empirical* data on institutionalized infants, separated Bowlby's maternal deprivation syndrome into three components: 1) the initial distress reaction of infants when hospitalized; 2) cognitive outcomes of institutionalization; and 3) emotional outcomes of institutionalization. He proposed that the distress reaction is a short-term response caused by the disruption of the child's total life circumstances (i.e., displacement into an unfamiliar and unpredictable environment and disruption of all customary relationships), rather than a response to only the separation from mother. He noted that, in a setting providing adequate stimulation and the possibility of forming compensatory relationships with stable and responsive caretakers, the depression and detachment of the child's initial reaction to institutionalization disappear. Since these compensatory experiences are provided by good quality day care, the depression and detachment characteristic of institutionalized infants should not follow entry into day care. Carefully comparing data from mother-present, mother-absent studies, Rutter concluded that the conditions leading to intellectual retardation involve a lack of adequate and appropriate social, perceptual, and emotional stimulation, rather than simply lack of attachment to a maternal figure. He further demonstrated that emotional disorders associated with institutionalization actually stemmed *from the failure ever to establish* a close attachment to a mothering figure, *rather than from the disruption of an already established bond.*

Thus Rutter's reassessment of the maternal deprivation syndrome suggests that privation, rather than deprivation, of a wide range of stimulating conditions which are not necessarily tied to the relationship with mother, leads to the adverse developmental outcomes observed in institutionalized infants. Within this context, the high level of environmental stimulation and the opportunity to develop stable relationships with substitute caretakers provided by good quality day care would be expected to lead to developmental outcomes well within the normal range.

In the same way that Bowlby mistakenly equated separation from mother with the multiple deprivations involved in institutionalization, Fraiberg (1977) erroneously equates the deplorable child care experiences of poor children with the effects of maternal employment. She accurately identifies inadequate child care as the antecedent of "failure to thrive in infancy" and later developmental disturbances. Indifferent and unstable caretakers in overcrowded and unsupportive environmental circumstances will undoubtedly impair a child's ability to form attachments. However, alternate child care need not systematically deny the emotional needs of children.

Fraiberg inappropriately links maternal employment to "the diseases of non-attachment," which include failures to form personal attachments, conceptual learning problems, and disorders of impulse control such as criminal psychopathy (Fraiberg 1977). She does so because she believes that the bonding necessary for avoiding "the diseases of non-attachment" must take place between mother and infant. She fears that maternal employment during infancy will preclude the formation of these bonds. Thus she advises that a group experience be postponed until age three and limited to half time until the child reaches age six.

Rutter also considered the conditions leading to the development of attachment (1974). He found that the development of attachment did not relate to the amount of time spent with the child or to the activities in which the pair participated. He specified that bonding, caretaking, and play were three different functions which might or might not be performed by the same person. He concluded that the minimal conditions required for attachment to develop were that 1) the same person had contact with the child over a prolonged period of time, and 2) that the person respond with high frequency and intensity to both explicit and subtle signals in the child.

Rutter found that children varied in their response to both daily and prolonged separations, and that no clear relationship between separation and bond disruption could be demonstrated. Depending on the maturational level of the child, and the nature of the substitute environmental conditions, certain separations could facilitate independence and autonomous functioning.

Thus Rutter's conclusions indicate that day care experience will not preclude the formation of the mother-infant bond, nor disrupt it once the attachment has been established. Rather, Rutter's review suggests that the daily separations and interpersonal experiences with substitute caretakers may actually serve as positive catalysts for developing more flexible social interaction skills and autonomous functioning. This position is much more supportive of alternate child care arrangements and suggests the need for a shift from focusing on the negative effects of separation from mother to the possibility of positive effects of that separation and of the exposure to multiple attachment figures. Rutter's work points to the need for future research studies to divest the mother-infant relationship of its mystical, exclusive quality and to include the full range of relationships available to infants.

Day Care as a Global Variable

Day care research has not attempted to characterize the child care environments provided by center care but has treated the day care experience as a homogeneous and global variable. Environmental inventories have not been used to describe systematically the phenomenology of the infant's daily experience in a center as it contrasts with that in a home care environment. Thus even if consistent differences between day care and home care groups had emerged, the salient environmental aspects responsible for those differences could not have been identified. Inventories to contrast home care, family care, and center care must be developed. These inventories should include such aspects as:

1) the physical environment—amount and organization of space; noise level; the number, type, and variety of toys provided;
2) caregivers—number, race, sex, age, ethnic origin, education and training qualifications, child-rearing attitudes, stability;
3) children—number, race, sex, ethnic origin, temperament, age groupings (age-segregated or infant, toddler, preschool mix);
4) interactions—frequency of each type: child-child, child-caregiver; physical vs. verbal, caretaking vs. affectionate.
5) daily routine and activities—length of day, naps, mealtimes, trips away from center, visitors (both adults and older children);
6) curriculum—structured vs. unstructured, familiarity vs. strangeness of materials, simplicity vs. complexity of teaching approach, stress on verbal, motor-manipulation, or social skills;
7) relationship of center to other family support systems—integrated into school or child guidance center vs. isolated center, proximity to clients' homes.

Several measures for assessing environmental conditions have recently been developed. These include the Home Stimulation Inventory (Wachs 1976), the Purdue Home Stimulation Inventory (Wachs 1976), and the Home Observation Index for Measurement of the Environment (Elardo 1977). These measures vary in the extent to which the criteria used to rate the environment are observable and objective, and thus their conclusions are also variable. However, two conditions have repeatedly been shown to correlate negatively with high rates of development: 1) auditory overstimulation, and 2) overcrowding resulting in lack of a quiet refuge to which an infant can regularly escape (Wachs 1976; Elardo 1977; Escalona 1973). In contrast, Wachs (1976) has found that toys giving audio-visual feedback correlate positively with high rates of development.

Interaction research has recently emerged as an approach which attempts to characterize the continuous, ongoing nature of infant-caregiver interaction (Lewis and Rosenblum 1974; Sander et al. 1972; Burns et al. 1972; Bakeman and Brown 1977; Gewirtz and Boyd 1976; Goldberg and Lewis 1969; Lewis 1972; Lamb 1977; Moss 1967). Two interesting themes have been developed from the studies in this field: 1) development of new models to measure the interaction itself as a dependent variable; and 2) documentation of the active role of even very young infants in initiating and regulating the interaction.

Direct study of this interaction requires new types of measurement models. Rather than considering only the frequency of single behaviors by the child and caregiver, new techniques such as sequential analyses and conditional probability matrices have been developed to describe the interactive, dynamic, and changing phenomenon of the dyadic relationship.

The interaction researchers emphasize the ability of even very young infants (four weeks) to regulate the amount of perceptual and social stimulation presented to them. They also point out that successful interaction requires the caregiver to adapt his or her behavior to the child's capacity for attention and need for withdrawal. A further necessary step is to examine interaction with alternate caretakers and peers.

Lack of a Developmental Framework

Day care research has not explored the effects of day care within a developmental framework. The needs and capacities of a child change over time, so that a child's reaction to a particular experience at one stage of development may differ from his reaction at another stage. Planners of center environments and curricula have not considered that environmental conditions that enhance development at one stage may be irrelevant to, or destructive of, optimal functioning in another developmental phase. For instance, a quiet and relatively low-stimulus environment may be more supportive of development in the first two or three months of infancy, while more intense and directed external stimulation may be needed by the older infant.

The question of age at entry is a specific developmental issue of particular importance which has not yet been investigated in day care research. The work of Sander and coworkers (1972) concerning the effects of different types of caretaking regimes on neonates is presented below as an example of a beginning approach to exploring age-at-entry issues.

In a more general context, although much of the day care research has focused on assessing separation behavior as an index of maternal attachment, the literature has lacked a theoretical orientation within which to interpret the developmental maturity of the separation behavior. Separation protest may indicate a normal, precocious, or regressive emotional relationship to mother, depending on a child's developmental level. Unfortunately, there is little empirical information available for assessing an infant's developmental level. A brief review of Margaret Mahler's work is presented below as one theoretical orientation which could be useful for generating future hypotheses and measurement instruments.

Mahler and her coworkers (Mahler, Pine, and Bergmann 1975), in a longitudinal, observational study of twelve mother-child pairs, have attempted to define patterns of functioning normally found at different levels of maturity during the first eighteen to twenty months of life.

Mahler specifies the first two years of life as the period of the "psychological birth of the human infant." During this "separation-individuation phase," she sees the child confronted with two developmental tasks: 1) to establish a sense of separateness and the ability to function autonomously, and 2) to develop individual personality characteristics. According to Mahler, the child first experiences its intrapsychic separateness from mother as the prototype for its relationship with the world in general. The mother acts as a "shielding membrane," a catalyst for development and as a stable home base from which to explore the external world and to test the child's own capacities (Mahler, Pine, and Bergmann 1975).

Mahler systematically delineates subphases in the child's development of attachment to mother, its subsequent disengagement from mother, and its development of autonomy and individual characteristics. Although she does not provide a measurement instrument, she does specify behavioral landmarks for each phase from which an assessment scale could be derived.

Mahler's work has not been integrated into the mainstream of developmental research because it is couched in a maze of psychoanalytic theorizing about inferred intrapsychic states. In addition, she and her coworkers have made no attempts to provide empirical evidence for their hypotheses through the use of large, representative samples and the conversion of their observations into data which can be analyzed statistically. The value of Mahler's theoretical formulations, however, is that they are based on direct observations. If her hypotheses could be replicated on larger samples, developmental norms could be defined, and rates and patterns of development under different child-rearing regimes could then be compared. Although

Mahler shares Bowlby's bias concerning the exclusivity of the attachment to mother, her developmental outline could be used in the context of multiple attachment figures.

The appropriate age of entry into day care is another developmental issue needing investigation. For example, very little data now exist concerning the effects of a group environment with multiple caretakers on neonates. Sander and coworkers (Sander et al. 1972; Burns et al. 1972) explored the effect of different environments on neonatal behavior during the first two months of life. They found that babies cared for in a traditional neonatal nursery setting with multiple caretakers showed more distress during feeding in the first ten days of life than an equivalent group in a rooming-in arrangement with one surrogate mother, or a group at home with their biological mothers. These authors found that the highest level of distress behavior during feeding occurred in a group which experienced one surrogate mother for the first ten days and then a new surrogate mother for days 11 through 28. The *shift* in caretakers accounted for significantly more variance in distress behavior than the specific caretaking arrangements of nursery, rooming-in, or home care (Burns et al. 1972). These findings suggest that infants develop an early synchrony with their primary caretaker which may be disrupted with a shift in caretaker or environment.

Klaus and Kennell (1976) stress the importance of the earliest hours after birth in the formation of the parents' attachment to the infant. The first two months may similarly represent a transitional adjustment period during which attachment is solidified and the baby and parents work together to reach a new family equilibrium. The effects of different child care arrangements on this transitional period are not known.

Use of Traditional Infant IQ Tests

Day care research has, for the most part, relied upon traditional infant IQ tests to assess intellectual outcomes. The use of these tests represents a conceptual as well as a methodological limitation because these tests are conceptually unsuited to measuring intellectual functioning in infancy. Piagetian assessment scales are measurement tools which are more appropriate to infant cognitive functioning and so should be incorporated into the day care field.

The Piagetian scales have several advantages over traditional infant IQ tests. They specify a series of skills at a given developmental level which may stablilize, change, or disappear as development continues. The scales permit intra-infant comparisons—i.e., how a child is progressing in various skills over times. Groups can be compared in terms of age at which achievements on various scales are reached. By relating the variations in ages at which infants living under different environmental circumstances achieve behavioral landmarks, one can begin to identify specific conditions that enhance or delay development. Since the scale items have conceptual significance, the circumstances that promote development of particular skills can be specified.

Corman and Escalona (1969) and Uzgiris and Hunt (1975) have designed ordinal scales of cognitive development within a Piagetian framework. Only the Uzgiris and Hunt scales will be presented here because these scales are more complete and are more often used in research studies.

Uzgiris and Hunt (1975) conceptualized six branches of psychological development which comprise sensorimotor intelligence: 1) the concept of the object, 2) means for achieving desired ends, 3) vocal and gestural imitation, 4) operational causality, 5) the construction of object relations in space, and 6) schemes for relating to objects. Each branch is measured by a scale containing a number of eliciting situations arranged in a sequence corresponding to Piaget's sequence of stages of sensorimotor development. Associated with each situation is a particular set of actions which are considered indicators of the attainment of a sequential step in a given branch of development.

Several methodological problems are inherent in these scales. Standardization is difficult to achieve because 1) the scales are usually presented in the child's own home, 2) materials used in the eliciting situations are not standardized, 3) the order of presentation of situations can be varied according to the child's interest, and 4) although situations may be repeated a number of times, the scoring reflects only the child's optimal performance. However, Uzgiris and Hunt report high interobserver agreement and intersession stability. The Uzgiris and Hunt scales have now been used in a great many research studies. The data have consistently replicated Piaget's theory of an invariant sequence in intellectual development (Escalona 1968; Uzgiris and Hunt 1975).

In an area of research related to studying the effects of day care, Hunt (1976) reviewed several articles reporting the mean age of acquisition of the highest level of object permanence and vocal imitation. In one study comparing orphanage- and home-reared children on the variable of child-caretaker ratio, a strong relationship was found between this ratio and the age at which object permanence and vocal imitation were attained. The mean age of acquisition (in weeks) was as follows:

Caretaker Ratio	Object Permanence	Vocal Imitation
10 to 1	195	177
3 to 1	154	160
Home-reared	130	122

Hunt also cites the results of two other studies, an enrichment program in a Mt. Carmel, Illinois, day care center in which mothers received training, and the assessment of a middle-class sample in Worcester, Massachusetts. The mean acquisition ages (in weeks) were:

	Object Permanence	Vocal Imitation
Mt. Carmel, Ill.	73	144
Worcester, Mass.	98	94

Comparison of the object permanence scores of the Mt. Carmel sample and the orphanage-reared children with a 10 to 1 caretaker ratio yields a difference of over two years in the development of top-level functioning. This extraordinary range indicates the plasticity of development of these functions and the kind of impact enrichment efforts can have. The comparison of the Mt. Carmel and Worcester data suggests that the enrichment program was well suited to improving object permanence, but not as efficient in the enhancement of vocal imitation. Intervention can thus be designed to have specific effects.

Day care centers that have developed cognitive curricula to enhance intellectual development in normal children or to provide compensatory experience for at-risk children have been singularly unsuccessful in producing significant long-term effects (Ricciuti 1976). The programs vary tremendously in the type of curriculum presented. The Piagetian scales could provide a conceptual framework for the development of day care curricula. Hunt (1976) stresses "the problem of the match" between the environment and the child. He proposes that different environmental factors are important at different ages. The crucial issue is to present the child with demands that are appropriately matched to his or her abilities. If the demands are too difficult, the child is apt to respond with distress and withdrawal. On the other hand, too little stimulation generates boredom, which leads to apathy and developmental retardation.

Despite the difficulties in the standardization of the Piagetian scales and the small samples used in many of the studies cited above, taken as a whole the data point to the utility of these scales in identifying advancement or retardation in the rate of development. If combined with descriptive data techniques specifying environmental circumstances, they can provide evidence suggesting those circumstances most effective in fostering specific aspects of cognitive development.

Failure to Consider Individual Differences

Although the impact of day care will unquestionably vary depending on the characteristics of individual children, day care planning and evaluation have not dealt with this issue. As the research has treated the day care experience as a homogeneous variable, it has similarly considered only gross variation in children, such as high-risk vs. normal populations. Data on individual differences may indicate that center care may not be appropriate for certain types of children. Similarly, varying kinds of environmental organization within center care, e.g., structured vs. unstructured curriculum, large vs. small group experience, may be differentially helpful to specific types of children. The Thomas, Chess, Birch studies (1963, 1968, 1977) and Escalona's work (1968) consider the contribution of the individual child's characteristics to the course of its development.

Thomas, Chess, Birch (1963, 1968, 1977) attempted to identify components of behavioral individuality which can be identified during the first months of life and remain persistent influences on the psychological organization of the child. They derived nine categories of temperamental characteristics.

Analysis of the data revealed three major clusters of temperamental traits. The first group is characterized by regularity, positive approach to new stimuli, high adaptability to change, and mild or moderately intense mood which is generally positive. These youngsters, who comprised 40 percent of the sample, are apt to be called the "Easy Children." At the opposite end of the temperamental spectrum are the "Difficult Children." These children, 10 percent of the original sample, show irregular sleep and feeding schedules; slow acceptance of new foods; prolonged adjustment periods to new routines, people, or situation; and frequent and loud periods of crying. Frustration typically provokes a temper tantrum. The third constellation is marked by a combination of initial responses to new stimuli of negative but mild intensity, and slow adaptability after repeated contact with new experiences. These children, comprising 15 percent of the sample, are referred to as the "Slow-to-Warm-Up Children." The children in the remainder of the sample had combinations of temperamental traits that did not fall into consistent patterns.

An analysis of the interaction between environmental demands and temperamental characteristics suggested that developmental outcomes depended on "the goodness of fit" between environment and temperament (Thomas and Chess 1977). The advantage of this conceptualization is that the environmental situations and demands which are likely to create stress for a child with a specific temperamental pattern can then be specified. For a Difficult Child, the stressful demands are those associated with socialization, e.g., demands for impulse control and conformity to the rules of family, school, and peer group. For a Slow-to-Warm-Up Child, the excessively stressful situation is one in which rigid demands are made for rapid adaptation to new situations. Even an Easy Child can develop behavior disturbances when the demands of the extrafamilial environment (school or peer group) contrast sharply with those of the home, and the child cannot develop a behavior pattern which reconciles the conflicting demands.

Especially relevant for day care planning are the Thomas, Chess, Birch (1969) findings that point to the importance of screening children so that their temperaments can be identified. Caregiver attitudes and environmental conditions consonant with each child's needs can then be provided. The age at entry and composition of groups may also require manipulation for individual children. For instance, half-time attendance for a "Slow-to-Warm-Up Child" may speed the child's eventual adjustment to a group setting. Similarly, the number of "Difficult Children" within a single group may need to be limited or supplemented by additional caretakers. Thomas and Chess provided a program of parent guidance to enhance parent-child interactions (1977). They found that the parents needed to know and respect their child's temperament before they could effectively monitor their own inappropriate attitudes and behavior. Parent and caretaker consultation would also be an appropriate part of day care center programs.

Escalona (1968) also attempts to describe the individual differences in the behavior styles of normal infants. She explored the impact of activity level on development and found that low activity level facilitated oral sucking behavior which became incorporated into a capacity for self-soothing. Because of their early development of self-soothing techniques, inactive babies thus tended to show less acute distress and to protest less vigorously than active babies. Escalona further found that active infants tended to mobilize their most advanced behavior in response to slight environmental stimulation, whereas inactive infants required strong and specific stimulation to engage in their more complex behavior repertoires.

Escalona's data suggest that while development generally proceeds at an equal rate in active and inactive infants, the conditions necessary to support developmental progress differ as a function of activity level. In general, active babies are less dependent on the environment for the stimulation necessary to maintain developmental progress, while inactive infants are less dependent on the environment for overcoming distress. The level of background stimulation given active infants in an ordinary home is generally enough to induce high-level behavior, even if the infant is given little attention beyond routine care. Routine caretaking contacts are stimulating enough to elicit the child's most mature level of functioning. Similarly, the presence of objects and toys within reach and sight can elicit object-oriented behavior from the active infant. Inactive babies, in contrast, need more specific provocation to stimulate more complex body coordinations, object manipulations, and social interactions. Thus the inactive baby, to make the same progress as the active baby in visual-motor coordination, vocalization, and communication, needs more attentive and stimulating caregiving routines.

Escalona points out that in some homes and institutional settings, caretakers approach children only when they appear to be in need. In such a situation, inactive infants will be approached and played with far less often than active infants. Since inactive infants can soothe themselves, caretakers may not always intervene when these infants do show distress because they know that the babies are likely to settle down on their own. The developmental consequences of such an environment for inactive infants can become severe in that these infants who most require specific adult stimulation are less likely to receive it.

Escalona's work, like the Thomas, Chess, Birch studies, underlines the necessity for the planning of day care environments to be sensitive to individual differences in children.

Differences Between Families Who Choose Center Care, Family Care, and Home Care

Families who plan to use day care services may differ significantly from those who prefer to rear their children at home. Similarly, the choice of family vs. center care may vary systematically with family characteristics. Therefore differences between home care vs. family care vs. center care youngsters may be attributable primarily to the family, rather than to caretaking arrangements. Day care research has not systematically examined the differences between groups *before* attempting to evaluate differences in children *after* a day care experience.

Hock (1976) found that day care mothers differed from home care mothers in several psychological characteristics which correlated with the children's separation reaction at twelve months. The New York City day care project (Freeman 1977) discovered that two thirds of the Hispanic families in their study chose family day care rather than center day care. This project also found that 81 percent of the family day care households were self-supporting, whereas the center care families included a significantly higher portion of families on public assistance.

Exploration of family characteristics is necessary before observed differences can validly be attributed to the day care experience. In addition, information concerning family demographic data may reveal that the impact of day care varies, depending on family variables.

Absence of Interaction Hypotheses

The conceptual problems which have been discussed thus far point to the fact that many more independent variables must be built into the design paradigms of research studies before the impact of day care can be adequately assessed. Research design must incorporate interactions between 1) family demographic characteristics such as low-risk vs. high-risk populations, ethnic origin, single- vs. two-parent families, extended vs. nuclear families, working (part or full time) vs. nonworking mothers; 2) the child's individual characteristics, such as sex, birth order, developmental level, temperament constellation; and 3) the day care program's characteristics, such as center vs. family care, high vs. average vs. low quality, part time vs. full time, structured vs. unstructured curriculum.

TWO STUDIES

The criticisms that have been directed toward day care research in general are not totally relevant for two projects currently in process. These more recent attempts to evaluate the effects of day care represent substantial improvements in research design and conceptualization. They are discussed separately below as examples of how the suggestions presented above can be implemented.

STANFORD DAY CARE PROJECT

The Stanford day care project (Ambron 1977) consists of 1) an original study designed to examine the effects of center and family day care of varying quality on the emotional and social development of one- and two-year-old children, and 2) a follow-up study which will post-test the original sample four months after the conclusion of the original study. The study is not complete at this time, so results cannot be reported here, but an outline of the study design is given in reference to methodological and conceptual issues raised earlier.

Methodological improvements include:

SAMPLING TECHNIQUE. The Stanford project has attempted to increase the generalizability of its findings by utilizing samples which are more representative than those of past studies. The day care programs being evaluated are of varying quality and include both center and family care. The children participating in the study represent a range of ethnic groups (70% white, 15% Chicano, and 15% black). Their socioeconomic status ranges from middle-middle class to families receiving public assistance. The sample size of 45 to 50 children in each group is large enough to yield significant differences. Although the members of each group have not been assigned randomly, the groups are matched on race, ethnicity, and SES.

MEASUREMENT TECHNIQUES. Several attempts to achieve ecological validity have been incorporated into the design of this study. The longitudinal nature of the pre-test, post-test, and follow-up design addresses the question of whether differences which emerge have short-term stability. Theoretical constructs such as "the quality of attachment" are assessed by multiple measures in several contexts (laboratory and real-life settings) and on six different occasions over a nine-month period.

Cognitive functioning is not assessed by traditional infant IQ tests. Behavioral measures of problem-solving ability, persistence, inner (private) speech, delay of gratification, and ability to follow instructions are included as measures of cognitive development, but these do not appear to be standardized assessment instruments. Although "daily diaries" describing aspects of the child's experience in terms of interactions, routines, and so on are being collected, Ambron does not specify whether this information will be documented in a standardized fashion.

CONTROL OF VARIANCE. Efforts to account for extraneous variance have been made by including some characteristics of family (SES, parents' educational level, father present, number of siblings) and child (age, sex, ethnicity, previous experience with alternate caregivers and with separation from mother) as independent variables. Specific interaction hypotheses are not presented. However, the inclusion of multiple independent variables suggests that the data analysis will use an interactive model.

STATISTICAL TECHNIQUES. Ambron plans to use multiple regression and analysis of variance techniques.

The Stanford project also represents some improvement in conceptualizing the issues involved in assessing child development outcomes.

MATERNAL ATTACHMENT. Although the question of adverse effects on the mother-child bond remains of concern to the Stanford researchers, improvements in the assessment of attachment have been incorporated into the study. The Ainsworth "strange situation" technique is supplemented by observations of attachment behaviors at home. In addition, social responsiveness and reciprocity to mother and to strangers, not merely separation protest, are included in the assessment of attachment.

DAY CARE AS A GLOBAL VARIABLE. The Stanford study includes only gross variations in day care, i.e., high or low quality and family vs. center care. Systematic documentation of salient variables of the day care programs is not included. This lack may be remedied in future studies, since the necessary information is being collected in the form of "daily diaries."

A DEVELOPMENTAL PERSPECTIVE. Although age at entry into day care is included as an independent variable, and each child is being pre-tested before entry into day care, careful attention is not being paid to developmental issues. This is particularly true of the approach to assessment which does not attempt to evaluate the child's emotional or cognitive functioning within a developmental context.

INFANT IQ TESTS. Assessment of intellectural development is not a major focus of this study. Some limited attempts to characterize the child's cognitive functioning in terms of problem-solving ability and ability to follow instructions have been included.

INDIVIDUAL DIFFERENCES. Gross variations in children such as age, race, sex are specified as independent variables. In addition, a child's individual prior history with separation and substitute caretakers is also considered as a source of individual variation. However, more detailed differentiation of children in terms of temperament or reaction tendencies has not been attempted.

DIFFERENCES BETWEEN FAMILIES CHOOSING CENTER VS. FAMILY VS. HOME CARE. This conceptual category is adequately considered in the Stanford study. Demographic characteristics such as race, ethnicity, SES, educational level, size of family, and child care history of the family are built into the research design.

INTERACTION HYPOTHESES. Although Ambron does not present specific interaction hypotheses, she has included multiple independent and dependent variables in the project, so that interaction analysis of the results should be forthcoming.

NEW YORK CITY INFANT DAY CARE STUDY

The New York City study (Golden 1977; Rosenbluth 1977; Freeman 1977; Brownlee 1977) was initiated to assess the effects of existing group and family day care programs on low-income youngsters and their families. Children who entered day care between two and twenty-one months of age were studied longitudinally until age three. Children reared at home were compared with the day care group cross-sectionally at age three. The child's psychological development, nutrition, and physical growth were assessed. The effect of the day care experience on the family was also examined.

The design of the study is outlined below.

Methodological improvements:

SAMPLING. The New York City project approaches an epidemiological study in that the size and composition of the sample represent a major segment of the population in New York City utilizing publicly funded day care. The study included 400 children from 32 public, private, and community-operated group and family infant day care programs and 20 preschool day care programs. The quality of the programs ranged from excellent to poor. The families studied were urban, low income, primarily black and Hispanic. The effects of day care for this population were the particular focus of the study. The wide range of programs sampled and the large number of children observed enhance the generalizability of results.

MEASUREMENT TECHNIQUES. This study included multiple assessments of the infants at six month intervals from six months to eighteen months and a final assessment at thirty-six months of age. Standardized IQ tests were supplemented by observations in real-life settings (behavior ratings), as well as by experimental procedures (play interview situation). The longitudinal design and repeated testing on several measures provided data representative of a child's functioning in a variety of situations. Social competence (as measured by scales designed by Burton White of Harvard which have not been reviewed by this author) rather than maternal attachment was a major focus of this study.

The New York City project included an extensive attempt to devise measurement instruments for describing environmental aspects of the programs. Checklists of equipment and behavioral interactions were devised from naturalistic observations at six-month intervals.

CONTROL OF VARIANCE. The New York City project is particularly strong in its analysis of the family characteristics which interact with the impact of day care to influence child development (Freeman 1977). This analysis indicated that the majority of Hispanic families choose family rather than group day care for infants. Thus the effects of Hispanic culture must be differentiated from the effects of family day care. Individual differences in children other than age at entry are not included as independent variables.

STATISTICAL TECHNIQUES. The preliminary reports available to this author do not specify the techniques of data analysis. However, the design suggests the use of multivariate statistics.

Conceptual aspects of design:

MATERNAL ATTACHMENT. The preliminary reports published do not include a single measure of attachment behavior. Rather, the child's social competence with peers and adults is the major aspect of psychological development being assessed. The general orientation of the study is much more neutral than prior studies which focused mainly on the possibility of negative effects of day care.

DAY CARE AS A GLOBAL VARIABLE. The New York City project represents an improvement in attempting to specify major components of program settings. The physical environment, caregiver behavior with the child, and the child's behavior were systematically recorded at six month intervals. Indices which characterize the child's experience, such as cognitive/language stimulation, were developed to compare group and family day care settings. The home environments of the non-day-care sample apparently were not similarly documented.

A DEVELOPMENTAL PERSPECTIVE. This study includes more of a developmental framework than does the Stanford project. Assessments are made at six-month intervals which correspond roughly to developmental periods. The cognitive assessment was specifically designed to compare both sensorimotor functioning at eighteen months and symbolic, verbal skills at thirty-six months. Age at entry is embedded within a developmental context, since the data on intellectual functioning are analyzed on the basis of day care entry prior to or after fourteen months of age. It is not clear whether the social competence measures will be evaluated within a developmental framework.

INDIVIDUAL DIFFERENCES. The issue of individual differences is not addressed in this study.

DIFFERENCES BETWEEN FAMILIES CHOOSING CENTER VS. FAMILY VS. HOME CARE. The New York City study represents an in-depth analysis of family differences in terms of race, ethnicity, family structure, family functioning, and economic resources. In addition, this study addresses a major unresearched issue in terms of the effect of day care on the family. The stability of the family structure and the economic status of the family will be assessed at the end of the study to determine whether day care had a positive, negative, or neutral effect on the family as a whole.

INTERACTION HYPOTHESES. Several interaction hypotheses are specified: the effect of day care as a function of type of care and age at entry on intellectual development; and the interaction between type of program and family demographic variables. Additional interactive relations will probably be examined as the data analysis proceeds.

Although the New York City and Stanford projects do not incorporate all the possible methodological improvements, or address all the unresearched issues, they do represent considerable improvement relative to the majority of past studies. The data emerging from these two current projects should, therefore, contribute meaningful information concerning the effects of infant day care.

SUMMARY OF MAJOR FINDINGS

The above summary was prepared before the publication of the final report of the New York study. We here summarize the findings from Golden et al. (1978).

The New York City infant day care study was longitudinal, comparative field study of 31 service-oriented group and family infant day care programs, and the effects of these programs on 400 children and their families. The primary contribution of this study is that it provides large-scale empirical data on issues for which research evidence has not previously been available. The major findings are outlined below in the context of *popular misconceptions* about infant day care which these new data dispel.

Infant day care may adversely affect the psychological development of children.

On all measures of intellectual, social, and emotional functioning, children attending infant day care programs for several years did as well or better than equivalent samples of home-reared children.

Infant day care may adversely affect the family as an institution.

The families using infant day care programs did not appear to be greatly affected by these programs. No significant differences in the longitudinal sample, in terms of socioeconomic status, economic resources, or family functioning emerged over the several years of the study. At completion of the study, the families who had used infant day care for several years did not differ significantly from families who had recently entered the programs.

Age at entry is an important variable interacting with the effect of day care on psychological development.

No relations emerged between age at entry and any of the outcome measures of psychological development at 36 months.

Differences between the group and family day care settings may have serious consequences for psychological development.

The major differences observed between group and family programs related to nutrition and health care, rather than to psychological development. The group programs were found to be superior to family programs in providing higher quality food and health services. This finding was due to the contrasting role which the New York City Health Department assumed in the two types of day care programs, rather than to intrinsic differences in the group vs. family settings. In the group programs, the Health Department closely supervised and, in some cases, directly participated in the provision of these services. In the family programs, in contrast, the responsibility was left to the individual provider mothers and the children's families.

The two types of programs were found to be basically equivalent in their effects on the children's psychological development. There was some evidence to suggest that group programs enhanced intellectual performance, and that family programs positively affected social competence—but the case is not conclusive.

Families using public day care services in an urban setting are disorganized welfare families.

The study found that the majority of families using public infant day care services in New York City were relatively intact, fairly well-functioning, poor, working families. These families worked even though they did not earn much more than they could get from public assistance. When public infant day care services were not available, these families arranged for private child care which was costly and at times inadequate. These data contrast with the commonly accepted negative stereotypes of low-income minority families.

Public infant day care services would be helpful in decreasing the number of families dependent on public assistance.

The authors state "Infant day care programs do not seem to get families off welfare" (p. 185). This statement is based on the fact that in the sample of families using infant day care services over several years, the proportion of families totally dependent on public assistance (14%) remained constant. However, the large majority (70%) of this sample was self-supporting before entering the infant day care programs. Since publicly funded infant day care services in New York City generally require mothers to work, only a small number of families are accepted who cannot work and also cannot care for their children. These families may remain unemployed for reasons such as disability, mental retardation, etc. Therefore, the provision of day care services should not be expected to change their welfare status.

Given the characteristics of the study sample, the New York City infant day care study is not a good test of whether day care services can help the large majority of families who use public assistance become self-supporting. Thus the conclusion that day care does not help families get off welfare is not warranted by the findings of this study. In order to explore this research question adequately, day care services would have to be provided to large numbers of families on public assistance. The study did find that a significantly larger proportion of families who kept their children at home until age three were on public assistance than those families who enrolled their children in infant day care between the ages of one and two. This finding possibly suggests that increasing the availability of infant day care services might have an impact on the number of families on welfare—but other conclusions are also possible.

RESULTS

Nutrition, Physical Health, and Growth

Highly significant differences were found in the nutritional value of the food provided by the group and family day care programs. At all ages (six months through thirty-six months), the group day care programs provided more positive nutritional foods, while the family day care children were given more negative ("junk") foods. Similarly, the quality of health care, in terms of immunization status, knowledge of current medical problems, and follow-up of prior medical problems, was significantly better in the group day care programs.

These differences in nutritional and health care were due to the different role which the New York City Health Department played in the two types of programs. In the group programs, the Health Department participated in menu planning and regulated food service practices, provided direct on-site pediatric services, and supervised medical follow-up and record keeping. In the family programs, the individual provider mothers were free to determine the food provided to the children, and the parents had to arrange for regular pediatric examinations on their own.

Despite the consistent differences in the quality of foods provided by the two programs, no significant differences were observed in the physical growth patterns or incidence of medical abnormalities between the group and family day care children. The lack of relation between the nutritional measures and later physical growth was probably due to two limitations in data collection: 1) only the type of food offered in the day care setting, rather than the amount actually consumed by the child, was recorded; and 2) no attempt was made to study the food eaten at home. Thus the nutritional measures may not reflect the children's eating patterns.

In regard to physical safety, more physical hazards for eighteen- and twenty-four-month-old children were observed in the family day care homes than in the group centers. However, the safety practices of the caregivers in the two settings did not differ.

Psychological Experiences and Development

The effects of infant day care were assessed in three different contexts. Family and group day care programs were compared in terms of the psychological experiences provided to each child. The psychological development of family day care, group day care, and home-reared children was evaluated at eighteen and thirty-six months. Both the psychological experiences and psychological development were studied as a function of age at entry. In addition, the psychological experience measures for each child were correlated with that child's developmental measures at thirty-six months to determine whether differences in experience which cut across type of program setting were related to positive developmental outcomes.

The psychological experiences provided in each setting were characterized in terms of physical environment—the type of materials and amount of space available for play; caregiver behaviors—the amount of individual attention, cognitive-language and social-emotional stimulation provided to the child; and the child's behavior—cognitive-language and social-emotional functioning. These experience measures were obtained for each child at twelve, eighteen, and twenty-four months by means of all-day naturalistic observations.

Group programs were found to be significantly better than family programs in the physical materials and play space available to the children. However, the organization of the physical environment was not related to later measures of psychological development. In contrast, the family programs had a higher caregiver-child ratio and provided significantly more opportunities for social interaction with and individual attention from caregivers. These differences in caregiver-child interactions were observed throughout the day and particularly during the noon meal. The amount of individual attention received from caregivers at eighteen and twenty-four months was significantly correlated with the child's social competence with adults at thirty-six months.

The two programs did not differ significantly on the other two measures of caregiver behavior, i.e., cognitive-language or emotional-social stimulation; nor on the similar measures characterizing children's behaviors. Age of entry into day care program was not related either to caregiver behavior or to children's behavior.

Psychological development at eighteen months was assessed only in terms of intellectual functioning on the Bayley Mental Scale. There were no significant differences between group and family day care children at this age; however, group day care children scored significantly higher than a comparable sample of home-reared children.

At thirty-six months, psychological development was evaluated in three different contexts: a standard test situation, a play interview, and naturalistic observation. Outcome measures included the Stanford-Binet Intelligence Scale, the Peabody Picture Vocabulary test, and behavior ratings of language competence, cognitive style, social competence with adults and peers, and adequacy of emotional functioning.

With the exception of the Stanford-Binet, there were no significant differences between family day care, group day care, and home-reared children on the measures of psychological development at thirty-six months. On the Stanford-Binet, the group day care children scored significantly higher than both the family day care and the home-reared samples, while there were no differences between the family day care and home-reared groups.

Age at entry into day care was not related to performance on the Bayley Mental Scale at eighteen months, or to any of the psychological development measures at thirty-six months.

When the psychological experience measures were correlated with the later measures of psychological development, no relations emerged between performance on the two standard intelligence tests (the Stanford-Binet and the Peabody Vocabulary Test) and any of the psychological experience measures. In contrast, individual differences in caregiver behaviors, at eighteen and twenty-four months, correlated significantly with individual children's language competence, social competence with adults, and emotional functioning at thirty-six months. Thus although caregiver behaviors were not found to vary systematically between types of day care programs, the quality of the caregiving which the children received was related to later measures of social and emotional functioning.

Family Development

The infant day care programs had no observable long-term or short-term effects on the socioeconomic status, economic resources, or family functioning of the families studied. At the completion of the study, the families who had been using day care services for several years did not differ significantly from families who had been in the programs for only one month.

POLICY RECOMMENDATIONS MADE

1. *Meet the vast, unmet need for subsidized, licensed infant day care.*

The current study found that public infant day care programs in New York City were used primarily by poor working families. If public programs were not available, these families arranged for private child care which was often unsatisfactory and costly. The results of the New York City infant day care study indicate that children attending infant day care programs for several years did as well or better than comparable samples of home-reared children on measures of cognitive, social, and emotional development. Thus, at the least, public infant day care programs provide reliable, low-cost child care which does not adversely affect the children.

2. *Supply family day care for children under two years of age.*

Children in family day care experienced more opportunities for social interaction with caregivers and more individual attention than did children in group day care. These experiences were related to positive developmental outcomes at three years of age. In addition, family day care has generally been less expensive than group care (although the improvements in nutrition and health care suggested below would reduce the cost differential), and may be more convenient for mothers.

3. *Increase the New York City Health Department's role in family day care.*

Group day care programs were found to be superior to family programs in nutrition, health care, and physical safety. This superiority was a result of the direct role the Health Department played in supervising meal planning, medical services, and organization of the physical environment for the group centers. A similar role should be assumed by the Health Department in the regulation of family day care programs.

4. *Supply group day care for children two years and older.*

Since children in group day care obtained higher IQ scores at thirty-six months of age than either home-reared children or children in family day care, the authors conclude that the group setting may be a more effective learning environment for children two years and older. However, the study did not record the psychological experiences provided in the two day care settings after twenty-four months of age. Thus, the specific components of the group experience that contributed to the higher IQ test performance are not known. The authors hypothesize that the use of licensed nursery school teachers as full-time teachers in the group day care programs may have provided more effective cognitive-language stimulation than the semi-weekly visits by paraprofessional education aides provided in the family day care programs.

The study conclusion that group day care "succeeded in preventing the decline in intellectual performance which low-income children generally manifest by three years of age" (p. 190) does not seem entirely warranted. While it is true that the IQ scores of the group day care children did not decline between eighteen and thirty-six months, if the thirty-six-month scores are examined in light of *initial* IQ scores, a decline over three years is observable in all three groups of children.

	Initial Bayley I.Q.	18 month Bayley I.Q.	36 month Stanford-Binet I.Q.
Longitudinal group day care	108	100	99
Longitudinal family day care	112	98	92
Cross-sectional		92	92

The decline in the IQ test performance of the group day care children appears to have been attenuated, but not prevented.

The meaningfulness of the differences in scores at thirty-six months must be cautiously interpreted since although a 7-point difference is statistically significant, it is moderate in size; and no significant differences were found on any of the other cognitive measures (including other measures of verbal intelligence) at thirty-six months. The stability and replicability of this finding need to be established.

If the more structured learning environment of a group program results only in higher test performance and not in more generalized intellectual functioning, then this recommendation may not be appropriate. In the other instances of qualitative differences between family and group day care, e.g., amount of individual attention from caregivers, family day care was found to be superior. Thus further research is necessary before the effect of different types of day care on intellectual development can be more completely understood.

5. *Move toward integration of group and family day care programs.*

Since the authors recommend that children be transferred from family to group day care at age two, a mechanism must be developed to ensure continuity of care.

6. *Additional recommendations*

Selection of caregivers:

Individual differences in caregiver behavior proved to be more important to later psychological development than type of setting. While recognizing the importance of training and supervision of caregivers, the authors propose that careful selection of women who already possess the appropriate personality characteristics may be more effective than attempting to train less suitable women.

Continued program evaluation:

New procedures or training programs should be evaluated to determine their effectiveness. Selected aspects of programs should be monitored on an ongoing basis.

Follow-up of New York City infant day care study:

The long-term impact of infant day care should be studied. The stability of the findings in the current study, particularly the IQ differences observed at thirty-six months, would be an important consideration in policy planning.

CONCLUSIONS

The current research on day care suggests the following conclusions:

1. No empirical evidence exists to indicate that good quality infant day care has adverse consequences on maternal attachment, or intellectual or social development.
2. Facilitative effects have emerged only in terms of attenuating the IQ test score decline usually observed in children from high-risk environments.
3. The only current, valid, overall conclusion, then, is that good quality day care, as evaluated by existing techniques, appears to have a neutral effect on development.

However, available research is limited in both quantity and depth. Unresearched or poorly researched issues include:

1. The effect of poor quality care.
2. The effect of day care on the neonatal period for both infants and parents.
3. The effects of day care on language development.
4. The effects of day care in a long-range longitudinal context.
5. The differential effect of family vs. center care.
6. The impact of day care on the family as a whole.
7. The differential impact of different types of programs for different types of children and families.
8. The impact of day care on society.
9. Many possible positive effects of day care.

To the extent that effects of day care would be overriding considerations in policymaking, one must note the limitations of existing research data and the number of issues which have not yet been investigated. Extensive, high-quality research efforts (such as the New York City and Stanford studies) which continue to explore the consequences of different types of child care should thus be a policy priority.

NOTE

Several interrelated studies, funded by the Administration for Children, Youth, and Families of HEW (now HHS) and implemented by Abt Associates and Stanford Research Institute, are clarifying the state of the art and making some progress. A research report from Abt Associates concludes as follows:

> The Preschool Inventory [developed by Bettye Caldwell for the Educational Testing Service] appears to be a reliable indicator of school-related cognitive skills, and as such will be a useful outcome measure in the NDCS. The Pupil Observation Checklist [developed in the research] captures some important aspects of children's test-taking behavior; data from the POCL may aid in interpreting other test scores and in cross-validating some observation data, notably *task persistence* scores from the Child-Focus Instrument [developed by Elizabeth Prescott and her colleagues]. Other measures of socioemotional and cognitive development have proved to be of questionable value for use with the NDCS population. Therefore, the latter tests have been dropped from the Phase III battery, while several new tests have been added. . . . (Abt Associates, *National Day Care Study: Second Annual Report, 1975–76* [Cambridge, Mass., 1977], pp. 101–2.)

[Subsequent to the Silverstein review, the study was completed as Abt Associates, *Report of the National Day Care Study*, in six volumes (Cambridge, Mass., 1979), published and distributed by the Department of Health, Education, and Welfare.]

BIBLIOGRAPHY

Ainsworth, M. D. S. 1972. "Attachment and Dependency: A Comparison." In J. Gerwitz, ed., *Attachment and Dependency*. Washington, D.C.: Winston & Sons.

Ainsworth, M. D. S., and S. Bell. 1970. "Attachment, Exploration, and Separation: Illustrated by the Behavior of One Year Olds in a Strange Situation," *Child Development* 41:50-67.

Ainsworth, M. D. S., and B. A. Wittig. 1969. "Attachment and Exploratory Behavior of One Year Olds in a Strange Situation." In B. M. Foss, ed., *Determinants of Infant Behavior*. London: Methuen. 4:111-36.

Ambron, S. 1977. "Stanford Daycare and Early Social Development Project: Follow-up Study Proposal." Working paper, Stanford University.

Anthony, E. J., and T. Benedek, eds. 1970. *Parenthood: Its Psychology and Psychopathology*. Boston: Little, Brown.

Badger, E., S. Elsass, and J. Sutherland. 1974. "Mother Training as a Means of Accelerating Childhood Development in a High Risk Population." Paper presented at Society for Pediatric Research, Washington, D.C.

Baer, M. 1954. "Women Workers and Home Responsibilities." *International Labor Review* 69:338-55.

Bakeman, R., and J. Brown. 1977. "Behavioral Dialogues: An Approach to the Assessment of Mother-Infant Interaction." *Child Development* 48: 195-203.

Baratz, S. S., and J. C. Baratz. 1970. "Early Childhood Interventions: The Social Science Base of Institutional Racism." *Harvard Educational Review* 40:29-49.

Bayley, N. 1965. "Comparisons of Mental and Motor Test Scores for Ages 1-15 Months by Sex, Birth Order, Race, Geographical Location, Education of Parents." *Child Development* 36:379-412.

Bell, S. 1970. "Development of Concept of Object as Related to Infant-Mother Attachment." *Child Development* 41:291-311.

Belsky, J. 1976. "Home and Laboratory: The Effect of Setting on Mother-Infant Interaction." Working paper, Cornell University.

Benedek, T. 1970. "The Psychobiology of Pregnancy." In E. J. Anthony and T. Benedek, eds., *Parenthood: Its Psychology and Psychopathology*. Boston: Little, Brown; pp. 137-52.

Biemiller, A., C. Avis, and A. Lindsay. 1976. " Competence Supporting Aspects of Day Care Environments—A Preliminary Study." Paper presented at Canadian Psychological Association, Toronto.

Bingham, N. E. n.d. "Observations of Infant Social Experience in Family and Center Day Care Settings." Dissertation in progress, Cornell University.

Blehar, M. 1974. "Anxious Attachment and Defensive Reactions Associated with Day Care." *Child Development* 45:683-92.

Bowlby, J. 1951. *Maternal Care and Mental Health*. Geneva: World Health Organization.

—1969. *Attachment and Loss*, vol. 1. New York: Basic Books.

—1973. *Attachment and Loss*, vol. 2. *Separation*. New York: Basic Books.

Brazelton, T., B. Kaslowski, and M. Main. 1974. "The Origin of Reciprocity: The Early Mother-Infant Interaction." In M. Lewis and L. A. Rosenblum, eds., *The Effect of the Infant on its Caregiver*. New York: Wiley; pp. 29-46.

Brazelton, T., E. Tronick, L. Adamson, A. Heidelise, and S. Wise. 1975. "Early Mother-Infant Reciprocity." *In Parent-Infant Interaction*. CIBA Foundation Symposium 33. New York: Associated Scientific Publishers; pp. 137-69.

Bronfenbrenner, U. 1967. "Response to Pressure from Peers Versus Adults Among Soviet and American School Children." *International Journal of Psychology* 2:199-207.

——1970a. *Two Worlds of Childhood: U.S. and U.S.S.R.* New York: Russell Sage.

——1970b. "Reaction to Social Pressure from Adults Versus Peers Among Soviet Day School and Boarding School Pupils in the Perspective of an American Sample." *Journal of Personality and Social Psychology* 15: 179-89.

——1974. *Is Early Intervention Effective? A Report on Longitudinal Evaluations of Preschool Programs*, vol. 2. Washington, D.C.: HEW, Office of Child Development.

——1975a. "Research on the Effects of Day Care on Child Development." In *Toward a National Policy for Children and Families*. Washington, D.C.: Advisory Committee on Child Development, National Academy of Science; pp. 117-33.

——1975b. "Reality and Research in the Ecology of Human Development." *Proceedings of the American Philosophical Society* 119:439-69.

——1976. "Ecological Validity in Research on Human Development." Paper presented at the American Psychological Association, Washington, D.C.

——1979. *The Ecology of Human Development*. Cambridge: Harvard University Press.

Bronfenbrenner, U., J. Belsky, and L. Steinberg. 1976. "Day in Context: An Ecological Perspective on Research and Public Policy." Paper prepared for the Department of Health, Education, and Welfare.

Brookhart, J., and E. Hock. 1976. "The Effects of Experimental Context and Experimental Background on Infants' Behavior Toward Their Mothers and a Stranger." *Child Development* 47:333-40.

Brownlee, M. 1977. "A Comparison of the Psychological Development of Children with Group and Family Infant Day Care Experience and Children Reared at Home for the First Three Years of Life." Paper presented at the Society for Research in Child Development Symposium.

Burns, P., L. W. Sander, G. Stechler, and H. Julia. 1972. "Distress in Feeding: Short-term Effects of Caretaker Environment of the First Ten Days." *Journal of the American Academy of Child Psychiatry* 11:427-39.

Caldwell, B. M. 1970. "The Effects of Psychosocial Deprivation on Human Development in Infancy." *Merrill-Palmer Quarterly* 16:260-77.

——1973. "Infant Day Care, the Outcast Gains Respectability." In P. Roby, ed., *Child Care–Who Cares: Foreign and Domestic Infant and Early Child Development Policies*. New York: Basic Books; pp. 20-36.

Caldwell, B. M., C. M. Wright, A. Honig, and J. Tannenbaum. 1970. "Infant Day Care and Attachment." *American Journal of Orthopsychiatry* 40:397-412.

Carey, W. B. 1972a. "Measuring Infant Temperament." *Journal of Pediatrics* 81:414.

——1972b. "Clinical Application of Infant Temperament Measurements." *Journal of Pediatrics* 81:823-28.

——1973. "Measurement of Infant Temperament in Pediatric Practice." In J. C. Westman, ed., *Individual Differences in Children*. New York: Wiley; pp. 293-306.

——1974. "Night Waking and Temperament in Infancy." *Journal of Pediatrics* 84:756-58.

Chess, S., A. Thomas, and H. G. Birch. 1967. "Behavior Problems Revisited: Findings of an Anterospective Study." *Journal of American Academy of Child Psychiatry* 6:321-31.

Clarke-Stewart, K. A. 1973. "Interactions Between Mothers and Their Young Children: Characteristics and Consequences." *Monographs of the Society for Research in Child Development* 38:6-7, Serial no. 153.

Cochran, M. 1976. "A Comparison of Group Day Care and Family Child-rearing Patterns." Working paper, Cornell University.

Cohen, D. J., and E. Zigler. 1977. "Federal Day Care Standards: Rationale and Recommendation." *American Journal of Orthopsychiatry* 47: 456-65.

Cohen, S. E., and L. Beckwith. 1977. "Caregiving Behaviors and Early Cognitive Development as Related to Ordinal Position in Preterm Infants." *Child Development* 48:152-57.

Coleman, R. W., E. Kies, and S. Provence. 1953. "The Study of Variations of Early Parental Attitudes: A Preliminary Report." In *The Psychoanalytic Study of the Child*, vol. 8, pp. 20-47. New York: International University Press.

Corman, H., and S. Escalona. 1969. "States of Sensorimotor Development: A Replication Study." *Merrill-Palmer Quarterly* 15:351-61.

Cornelius, S., and N. Denny. 1975. "Dependency in Day Care and Home Care Children." *Developmental Psychology* 11:575-82.

Crano, W. D. 1977. "What Do Infant Mental Tests Test? A Cross-legged Panel Analysis of Selected Data from the Berkeley Growth Study." *Child Development* 48:144-51.

Datta, L. 1969. "A Report on Evaluation Studies of Project Head Start." Paper presented at the American Psychological Association, Washington, D.C.

Deutsch, M., et al. 1971. *Regional Research and Resource Center in Early Childhood: Final Report.* Washington, D.C.: U.S. Office of Economic Opportunity.

Doyle, A. 1975a. "Infant Development in Day Care." *Developmental Psychology* 11:655-56.

———1975b. "The Effects of Daycare on Infant Development." Final report to Canada Council.

Doyle, A., and K. Somers. n.d. "The Effects of Group and Family Day Care on Infant Attachment." Working paper.

Dunn, J. 1975. "Consistency and Change in Styles of Mothering." In *Parent-Infant Interaction.* CIBA Foundation Symposium 33. New York: Associated Scientific Publishers.

Elardo, R., R. Bradley, and B. M. Caldwell. 1977. "A Longitudinal Study of the Relation of Infants' Home Environments to Language Development at Age Three." *Child Development* 48:595-603.

Elliot, V. 1973. "Impact of Day Care on Economic Status of the Family." In D. Peters, ed., *A Summary of the Pennsylvania Day Care Study.* University Park: Pennsylvania State University.

Escalona, S. K. 1968. *The Roots of Individuality.* Chicago: Aldine.

———1973. "Basic Modes of Social Interaction: Their Emergency and Patterning During the First Two Years of Life." *Merrill-Palmer Quarterly* 19:205-32.

Etaugh, C. 1974. "Effects of Maternal Employment on Children: A Review of Recent Research." *Merrill-Palmer Quarterly* 20:71-98.

Falender, C., and R. Heber. 1976. "Mother-child Interaction and Participation in a Longitudinal Program." Working paper.

Feine, R. J. n.d. "The Differential Structural Characteristics of Sentences Formed by Preschool Children in Family and Group Day Care Centers." Working paper.

Fowler, W. 1972. "A Developmental Learning Approach to Infant Care in a Group Setting." *Merrill-Palmer Quarterly* 18:145-75.

———1975. "How Adult/Child Ratios Influence Infant Development." *Interchange* 6:17-31.

Fowler, W., and N. Khan. 1974, 1975. "The Development of a Prototype Infant and Child Day Care Center in Metropolitan Toronto." #1 Year III Progress Report; #2 Year IV Progress Report.

Fraiberg, S. 1977. *Every Child's Birthright: In Defense of Mothering.* New York: Basic Books.

Freeman, H. 1977. "A Study of Families in Group and Family Infant Day Care Programs." Paper presented at the Society for Research in Child Development Symposium, New Orleans.

Garbarino, J., and U. Bronfenbrenner. 1976. "The Socialization of Moral Judgment and Behavior in Cross-cultural Perspective." In T. Lickona, ed., *Morality: A Handbook of Moral Development and Behavior.* New York: Holt, Rinehart, and Winston.

Garber, H., R. Heber, C. Hoffman, and S. Harrington. 1976. "Preventing Mental Retardation Through Family Rehabilitation." In *TADS Infant Education Monograph.* Chapel Hill, N.C.: TADS.

Gewirtz, J. L., and E. F. Boyd. "Mother-Infant Interaction and Its Study." In H. W. Reese, ed., *Advances in Child Development and Behavior.* New York: Academic Press.

Ginsburg, H., and S. Opper. 1969. *Piaget's Theory of Intellectual Development.* Englewood Cliffs, N.J.: Prentice-Hall.

Goldberg, S., and M. Lewis. "Play Behavior in the Year-old Infant: Early Sex Differences." *Child Development* 40:21-31.

Golden, M. 1977. "Overview: New York City Infant Day Care Study." Paper presented at the Society for Research in Child Development Symposium, New Orleans.

Golden, M., and B. Birns. 1976. "Social Class and Infant Intelligence." In M. Lewis, ed., *Origins of Intelligence.* New York: Plenum Press; pp. 299-352.

Golden, M., et al. 1978. *The New York City Day Care Study.* New York: Medical and Health Research Association of New York City, Inc.

Goldman, K. S., and M. Lewis. 1976. *Child Care and Public Policy.* Princeton, N.J.: Institute for Research in Human Development, Educational Testing Service.

Gouin-Decarie, T. 1965. *Intelligence and Affectivity in Early Childhood.* New York: International Universities Press.

Gratch, G., and W. Landers. 1971. "Stage IV of Piaget's Theory of Infants' Object Concepts: A Longitudinal Study."*Child Development* 42:359-72.

Gross, D. 1976. "Some Observations on the Group Care of Infants." Unpublished memorandum, Bank Street College of Education, New York.

Harnischfeger, A., and D. E. Wiley. 1975. *Achievement Test Score Decline: Do We Need to Worry?* Chicago: CEMREL.

Harrell, J. 1973. "Substitute Child Care, Maternal Employment, and the Quality of Mother-child Interaction." In D. Peters, ed., *A Summary of the Pennsylvania Day Care Study*.

Harrell, J., and C. Ridley. 1975. "Substitute Child Care, Maternal Employment, and the Quality of Mother-child Interaction." *Journal of Marriage and the Family*, pp. 556-65.

Heber, R., H. Garber, D. Harrington, C. Hoffman, and C. Falender 1972. *Rehabilitation of Families at Risk for Mental Retardation*. Madison: University of Wisconsin.

Hess, R., and V. Shipman. 1965. "Early Experience and the Socialization of Cognitive Modes in Children." *Child Development* 36:869-86.

Hock, E. 1976. *Alternative Approaches to Child Rearing and Their Effects on the Mother-infant Relationship*. Final report. Washington, D.C.: HEW, Office of Child Development.

Hunt, J., and N. Bayley. 1971. "Explorations into Patterns of Mental Development and Prediction from the Bayley Scales of Infant Development." In J. P. Hill, ed., *Minnesota Symposia on Child Psychology* 5:52-71.

Hunt, McV. J. 1976. "The Utility of Ordinal Scales Inspired by Piaget's Observations." *Merrill-Palmer Quarterly* 22:29-45.

Jacobs, B. S., and H. A. Moss. 1976. "Birth-order and Sex of Siblings as Determinants of Mother-infant Interaction. *Child Development* 47:315-22.

Kagan, J. 1976a. "The Effect of Day Care on the Infant." Paper prepared for the Department of Health, Education, and Welfare.

——1976b. "Emergent Themes in Human Development." *American Scientist* 64:186-96.

——1977. "The Child in the Family." *Daedalus* 106:33-56.

Kagan, J., R. Kearsley, and P. Zelazo. 1976. "The Effects of Infant Day Care on Psychological Development." Paper presented at the American Association for the Advancement of Science, Boston.

Keister, M. 1970. "A Demonstration Project: Group Care for Infants and Toddlers." Working paper.

Kerlinger, F. N. 1973. *Foundations of Behavorial Research*. 2nd ed. New York: Holt, Rinehart, and Winston.

Keyserling, M. D. 1972. *Windows on Day Care*. New York: National Council of Jewish Women.

Klaus, M. H., and J. H. Kennell. 1976. *Maternal-infant Bonding*. St. Louis: C. V. Mosby.

Kohn, M. 1973. "Social Class and Parent-child Relationships: An Interpretation." *American Journal of Sociology* 68:471-80.

Lally, R. 1973. "The Family Development Research Program." Working paper, Syracuse University.

——1974. "The Family Development Research Program." Working paper, Syracuse University.

Lamb, M. 1977. "Father-infant and Mother-infant Interaction in the First Year of Life." *Child Development* 48:167-81.

Lambie, D. Z., J. Y. Bond, and D. P. Weikart. 1974. *Home Teaching with Mothers and Infants.* Ypsilanti, Mich.: High/Scope Educational Research Foundation.

Largman, R. 1975. "Social-emotional Effects of Age of Entry into Full-time Group Care." Ph.D. diss. University of California at Berkeley.

Lay, M., and W. Meyer. 1973. *Teacher/Child Behaviors in an Open Environment Day Care Program.* Syracuse, N.Y.: Syracuse University Children's Center.

Lewis, J. 1975. "Family Development Center: A Demonstration Project." Working paper.

Lewis, M. 1972. "State as an Infant-environment Interaction: An Analysis of Mother-infant Interaction as a Function of Sex." *Merrill-Palmer Quarterly* 18:95-121.

——1973. "Infant Intelligence Tests: Their Use and Misuse." *Human Development* 16:108-18.

Lewis, M., and S. Lee-Painter. 1974. "An Interactional Approach to the Mother-infant Dyad." In M. Lewis and L. Rosenblum, eds., *The Effect of the Infant on Its Caregiver.* New York: Wiley; pp. 21-48.

Lewis, M., and L. Rosenblum 1974. *The Effect of the Infant on Its Caregiver.* New York: Wiley.

Lippman, M. A., and B. H. Grote. 1974. *Socio-emotional Effects of Day Care: Final Project Report.* Bellingham, Wash.: Western Washington State College.

McCutcheon, B., and K. Calhoun. 1976. "Social and Emotional Adjustment of Infants and Toddlers to a Day Care Setting." *American Journal of Orthopsychiatry* 46:104-8.

Macrae, J. W., and E. Herbert-Jackson. 1975. "Are Behavioral Effects of Infant Day Care Program Specific?" *Developmental Psychology* 12:269-70.

Mahler, M. S., F. Pine, and A. Bergmann. 1975. *The Psychological Birth of the Human Infant.* New York: Basic Books.

Meyers, L. 1973. "The Relationship Between Substitute Child Care, Maternal Employment, and Female Marital Satisfaction." In D. Peters, ed., *A Summary of the Pennsylvania Day Care Study.*

Moore, T. 1964. "Children of Full-time and Part-time Mothers." *International Journal of Social Psychiatry*, Special Congress Issue #2, pp. 1-10.
——1975a. "Stress in Normal Childhood." *Human Relations* 22:235-50.
——1975b. "Exclusive Early Mothering and Its Alternatives: The Outcome to Adolescence." *Scandinavian Journal of Psychology* 16:255-72.
Moskowitz, D. 1975. "Effects of Day Care Experience on Attachment and Exploratory Behavior." Master's thesis, University of Connecticut.
Moskowitz, D., and J. C. Schwartz. 1976. "Effect of Day Care Experience on Three-year-old Children's Attachment Behavior." Paper presented at the Eastern Psychological Association, New York.
Moss, H. A. 1967. "Sex, Age, and State as Determinants of Mother-infant Interaction." *Merrill-Palmer Quarterly* 13:19-36.
Naquera, H. 1973. "Day Care Centers: Red Light, Green Light, or Amber Light." Working paper, New York.
National Day Care Study: Second Annual Report 1975-1976. 1977. Cambridge, Mass.: Abt Associates Inc.
Parent-Infant Interaction. 1975. CIBA Foundation Symposium 33. New York: Associated Scientific Publishers.
Peaslee, M. V. 1976. "The Development of Competency in Two-year-old Infants in Day Care and Home Reared Environments." Ph.D. diss., Florida State University College of Education.
Peters, D. 1973. *A Summary of the Pennsylvania Day Care Study*. University Park: Pennsylvania State University.
Peterson, T. 1937. "A Preliminary Study of the Effects of Previous Nursery School Attendance Upon Five-year-old Children Entering Kindergarten." Iowa Studies in Child Welfare.
Piaget, P., and B. Inhelder. 1969. *The Psychology of the Child*. New York: Basic Books.
Policare, H. 1977. "A Comparison of the Psychological Experience of Infants in Group and Family Day Care." Paper presented at the Society for Research in Child Development Symposium, New Orleans.
Prentice, N., and J. Bieri. 1970. "Intellectual Development of Culturally Deprived Children in a Day Care Program: A Follow-up Study." Paper presented at the American Orthopsychiatric Association, San Francisco.
Prescott, E. 1973. "A Comparison of Three Types of Day Care and Nursery School-Home Care." Paper presented at the Society for Research in Child Development, Philadelphia.
Ramey, C., and D. Farran. 1975. "Infant Day Care and Attachment Behaviors Toward Mothers and Teachers." Paper presented at the American Psychological Association, Chicago.

— 1976. "Infant Day Care and Attachment Behaviors Toward Mothers and Teachers." Revision of Chicago APA paper. Unpublished manuscript, University of North Carolina.

Ramey, C., and J. Mills. 1975. "Mother-infant Interaction Patterns as a Function of Rearing Conditions." Unpublished manuscript, University of North Carolina.

—In press. "Social and Intellectual Consequences of Day Care for High Risk Infants." In R. Webb, ed., *Social Development: Family and Group Experience*. Baltimore, Md.: Johns Hopkins University Press.

Ramey, C., and B. Smith. 1976. "Learning and Intelligence in Disadvantaged Infants: Effects of Early Intervention." Paper presented at the Council on Exceptional Children.

Raph, J. B., A. Thomas, S. Chess, and S. J. Korn. 1964. " The Influence of Nursery School on Social Interactions." *American Journal of Orthopsychiatry* 38 : 144-52.

Ricciuti, H. 1974. "Fear and the Development of Social Attachments in the First Year of Life." In M. Lewis and L. Rosenblum, eds., *The Origins of Human Behavior: Fear*. New York: Wiley.

—1976. "Effects of Infant Day Care Experience on Behavior and Development: Research and Implications for Social Policy." Paper prepared for the Department of Health, Education, and Welfare.

Ricciuti, H., and R. Poresky. 1973. "Development of Attachment to Caregivers in an Infant Nursery During the First Year of Life." Paper presented at the Society for Research in Child Development, Philadelphia.

Riegel, K. F. 1975. "Subject-object Alienation in Psychological Experiments and Testing." *Human Development* 18:181-93.

Robinson, H., and N. Robinson. 1971. "Longitudinal Development of Very Young Children in a Comprehensive Day Care Program: The First Two Years." *Child Development* 42:1673-83.

Rosenbluth, L. 1977. "A Comparison of the Nutrition Provided to Infants in Group and Family Day Care in Their Day Care Setting." Paper presented at the Society for Research in Child Development, New Orleans.

Rossi, A. 1977. "A Biosocial Perspective on Parenting." *Daedalus* 106:1-32.

Rutter, M. 1972. *Maternal Deprivation Reassessed*. London: Penguin.

—1974. *The Qualities of Mothering: Maternal Deprivation Reassessed*. New York: Jason Aronson.

Sander, L. W., H. L. Julia, G. Stechler, and P. Burns. 1972. "Continuous 24-hour Interactional Monitoring in Infants Reared in Two Caretaking Environments." *Psychosomatic Medicine* 34:270-82.

Saunders, M. 1972. "Some Aspects of the Effects of Day Care on Infants'

Emotional and Personality Development." Ph.D. diss., University of North Carolina.

Saunders, M., and M. Keister. 1972. "Family Day Care: Some Observations." Working paper.

Schaffer, H. R., and P. E. Emerson. 1964. "The Development of Social Attachments in Infancy." *Monographs of the Society for Research in Child Development*; pp. 1-77.

Schwarz, J. C. 1975. "Social and Emotional Effects of Day Care: A Review of Recent Research." Paper presented to Conference on the Family and Social Change sponsored by the Society for Research in Child Development.

Schwarz, J., G. Krolick, and R. Strickland. 1973. "Effects of Early Day Care on Adjustment to a New Environment." *American Journal of Orthopsychiatry* 43:340-46.

Schwarz, J., R. Strickland, and G. Krolick. 1974. "Infant Day Care: Behavioral Effects at Preschool Age." *Developmental Psychology* 10:502-6.

Scott, H. 1974. *Does Socialism Liberate Women? Experiences from Eastern Europe*. Boston: Beacon Press.

Stern, D. N. 1974. "Mother and Infant at Play: The Dyadic Interaction Involving Facial, Vocal, and Gaze Behaviors." In M. Lewis and L. Rosenblum, eds., *The Effect of the Infant on its Caregiver*. New York: Wiley; pp. 187-214.

Thomas, A., and S. Chess. 1977. *Temperament and Development*. New York: Bruner/Mazel.

Thomas, A. S. Chess, H. G. Birch, M. E. Hertzog, and S. Korn. 1969. *Behavioral Individuality in Early Childhood*. New York: New York University Press.

Ulrich, R., S. Louisell, and M. Wolfe. 1971. "The Learning Village: A Behavioral Approach to Early Education." *Educational Technology* (February), pp. 32-45.

Uzgiris, I. C. 1973. "Patterns of Cognitive Development in Infancy." *Merrill-Palmer Quarterly* 19:180-205.

——1976. "Infant Development from a Piagetian Approach: Introduction to a Symposium." *Merrill-Palmer Quarterly* 22:3-10.

Uzgiris, I. C., and J. McV. Hunt. 1975. *Assessment in Infancy*. Urbana: University of Illinois Press.

Wachs, T. D. 1976. "Utilization of a Piagetian Approach in the Investigation of Early Experience Effects: A Research Strategy and Some Illustrative Data." *Merrill-Palmer Quarterly* 22:11-30.

Wachs, T., I. C. Uzgiris, and J. McV. Hunt. 1971. "Cognitive Development in Infants from Different Age Levels and Different Environmental Backgrounds: An Explanatory Investigation." *Merrill-Palmer Quarterly* 17: 283-317.

White, B. L. 1975. *The First Three Years of Life*. Englewood Cliffs, N.J.: Prentice-Hall.

Willis, A., and H. Ricciuti. 1974. "Longitudinal Observations of Infants' Daily Arrivals at a Day Care Center." Technical report, Cornell Research Program in Early Development and Education. Ithaca, N.Y.: Cornell University.

——1975. *A Good Beginning for Babies: Guidelines for Group Care*. Washington, D.C.: National Association for the Education of Young Children.

Winett, B. A., W. L. Fuchs, and S. Moffatt. 1974. "An Evaluative Study of Day Care and Non-Day Care Children and Their Families." Working paper, University of Kentucky.

Woolsey, S. H. 1977. "Pied Piper Politics and the Child-care Debate." *Daedalus* 106:127-45.

Yarrow, L. J. 1964. "Separation from Parents During Early Childhood." In M. L. Hoffman and L. W. Hoffman, eds., *Review of Child Development Research*, vol. 1, pp. 89-136. New York: Russell Sage.

Appendix B

THE STUDY METHOD

It is difficult to specify exactly when some studies begin. In the present instance, we were alerted to the issue while in the midst of a comparative study of social service systems[1] and when we had already decided that it would be useful to obtain some information about approaches in Eastern and Western Europe to family policy as field and as perspective. As we carried out the exploration involved in selecting countries and recruiting personnel for what became the International Working Party on Family Policy[2] the discussions confirmed the fact that the "under-three" question was central to debate and discussion of family policy in Europe. A modest feasibility exploration permitted us to develop the general design and reach agreements with research collaborators. The design itself and procedures grew out of the requirements of the topic and earlier experiments.

Our earliest effort had been an attempt to join together American observations (since we were to report to American audiences) with program explications by country experts, in a report on social services for families in Northern and Western Europe.[3] This proved to be a useful strategy in a journalistic endeavor where the goal was to report, not to add to knowledge in any basic sense. The subsequent studies had to be more systematic.

The eight-country social services study[4] was designed completely by us and carried out by teams which we recruited, financed, and coordinated. Funding requirements were such that we were compelled to focus the research questions, settle the basic methods, and draft research instruments before the team could be brought together for the first of three coordination meetings. We recognized at the time, and particularly later, that we paid a price for these constraints. On the other hand, we visited major programs in all countries with team members, both to achieve mutual clarification of data-collection expectations and to ensure first-hand acquaintance with programs we would later be writing about on the basis of data assembled by others.

By the time the present study was launched, we were convinced of: the urgency of keeping final formulation of issues and design as open as possible, pending team meetings, so as to allow an optimum contribution by country collaborators; the importance of team review and correction of data-collection guides before proceeding too far with field work; the critical need to maintain our practice of program visiting and independent discussions with administrators and policy experts in participating countries, to prepare us as critics and consumers of the reports assembled in each of the countries.

Before all this could occur, however, the countries needed to be selected. The process began with the conceptualization of the research question. In the course of our explorations of family policy we had come to realize that the question of what, if any, public policy position should be developed regarding the care of children under age three while parents worked was an issue in flux. There were differences among countries within Eastern Europe, as there were in the West. Moreover there was strong debate about some central questions: What were the impacts of different policies, once in place? What were the relative costs of different strategies? The idea of a "natural" experiment grew even as the question formulated itself. The exploration during the feasibility phase served both to provide sufficient detail to ensure proper characterization of each of the potential participant countries, and to test feasibility from the point of view of access to data and availability of qualified cooperating teams. Obviously, there were or could have been alternatives (Belgium, rather than France? Czechoslovakia, rather than Hungary? Another Scandinavian country?) However, we fortunately were able to select what, on the face of it, appeared to be the prototypical countries in each instance and to win cooperation, although the process was complicated and delayed in at least two instances.

Thus, by the time the total team met for its planning meeting we had general acquaintance with infant-toddler child care in each of the countries and we had drafted a first approximation of a series of instruments. However, the situation remained open.

The first team meeting (spring 1977) served to refine the question and to revise the instruments. Our visit to teams at work in the summer of 1977, by which time they had tested the approach against local circumstances, allowed us to achieve clarification and consensus. Final revisions on the instruments were mailed to all teams in August 1977. From that point, the collaboration was carried out through the mails. Receipt of materials from the teams was followed by requests for clarification and elaboration, and their responses to us.

The teams submitted their final reports as "source books," organized in accord with the instrument order, as soon as they were completed. (In the case of the two Germanys and France, the original reports were written in native languages. The French report was accompanied by a partial translation, and the report from the Federal Republic of Germany by a full translation. The other reports were translated before submission to us.)[5]

We completed our country visits in June 1978, having dictated a full volume of program description notes and explanations of policies and programs as provided by administrators, officials, and experts (none of which materials are here published, but all of which enriched our perspective and enabled us to raise relevant questions). Descriptions of the French and Swedish child care programs, based on this material, have been published elsewhere.[6]

In July 1978 the team met again in a conference center near Paris, devoting almost a full week to shaping and testing a series of potential hypotheses. The following fall and winter we drafted the final report, sent it to our colleagues for comment, and revised it again.

While the analysis in the volume suggests the categories of data collected, research readers may be interested in the organization of the seven study guides, constituting the final research instruments:

1. Baseline Data
   Demographic data, labor-force data, relevant trends in demography and labor force participation by mothers, supplementary socioeconomic data for context.
   Data as to where children are cared for during the day (ages 0-3, 3-6), as well as after-school arrangements.
2. Social Welfare Benefits which Assist Mothers—Parents—Families with Young Children
   Following an inventory of all relevant benefits (a checklist was supplied), each relevant benefit was reported on separately, and in some detail, in accord with an outline.

3. Programs and Services to Care for Children Outside Their Own Homes

Following an inventory of all relevant programs (a checklist was supplied), teams followed a detailed outline in reporting on the several models. Brief reports were requested on secondary programs, detailed reports on the four major possibilities (center-based child care, agency-operated family day care, privately operated family day care, preschools which admit children under age three). Teams provided program descriptions—action pictures—which the codirectors supplemented with their own observations.

4. The Policy Context (Two Data Guides)

While outlines were offered, the team was asked for a memorandum or an essay placing child care policy for children under three in overall policy context for the country. Here country orientations and the sense in which family policy is explicit or implicit needed to be recognized. A report on the current debate and issues was requested, and the positions of major political parties and interest groups were to be identified.

5. Research on Implementation, Effects, and Effectiveness

Teams were asked for a summary of the research considered important and of good quality in their countries, relating to effects on families, effects on children, user response, cost-benefit or cost-effectiveness findings, staff to child ratios, and parent participation. While the question was asked with reference to both child care programs and social benefits, available research deals almost solely with the former. Public opinion survey results were also requested.

6. Researchers' Assessments (Optional)

In this optional, open-ended section, the teams were offered the opportunity to sum up and present their perspectives on trends and developments.

No two team reports were alike in emphasis or orientation. Some were more full for some topics than for others. Correspondence, discussion, probing, independent work by the codirectors served to ensure at least the minimum required on almost all items for all countries. Gaps, where they remain, are reported in the text and reflect country circumstances.

In June 1979 the team assembled just before a reporting conference in Copenhagen at which, under the sponsorship of the World Health Organization and the Danish National Institute of Social Research, the preliminary results were offered to an audience of European experts, including representatives of major international organizations. Some months earlier we had completed a draft of the research report and had circulated it to all teams. Thus the meeting was an opportunity for the country researchers to offer corrections of fact and interpretation and to assess the overall report. The conference itself was a forum for a discussion of findings and their policy implications. All this provided the stimulus and guidance for final revisions by the codirectors and the writing of the present book.

It will be noted that the country studies took place in a variety of settings and were carried out by people from several disciplines. We have learned that applied policy work and program research in this and related fields is structured somewhat differently in each country, reflecting the state and status of the several behavioral and social sciences, and the relationship between research and practice. While there are several recognizable major traditions, no two countries are exactly alike.

The study called for an unusual combination: we were bringing together child development assessments of the impact of earlier child care programs with analysis of cash benefits and related entitlements. Our child care interests spanned both program concerns and cost-benefit questions. Somehow each country required representation on its staff from these two major interests: child development and policy analysis. This was variously accomplished by creating teams of two codirectors, each specialized in relation to one of the facets (FRG), or multidisciplinary teams in which tasks were taken on in accord with the general proclivity of the discipline (France), or by having the directors draw upon other expertise at the consultant level (Sweden)—or through various combinations of these arrangements in the other countries. Our principal study directors thus came from psychology, economics, public administration, education, medicine, sociology, social policy—and the principal consultants came from similar fields as well as from child care backgrounds.

The research was based in 1) a university-ministry collaboration; 2) a specialized research institute tied to a ministry; 3) a medically oriented but free-standing child and youth research institute; 4) a family sociology section of an academy of science; 5) a ministry-labor union expert collaboration; and 6) a research program in a professional school, based in a university.

This diversity proved to be enriching and made it possible to develop a view of social policy that joins care programs and cash benefits in one analysis and then focuses on results to society of various "packages."[7]

NOTES

1. A. J. Kahn and S. B. Kamerman, *Social Services in International Perspective* (Washington, D.C.: U.S. Government Printing Office for HEW, 1977).

2. S. B. Kamerman and A. J. Kahn, eds., *Family Policy: Government and Families in Fourteen Countries* (New York: Columbia University Press, 1978).

3. A. J. Kahn and S. B. Kamerman, *Not for the Poor Alone* (Philadelphia: Temple University Press, 1975).

4. Kahn and Kamerman, *Social Services in International Perspective*.

5. The country source books are available to researchers at the cost of reproduction. The full Swedish report, which includes a summary for the Swedish public of the general research, has been published as Ingemar Lindberg and Lena Nordenmark, *Familjepolitik små barn* (Stockholm: Publica, 1980).

6. S. B. Kamerman, *Parenting in an Unresponsive Society: Managing Work and Family Life* (New York: Free Press, 1980).

7. For some discussion of the potential contributions of such research, see: "Introduction to the Transaction Edition," *Social Services in International Perspective* (Rutgers, N.J.: Transaction Press, 1980).

INDEX